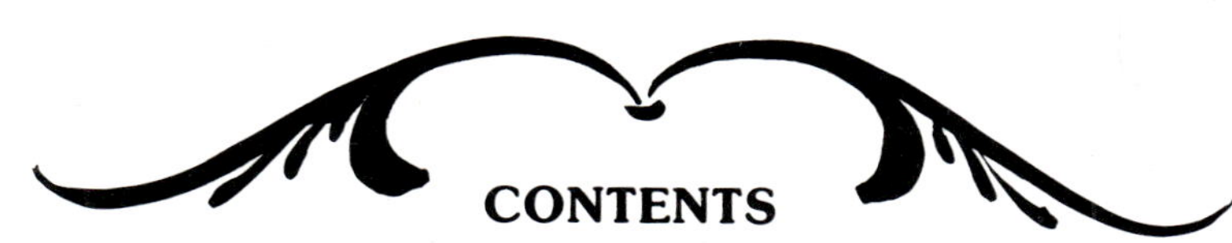

CONTENTS

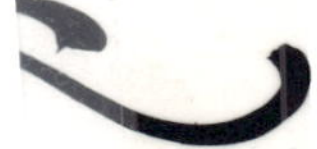

Jackie's Toy Box is full ... od humored nonsense. It is dedicated to two very spec ... stics, and whose antics and kindnesses are among my f...

P.S. Peggie and Angel have eac ... of you their grandsons' photos, I've decided to include their grandba ... Toy Box to share with you.

Library of Congress #82-70359
ISBN 0-941284-12-3

Printed by *United Litho*, Falls Church, VA
Color Separations by *Sun Crown*, Washington, D.C.
Typesetting by *Type Too Ltd*, Rockville, MD
Color Photography by *Dan Glass*, Bethesda, MD
B & W Photography by *Lynn Shaw*, Potomac, MD

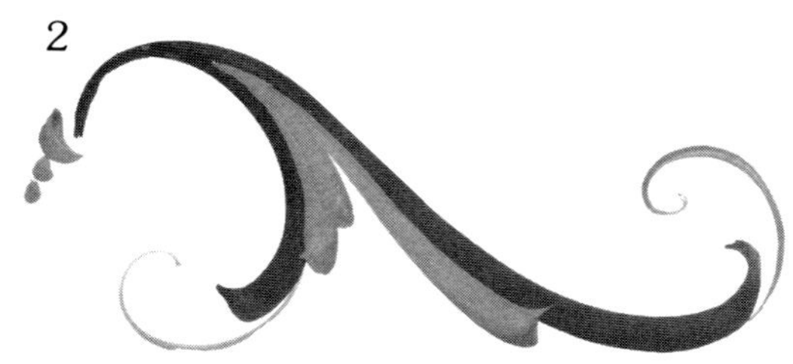

THE TRADITION OF DECORATIVE FOLK PAINTING

Decorative Folk Painting is a visual art which has enabled people from the earliest times, to express and share their innate creativity. Through the use of pigments and brushes, we decorate and personalize our surroundings, adding a touch of human warmth and artistry to our mechanized utilitarian world.

The realm of decorative painting is extensive, including a broad range of skills, and reflecting decorative arts from around the world. While our heritage of decorative art dates back to paintings on cave walls, the most immediate influence is European, having been brought to America by the early settlers in the form of painted chests, furniture, and other functional items. An in depth study, however, of decorative designs, strokes, and methods also reveals marked similarities with Oriental techniques which were imitated in Europe between the seventeenth and nineteenth centuries.

Decorative folk art holds appeal and excitement for all levels of talent and extremes of interest - from fabric and canvas painting to wall and floor stenciling; from glass, tin, and wood painting to gold leafing and freehand bronzing techniques. Whether the painting is done in oils, watercolors, or acrylics, and whether it is also done in conjunction with other decorative techniques such as woodburning, wood carving, or calligraphy is a matter of personal style and preference. Today's decorative artists draw inspiration from divergent ethnic art forms and media including Norwegian Rosemaling, German Bauernmalerei, Chinese brush painting, Russian Khokloma, Korean Tanchong, Pennsylvania Dutch Hexology, Mexican, Hungarian, and Swedish folk art, and so on. The scope broadens as we continue to re-discover old techniques, experiment with new ones, and pass our discoveries on to others through classes and instruction books.

Decorative folk art leaves realism and truth to the photographers and botanists. As folk artists, we paint to give expression to our creative natures. We need have no pretensions, no rules or regulations. We paint with the innocence of childhood (wherein it's possible to do *anything* one imagines) taking naive delight in decorating our surroundings with that which we feel in our hearts. We find pleasure in knowing that we are part of our country's continuing heritage of folk artists whose painted expressions, now sought by collectors and museums, are bold reminders of the age old happiness of creativity.

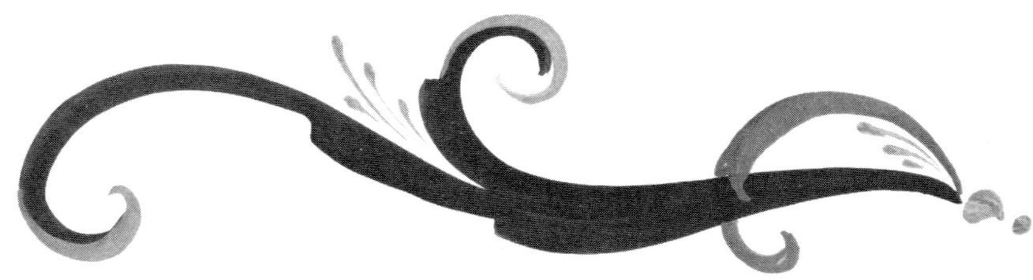

SUPPLIES

BRUSHES

In decorative painting, good quality **art brushes** (pictured on the left) are your most important tools. To try to work with poor or improperly cared for brushes is frustrating and unrewarding. The brushes shown, by Loew-Cornell, include Series 7550 Flat, size ½", Series 7300, sizes 10, 6, 2; Series 7000 Round, size 3; Series 465 Liner (or substitute Series 475), size 2. Although additional sizes are used in the book, these brushes provide an adaptable range of sizes from narrow to wide, suitable for getting started. Once you are hooked on decorative painting you will want to add other sizes within the series.

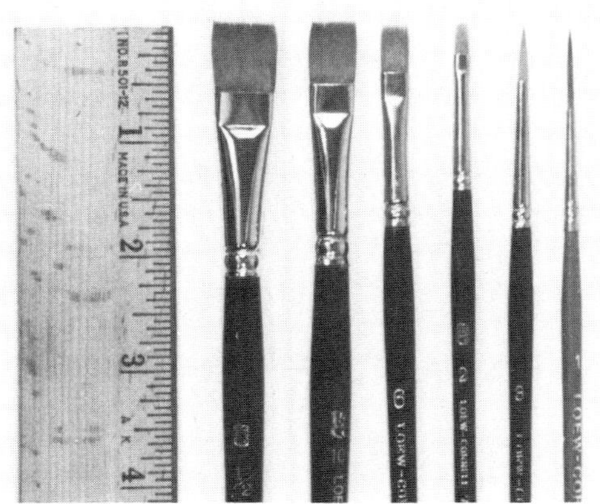

Art Brushes

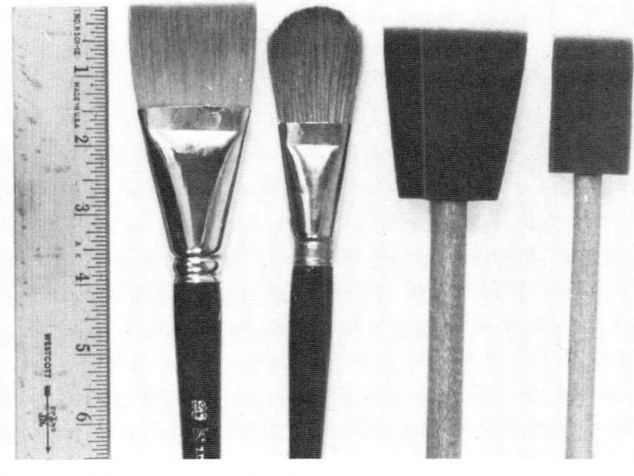

Surface Preparation Brushes

The **surface preparation brushes** (pictured on the right) include Loew-Cornell Series 7550 1½" wash brush, a large mop brush, and two foam or poly brushes, 1½" and 1". The mop brush is used in conjunction with antiquing. The other brushes are used for applying sealer, basecoat paints, and varnish. Although the foam brushes are inexpensive and disposable, I prefer the 7550 wash brush. It facilitates surface preparation, getting into tight places easily, and painting clean, even edges. It is more expensive initially, but, in addition to appreciating its quality, I find myself taking better care of it so it far outlasts countless foam brushes.

PAINTS, PALETTE, PALETTE KNIFE, BRUSH WASHER

The **paints** featured in this book are acrylics. Delta Ceramcoats, Plaid Folk Art Colors and Illinois Bronze Country Colors all work beautifully. Tubed acrylics or oils may also be used.

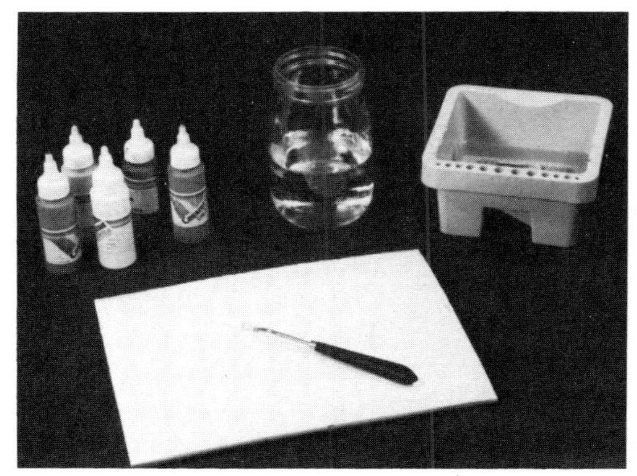

The **palette** pictured is a disposable one. The palette is a surface upon which paints are placed for intermixing and for loading into the brushes. For acrylics, a waxed surface is preferable as it does not crinkle under the waterbased paint. Disposable palettes consist of a pad of tear-off sheets. Other items which serve well as palettes include plastic meat trays, a piece of glass with edges taped for safety, or a white porcelain dish. The latter items may be easily cleaned by soaking in water for a half hour or so. Any dried acrylic is then easily peeled off. If a non-disposable palette is used with oil paints, it may be cleaned by wiping with a paper towel.

The **palette knife** is used for mixing colors together. It is also used for patching flaws and filling holes in projects with wood filler.

The **brush washer** contains water for cleaning acrylic paints from brushes. A jar can serve this purpose equally well. For working with oils, replace the water with turpentine or paint thinner.

TRACING PAPER, CHALK, CONTÉ PASTEL PENCIL

Tracing paper is used for copying designs and transferring them onto projects. It is also useful for practicing brush strokes on.

The **chalk** and **Conté Pastel Pencil** are used in designing and transferring patterns.

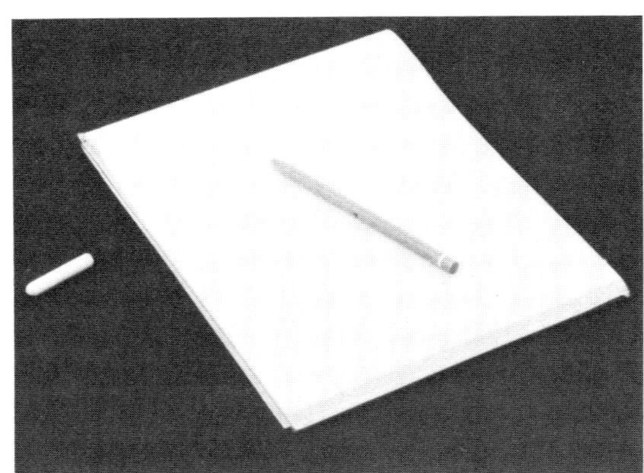

SURFACE PREPARATION SUPPLIES

(Available at hardware stores)

Woodfiller (or powdered wood putty) is mixed with water and used for filling holes and flaws in wooden projects.

Sandpaper is necessary to smooth the grain of wood and prepare it for the **sealer.** The nylon **"scrubbies"** and **abrasive sponges** shown are also ideal for smoothing surfaces. The **tack rag** is a sticky cloth used for removing fine dust. **Cheesecloth** (also found in the food preserving section of your grocery store and in some craft and variety stores) is used in antiquing and for some special effects.

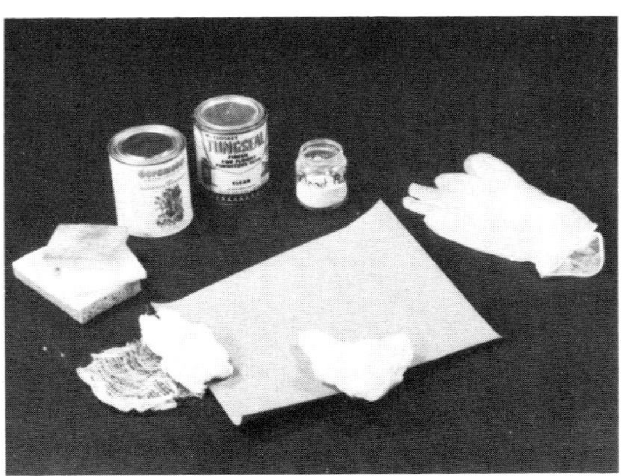

MISCELLANEOUS SUPPLIES

Other supplies you will find helpful: paper towels, stylus, bottle caps or 35mm film lids, natural sponge, jars, Ivory soap, cotton swabs, linseed oil, notebook for saving your practice sheets, Purex Cleaning Pads (for sanding - found in the grocery store near SOS pads and scouring powders).

Once you have assembled all the supplies, your next move is to decide what to paint on. That is easy. If it does not wiggle, giggle, or cry and if it is neither edible nor returnable - DECORATE IT!

ARRANGING YOUR WORK AREA FOR CONVENIENCE AND COMFORT

Find a layout for your supplies which is the most convenient and which requires the least expenditure of effort. For instance, paper towels for blotting wet brushes should be close to the water and near your painting hand. If you're right handed, your brushes should be close to your right hand - not halfway across the table out of easy reach. Access to the paints on your palette should be unobstructed. Some artists, particularly when working with a limited palette (only a few paints), always squeeze the colors onto their palette in the same order, so that their movements are automatic - not a moment is wasted in looking around for a certain color.

An extra jar of water is handy for acrylic painters to have nearby. Use this water for washing soap out of brushes. It is desirable that soap not contaminate your rinse water as it diminishes the adhesive quality of the acrylics.

See to it that you are comfortably seated at your work area. Some painters prefer sitting on a high stool, others opt for a comfortable chair. If you are working on your project on the work table, be sure you are at a height which does not require you to raise your shoulders in order to work. Otherwise you will tire quickly. In such a case, push your chair away from the table and hold your project in your lap, letting your arms hang freely by your sides.

Take mini breaks from time to time. A two-hour session is generally long enough to persevere at painting. Give yourself a stretch break for a few minutes. When you return to your painting, you will have a fresh perspective and renewed vigor. By taking refreshing little breaks, you should be able to continue painting day and night. This devotion to your new hobby gives the dust bunnies plenty of time to multiply, undisturbed in the corners. Children will outgrow clothing without your ever having to mend or iron it. Spouses will learn culinary and laundry skills in order to get from one day to the next. And all the money saved by resorting to quick, unimaginative meals can be stashed away to purchase painting supplies.

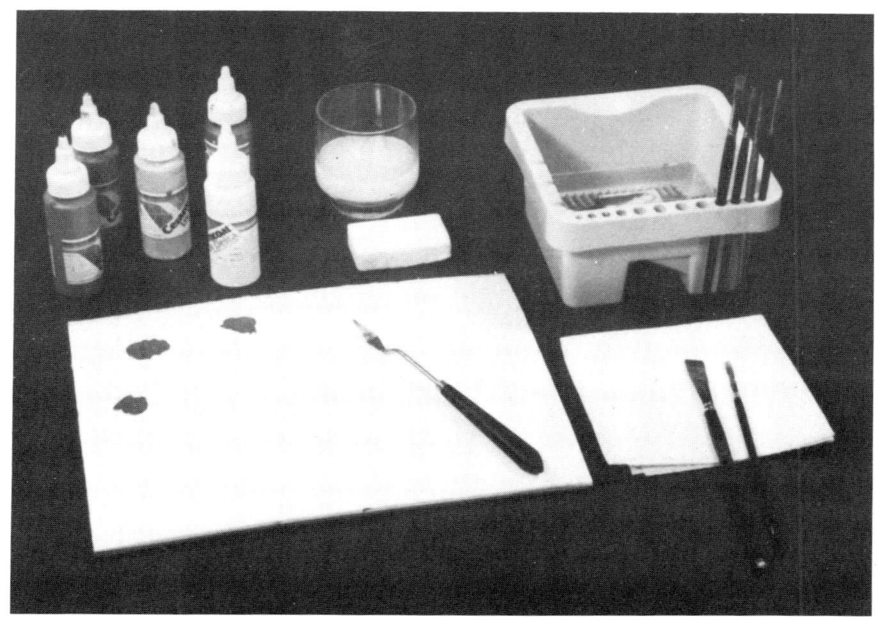

KEEPING YOUR ACRYLICS FRESH LONGER

While acrylics lend themselves so beautifully to decorative folk painting because of their rapid drying time, that very feature can be a bit frustrating when they dry out on your palette while you are still trying to work with them. This is particularly true of combinations of colors which you have worked laboriously to mix. It is possible to prolong their palette life.

1. Scrape paints into a condensed pile and cover with a small cap. I have found 35mm film container lids to be ideal. Once pressed down onto the palette, they seal tightly, preserving the paint under them for several hours. If you expect to be away from your palette for a long time, sprinkle a drop or two of water over the pile of paint before covering it.

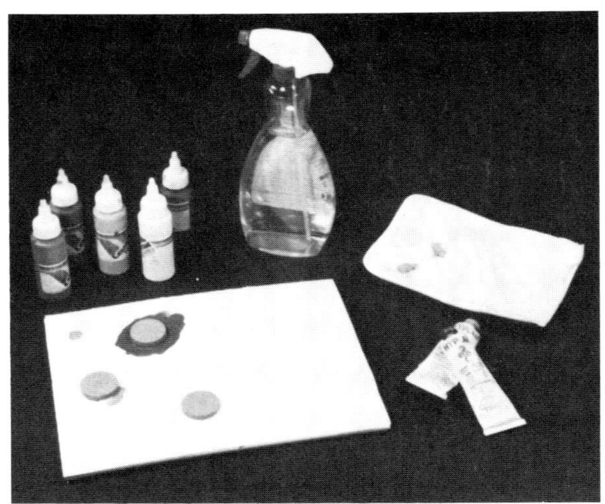

2. Mist water over your palette with an atomizer or spray bottle (such as those containing window cleaner or hair spray).

3. Use a styrofoam meat tray or other tray with raised sides, as your palette. Keep it covered with a damp paper towel. If you are using the stiffer tubed acrylics, squeeze them directly onto a damp paper towel.

CARE AND HANDLING OF BRUSHES

Your brushes represent a good investment. Treat them with care and respect, and they will work well for you and last longer.

1. Clean your brushes often and thoroughly. A quick swish through the water is **not** enough. Use Ivory soap and your fingers to gently work the soap into the hairs. Rinse. Continue soaping and rinsing until every trace of color is gone! Paint allowed to harden in your brush, even in minute amounts, eventually creates a hard "knot" up near the metal ferrule. This "knot" causes the hairs to separate and thereby reduces the effectiveness of the brush. A brush thus damaged can sometimes be partially restored by cleaning with a solvent such as nail polish remover or alcohol. This is a harsh measure so should be resorted to only when absolutely necessary. Keep solvent away from the handle as it will penetrate the lacquer and create a very sticky situation.

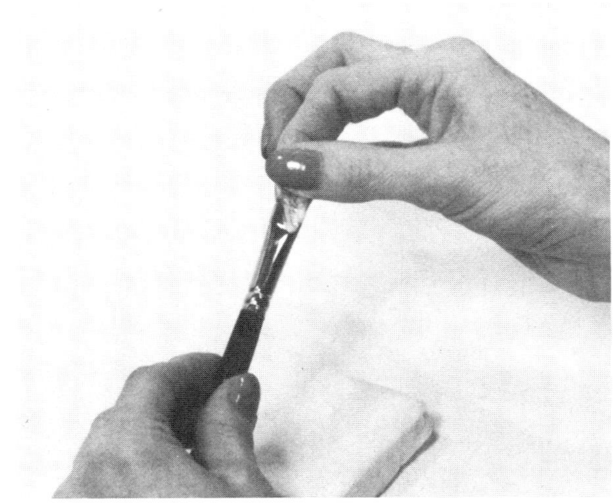

2. After thoroughly cleaning the brush, put more soap into it and re-shape the hairs. Draw round and liner brush hairs to a fine point. Shape flat brushes to a smooth chisel edge. Dry. The hairs should be quite stiff. This helps them to retain their crisp shapes, and minimizes damage in storage.

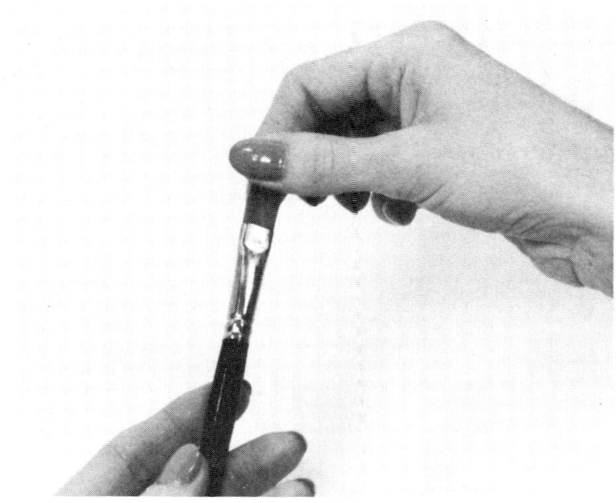

3. Store the brushes so the hairs will not be bent or crushed. Some possibilities include: a) weave them into a woven placemat which can be rolled up and tied with ribbon for storage or travel, b) fasten them to cardboard with elastic or rubber bands, c) stand them on their handle ends in a glass or jar, d) store them in commercially available cases specially designed to separate the brushes and keep them from shifting.

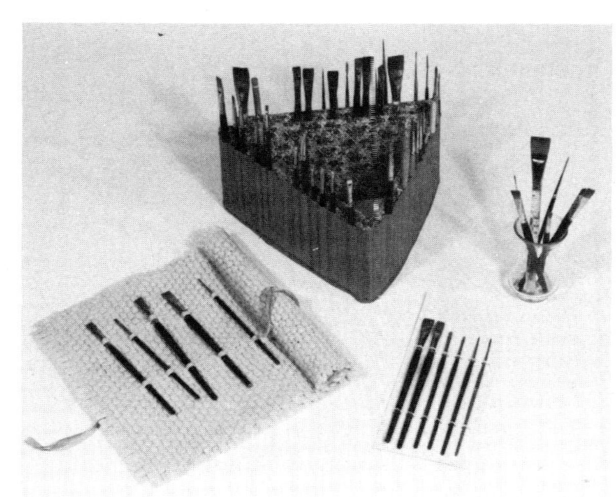

POP QUIZ

4. How many things can you find wrong with this picture?

a. Brushes have been left standing in water. They will soon be water-logged.

b. Brushes allowed to stand on their bristles get bent out of shape.

c. Water level is so high in the jar that it could eventually damage the wooden handle.

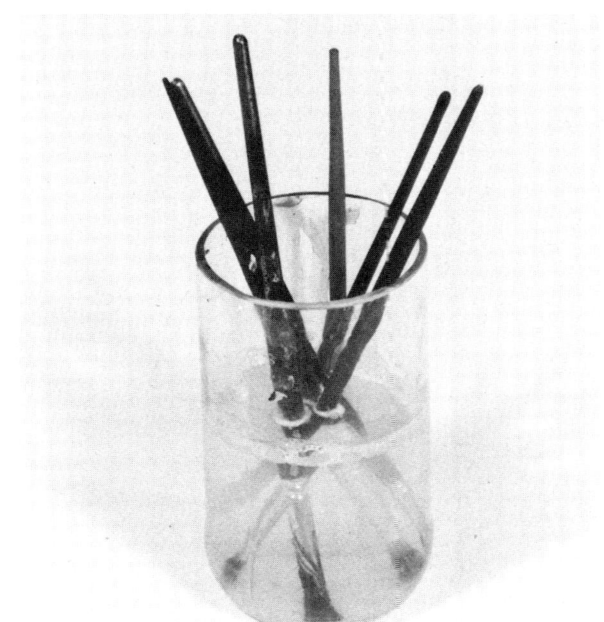

HINT: If you plan to paint for long periods, you'll find 2 or more sets of brushes handy. As a brush becomes waterlogged or lazy from extended use, clean it, shape it, and set it aside. Grab a reserve and carry on!

SURFACE PREPARATION

Pictured are six basic steps to follow in preparing wooden projects for decorative painting.

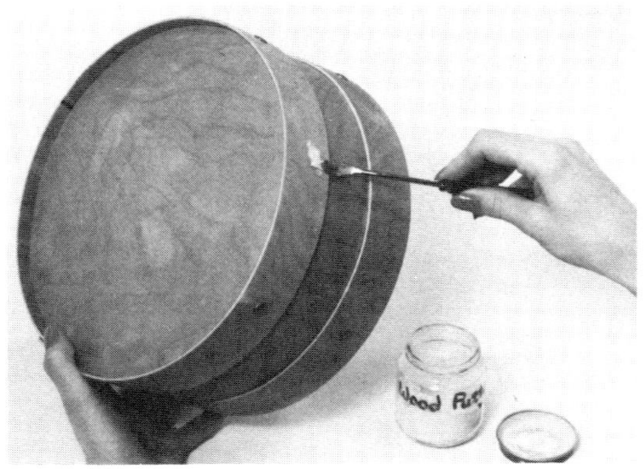

1. Fill holes and flaws with wood putty or wood filler.

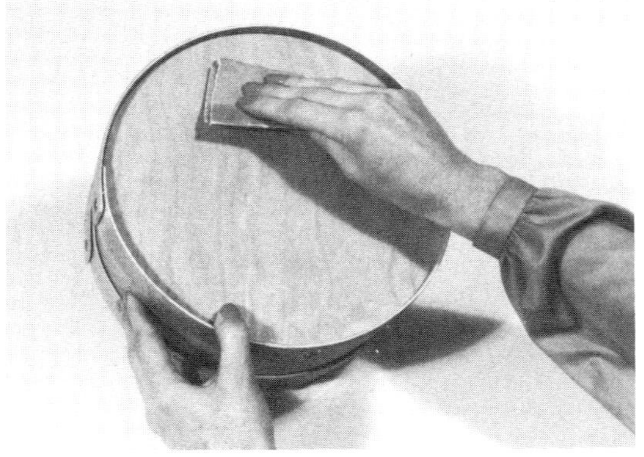

2. Sand, moving with the grain of the wood. If the wood is especially rough, begin sanding with a coarse textured paper. Follow this with a medium texture and, lastly, with a fine texture.

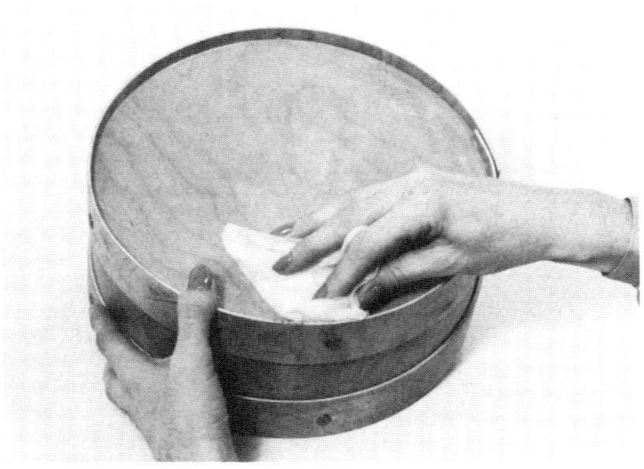

3. Remove dust thoroughly with a tack cloth.

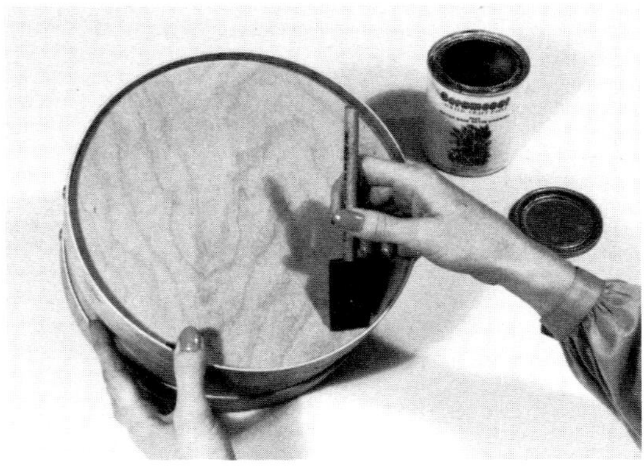

4. Seal the wood with any clear sealer or water based varnish. Sealing will raise the grain slightly. Dry, according to manufacturer's directions. (Water based varnishes and sealers dry within a few minutes).

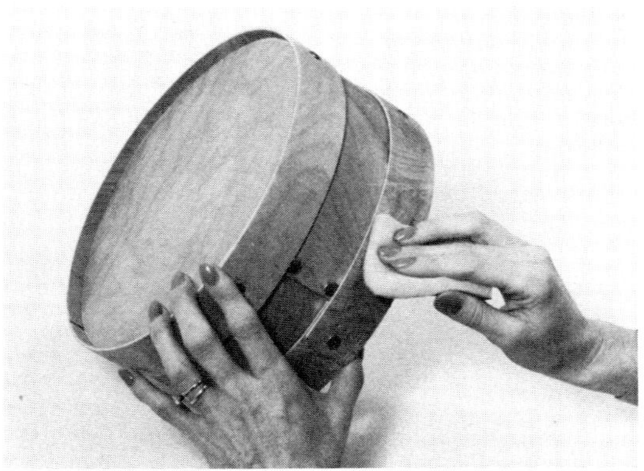

5. Sand very lightly with fine sandpaper, steel wool or abrasive "scrubbie." Again, remove all dust with a tack cloth.

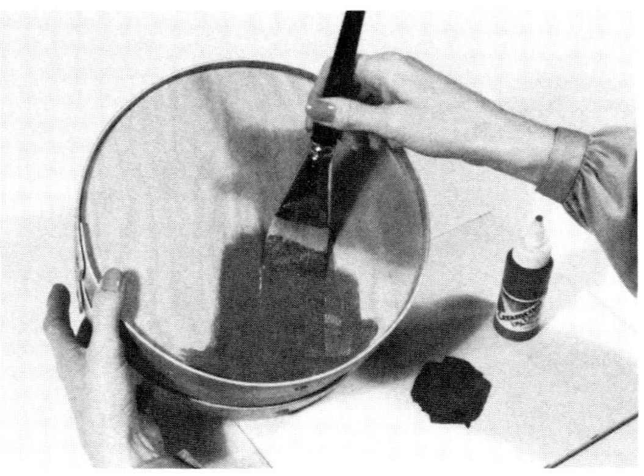

6. Basecoat with a background color of your choice. Several thin coats are preferable to a thick, uneven one.

TRANSFERRING PATTERNS

In order for you to develop your greatest potential as a decorative folk artist, it is preferable that you not limit yourself to the rigid confines of a pattern. To do so tends to stifle any creative endeavors you might otherwise be inclined to attempt. Realizing, however, that there are times when the slight suggestion of a pattern might serve as a "security blanket," I will share the following tips with you. Notice, however, the mention of "slight suggestion." This means that you are encouraged to trace the least amount of pattern possible leaving as much opportunity as you can for your own personal interpretation and embellishment.

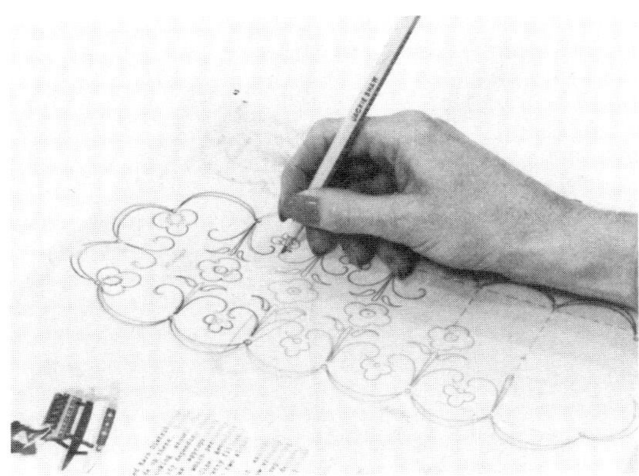

1. Copy the pattern onto tracing paper.

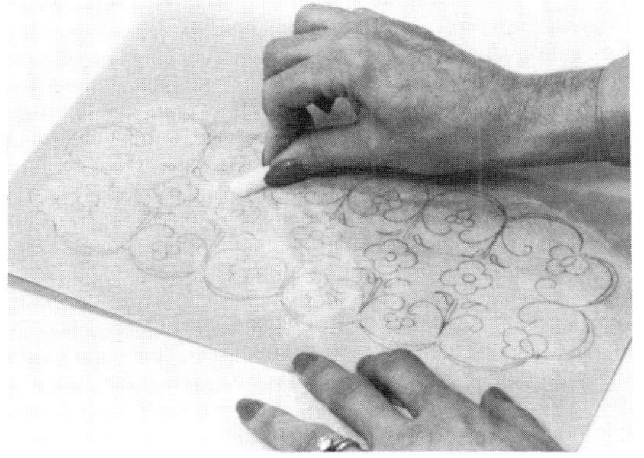

2. Rub chalk on the back of the pattern. Use a color which will barely show against your background and which will not muddy your work. Cheap chalk is best. (Do not use oil pastels.) Shake off excess chalk dust.

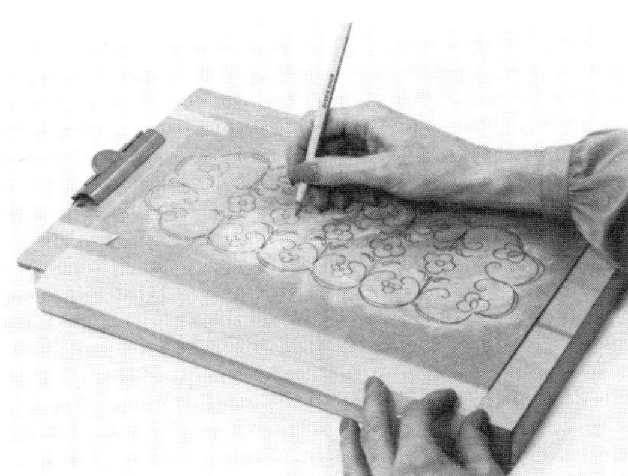

3. Tape pattern in place. Retrace pattern lines. Use a different color pen so you will be able to see where you have retraced. If you plan to use the pattern repeatedly, trace it onto Vidalon or Deluxe Vellum - a sturdier grade of tracing paper. You can protect the tracing by placing a piece of waxed paper over it before transferring it to your project. Retrace your pattern lines, through the waxed paper. You will be able to see, by the tracks in the waxed paper, where you have traced and where you have missed.

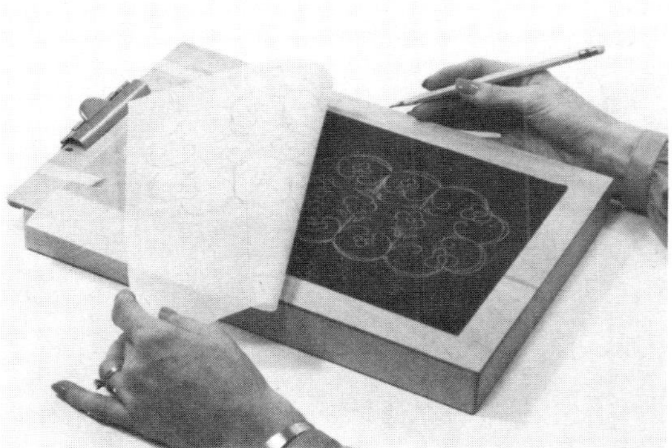

4. Before removing the pattern, lift it to see that all critical parts transferred clearly. The chalked pattern lines wipe away easily with a damp cloth upon completion of your painting.

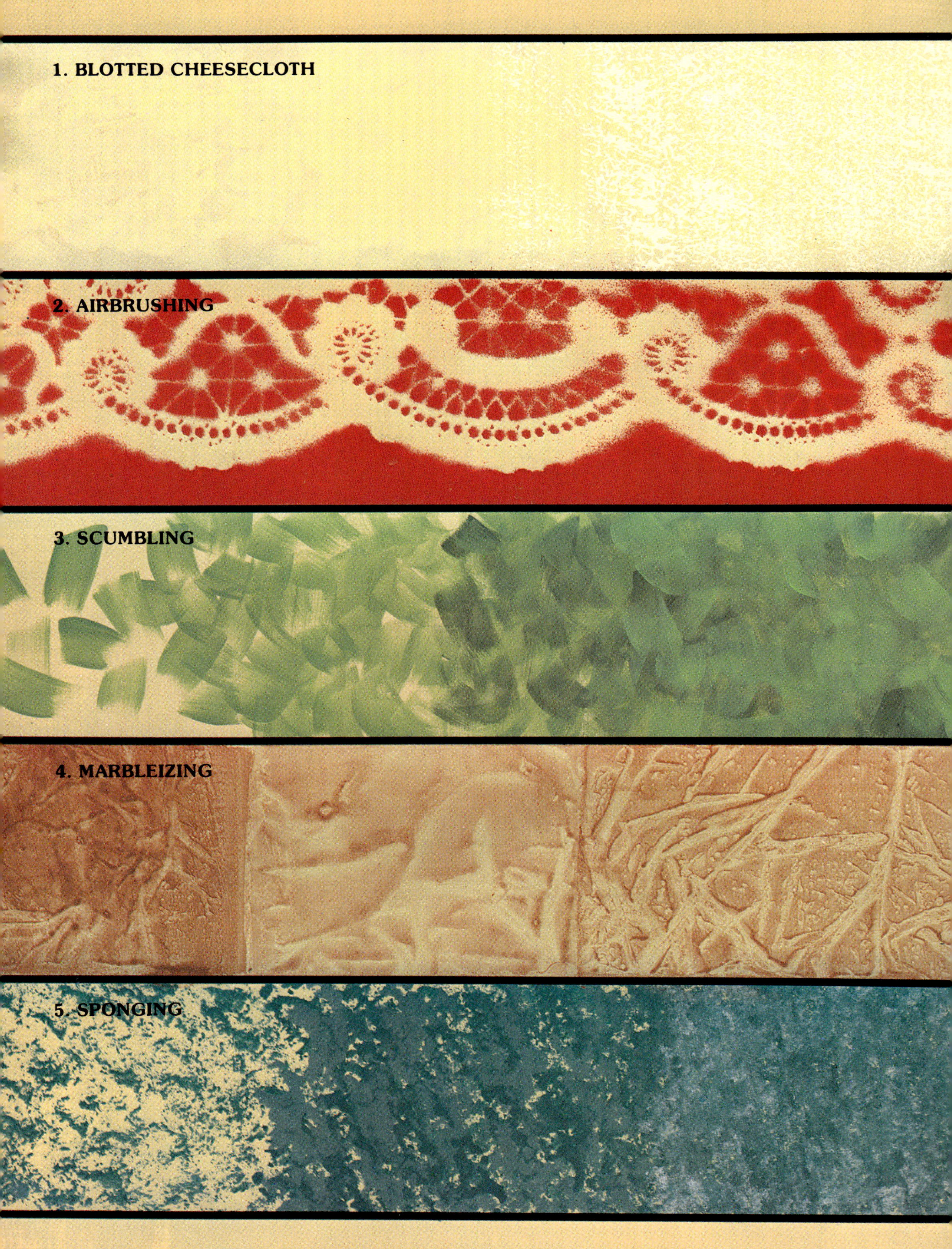
1. BLOTTED CHEESECLOTH
2. AIRBRUSHING
3. SCUMBLING
4. MARBLEIZING
5. SPONGING

SPECIAL EFFECTS

Five different techniques for creating special decorative effects are illustrated on the facing page.

1. **BLOTTED CHEESECLOTH.** With a large flat brush, dab on a layer of paint. Let dry. Add successive layers until coverage is adequate. Dry. Dip wadded cheesecloth into a lighter value of paint. Blot excess paint by pressing the cheesecloth several times onto a paper towel. Lightly dab the cheesecloth onto the previously painted area. This technique was used to suggest the fuzzy plush of the clown on the toybox (pages 56-61).

2. **AIRBRUSHING.** Use an airbrush and a stencil or mask (such as a paper doily) to create an interesting or unusual surface effect. Double-sided tape is ideal for holding the mask in place. Be sure to protect surrounding areas from over-spray. See the dollhouse (pages 78-83) for more on airbrushing.

3. **SCUMBLING.** This technique involves casual brush strokes going in various directions, often in several colors or values. In the sample pictured, light and dark values of a single color (green) were used. This technique was employed in decorating "Snap Dragon," (pages 46-47).

4. **MARBLEIZING.** Apply a basecoat. Dry. Select a color in a lighter or darker value than the basecoat and thin this color slightly with water (in the case of oils, use painting medium).

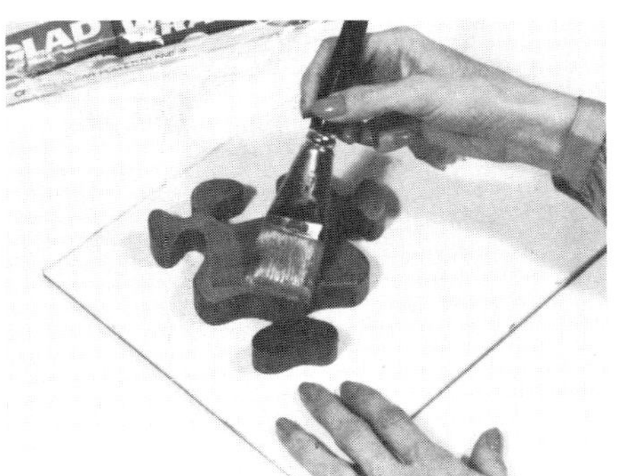

Apply the thinned paint quickly.

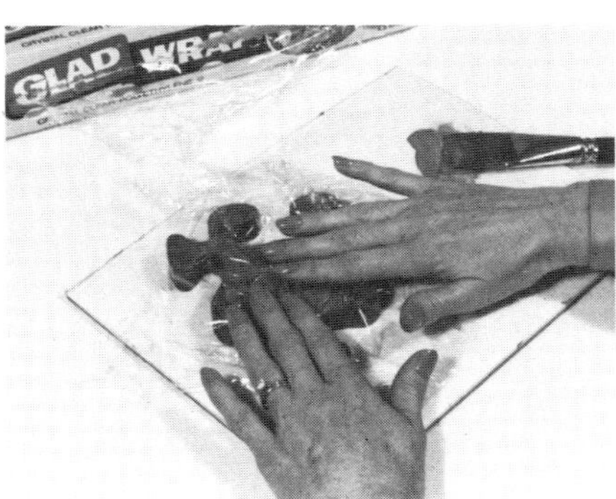

Cover immediately with wrinkled plastic wrap and smooth your hands across the plastic to "iron" in the wrinkles. Push wrinkles around with your fingers to create an interesting pattern.

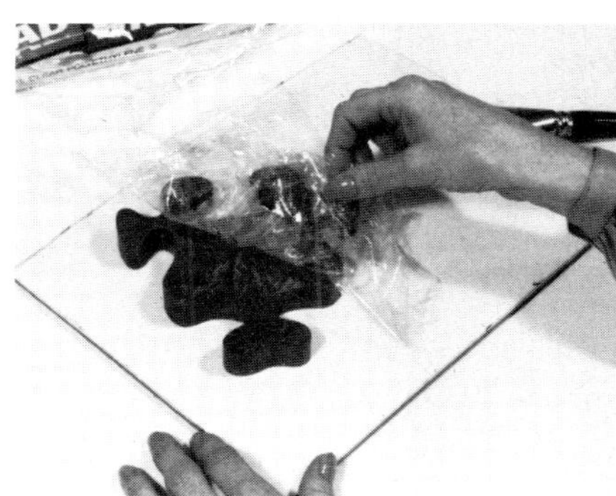

Remove plastic and admire the fun results.

In the color illustration, the example on the left had too little water so was too dry to be effective. The middle example was too wet. And the example on the far right was just right. Mr. Alley Gator (pages 45, 48) was marbleized.

5. **SPONGING.** For best results use a natural sponge. At first, one color is dabbed on, then a second one, and then others if desired. The Uni-stick Unicorn's handle was painted with 2 sponged colors (pages 48 and 50). The Crayonasaurus has a single sponged color (pages 42 and 48).

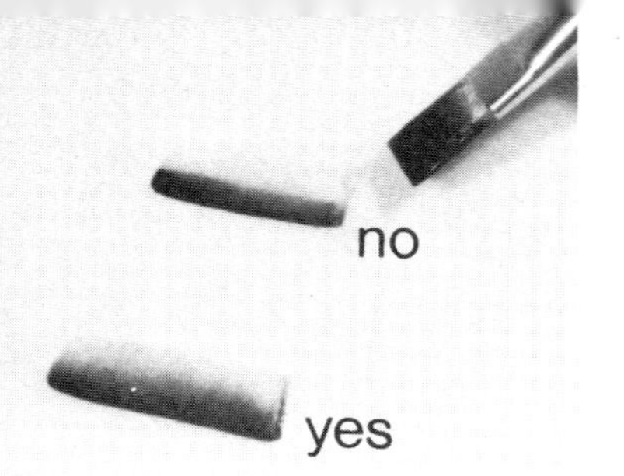

C. Sideloaded Stroke

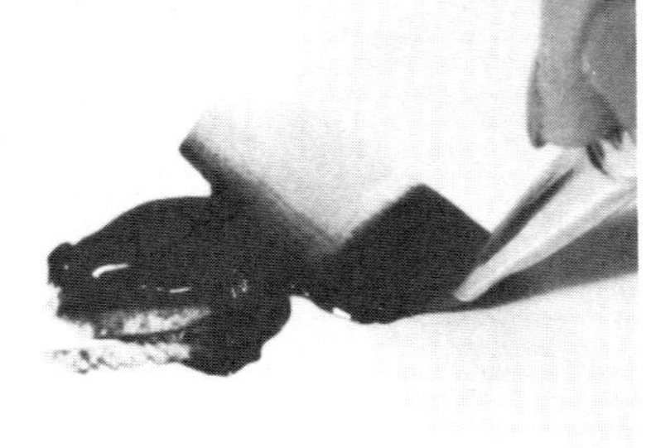

B. Sideload brush

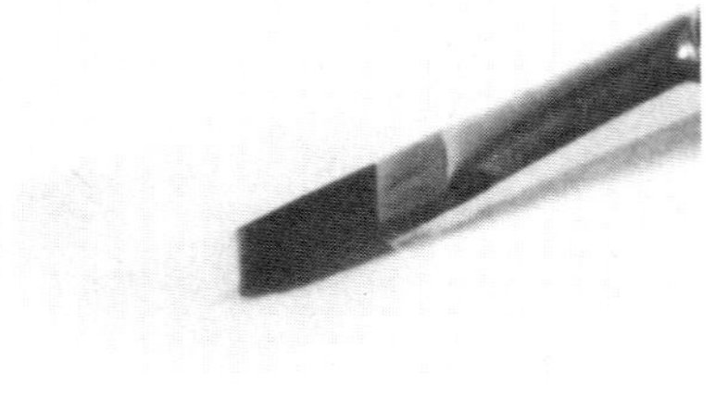

A. Blot on paper towel.

STROKES MADE WITH A FLAT BRUSH

SIDELOADING THE BRUSH

Blot excess water on towel. See figure A.

Slide edge of brush through edge of paint. See Figure B.

Blend stroke back and forth until color changes *gradually* from intense to pale. Note "yes" and "no" strokes in Figure C.

BROAD STROKE

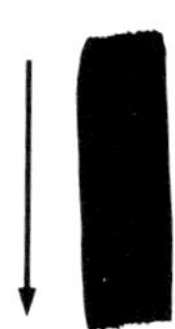

Pull a stroke using the full width of the flat brush.

See Figure D.

KNIFE EDGE

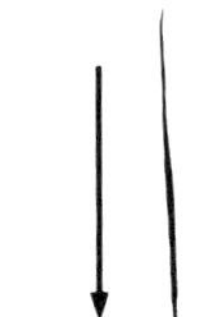

Hold flat brush perpendicular to surface.

Slide brush on the knife edge to form a thin stroke.

See Figure E.

LEAF STROKE

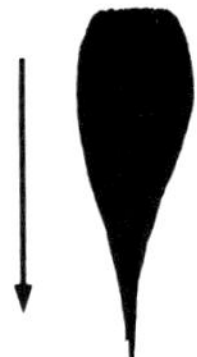

Begin this stroke like a broad stroke.

Gradually begin rotating the brush and releasing pressure to end the stroke on the knife edge. Stop. Lift off.

See Figures D and E.

CRESCENT STROKE

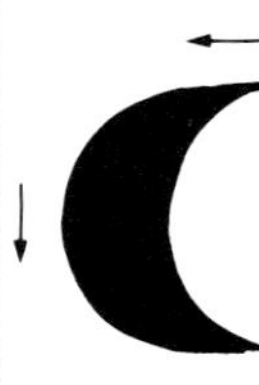

Begin on the knife edge.

Pull, apply gradual pressure.

Apply greatest pressure.

Begin releasing pressure.

Slide on knife edge. Stop. Lift off.

See Figure F.

MODIFIED CRESCENT

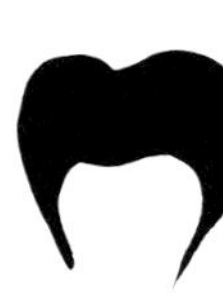

Form this stroke like the crescent stroke except for a slight release of pressure in the center. Re-apply pressure and complete the crescent.

See Figure G.

"S" STROKE

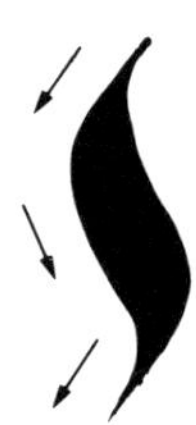

Slide on knife edge, applying gradual pressure.

Reverse directions, applying more pressure.

Release pressure and reverse directions.

Slide on knife edge. Stop. Lift off. See Figure H.

CIRCLE STROKE

It's easiest to begin this stroke a little out of control in order to have greater control at the end. Note in Figures I through L the changing positions of hand, fingers, and brush as indicated by the position of the flag.

D. Broad Stroke

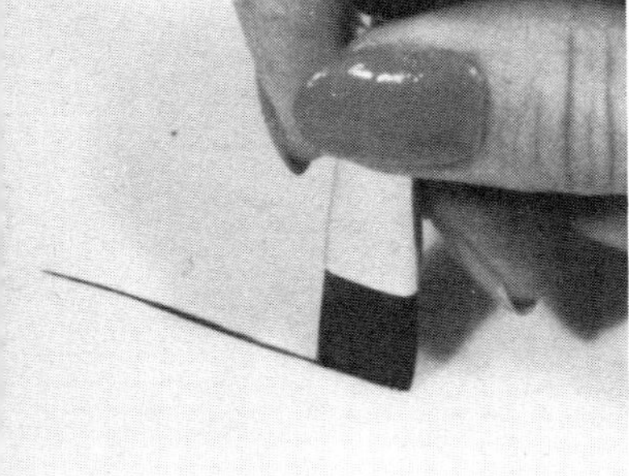

E. Knife Stroke

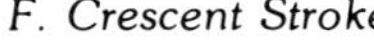

F. Crescent Stroke

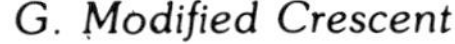

G. Modified Crescent

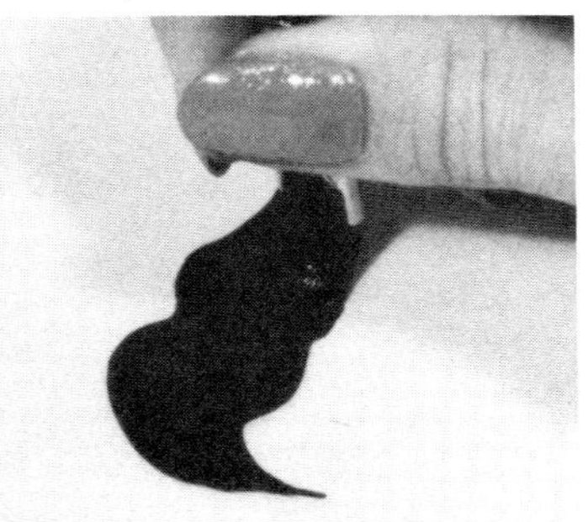

H. "S" Stroke

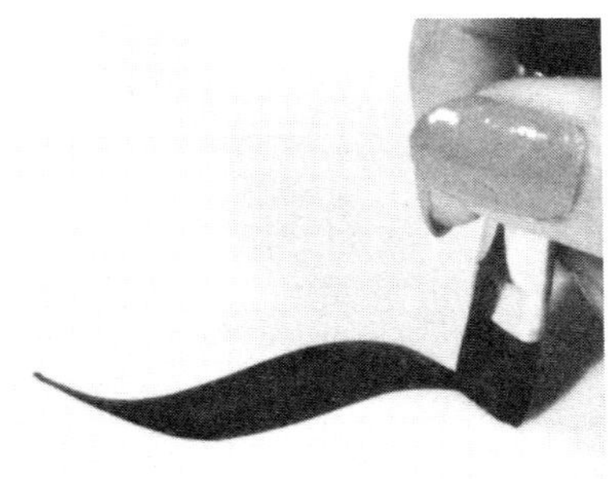

I. Circle Stroke - beginning

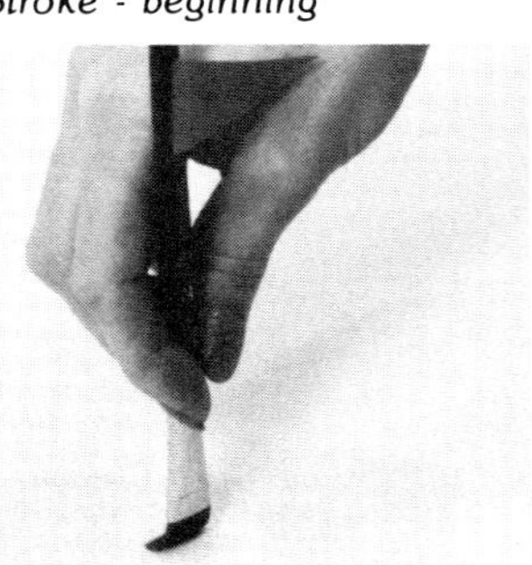

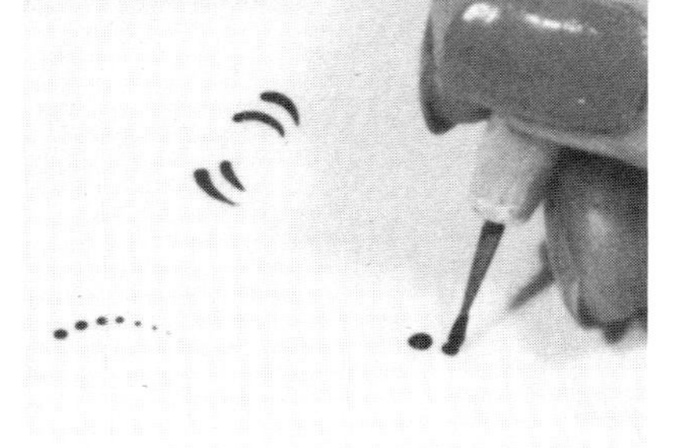

R. *Dots*

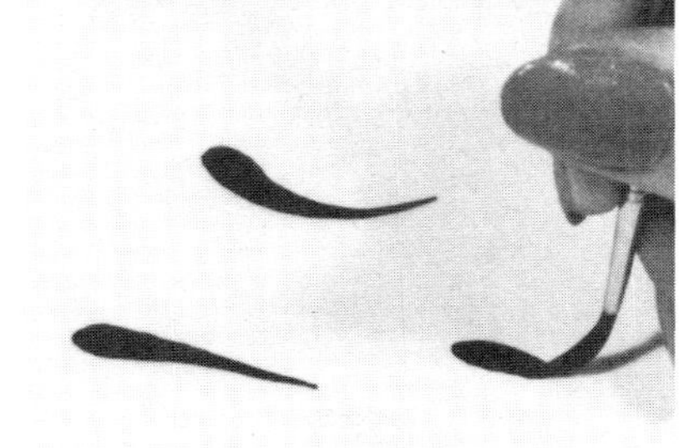

Q. *Comma Stroke*

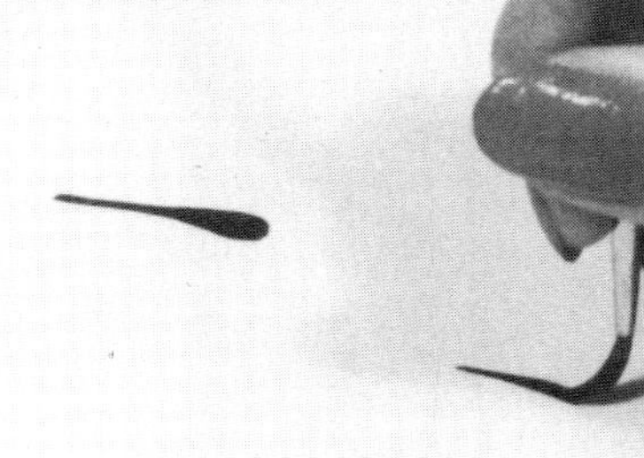

P. *Teardrop Stroke*

STROKES MADE WITH A LINER OR ROUND BRUSH

COMMA Press down and pause. Pull; gradually release pressure. Continue releasing pressure. Slow down; permit hairs to return to point. Lift off. See Figure Q. 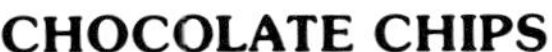	**TEARDROP** Point and pull. Pull, applying gradual pressure. Continue pulling and pressing. Press. Stop. Lift straight up. Variation: Drag tip of brush to form curlycue. See Figure P.
CHOCOLATE CHIPS Press down a "glob." Flick tip of brush thru top of blob, forming a point. This stroke works best if done quickly. See Figure N.	**DOTS** 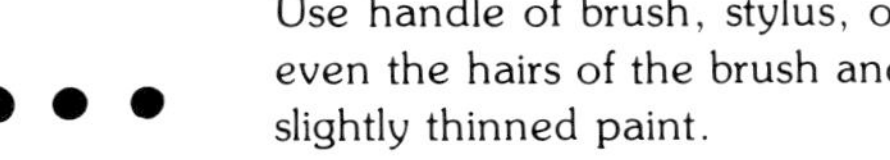 Use handle of brush, stylus, or even the hairs of the brush and slightly thinned paint. Dots painted in succession decrease in size. For uniform dot size, re-load for each dot. See Figure R.
LINE WORK 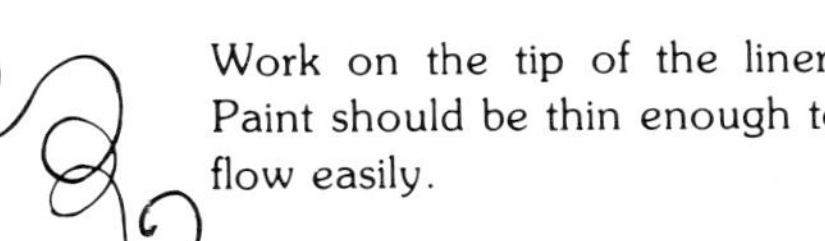 Work on the tip of the liner. Paint should be thin enough to flow easily. See Figure M. 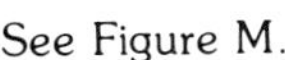	**FILL-INS**  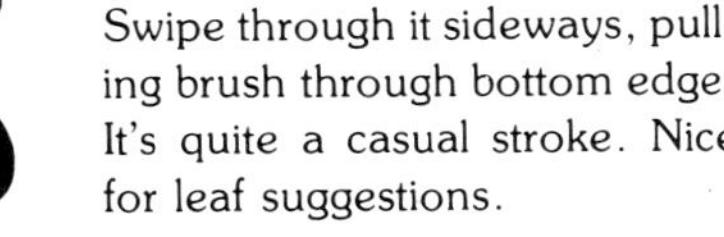 Press down a "glob." Swipe through it sideways, pulling brush through bottom edge. It's quite a casual stroke. Nice for leaf suggestions. See Figure O.
"S" STROKE 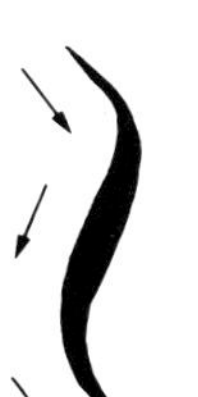 Point Pull, gradual pressure Reverse direction, more pressure Reverse direction, gradually release pressure. Pull. Point. Stop. Lift off. See Figure H.	**DIAMOND, CRESCENT, MODIFIED CRESCENT**  These strokes are made with the same pressure and release as the "S" stroke. See Figures F and G.  

O. *Fill-ins*

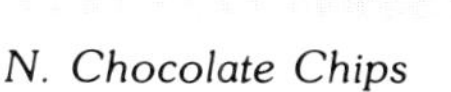

N. *Chocolate Chips*

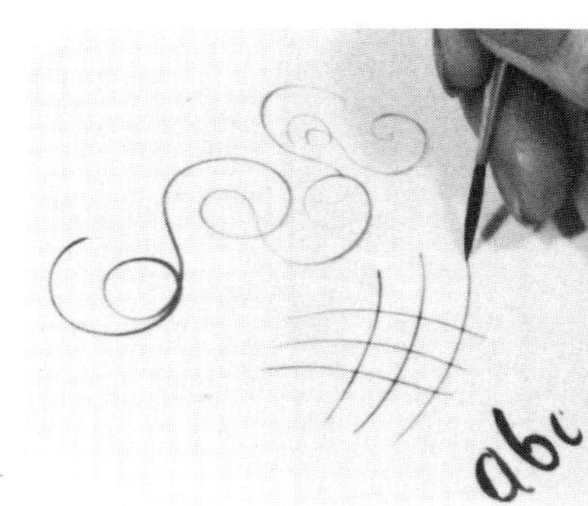

M. *Line Work*

J. *Circle Stroke - first quarter*

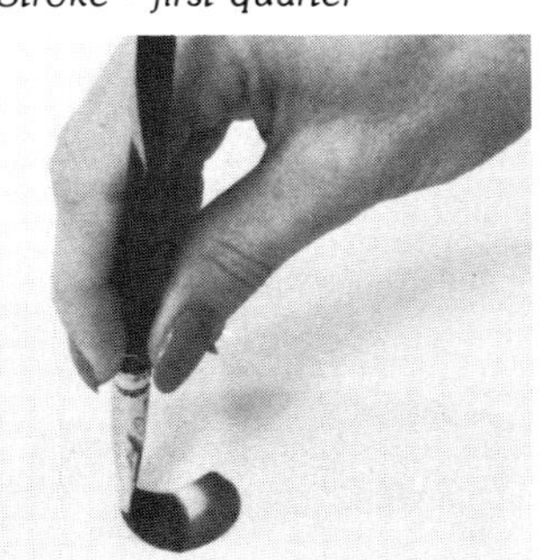

K. *Circle Stroke - first half*

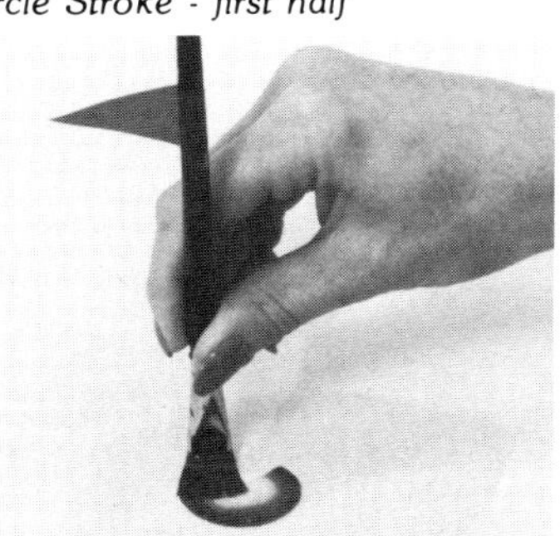

L. *Circle Stroke - completed*

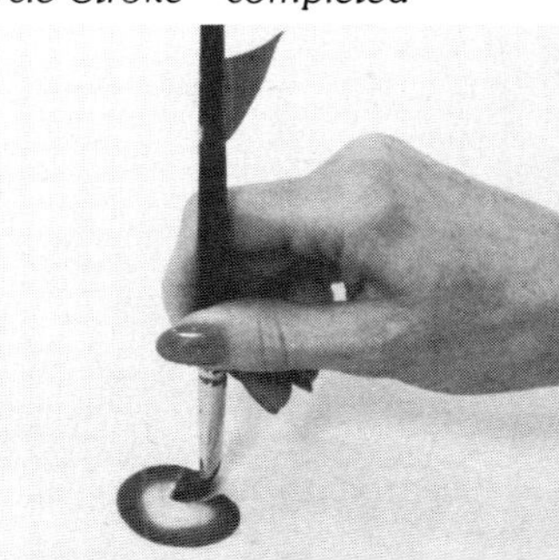

COLOR MIXING ON THE RUN

(A quickie lesson for when the urge to create - right now - is there, but the confidence of understanding color mixing and theory is not.)

The properties of color:

HUE - the name of a color. Is it red, green, orange?

VALUE - a color's relation to white or black or the greys in between. Is it light or dark?

INTENSITY - the saturation or pureness of color; the extent to which it is free from any other colorant. Is it bright or dull?

TEMPERATURE - an artistic, not a physical property. Warm colors (reds, oranges, yellows) appear to advance; cool colors (greens, blues, violets) appear to recede. Is it warm or cool?

Having a comfortable understanding of the properties of color will facilitate the ease with which you are able to develop your own color schemes.

PRIMARY COLORS: red, blue, yellow. All other colors can be mixed from these primary colors, and their relationship to one another can be readily understood by means of a **color wheel.**

SECONDARY COLORS: orange, green, violet. These colors are obtained by mixing together any two primary colors.

INTERMEDIARY COLORS: yellow-green, blue-green, blue-violet, red-violet, red-orange, yellow orange. These colors are obtained by mixing together a primary and a secondary color.

TERTIARY COLORS: citron, russet, olive. These colors are achieved by mixing any two secondary colors or, in actuality, all three primaries.

COMPLEMENTARY COLORS: are located diametrically opposite one another on the color wheel. Therefore the complement of a warm color (red) is a cool color (green). The effect of mixing a color with its complement is to dull, grey, or neutralize that color (i.e. reduce the intensity).

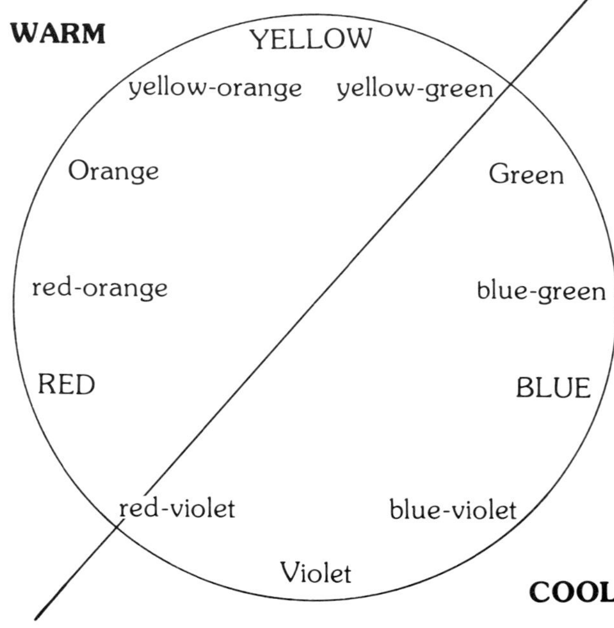

For more aid in understanding color theory and mixing refer to *There's A Rainbow In My Paintbox*, ©Jackie Shaw, 1977.

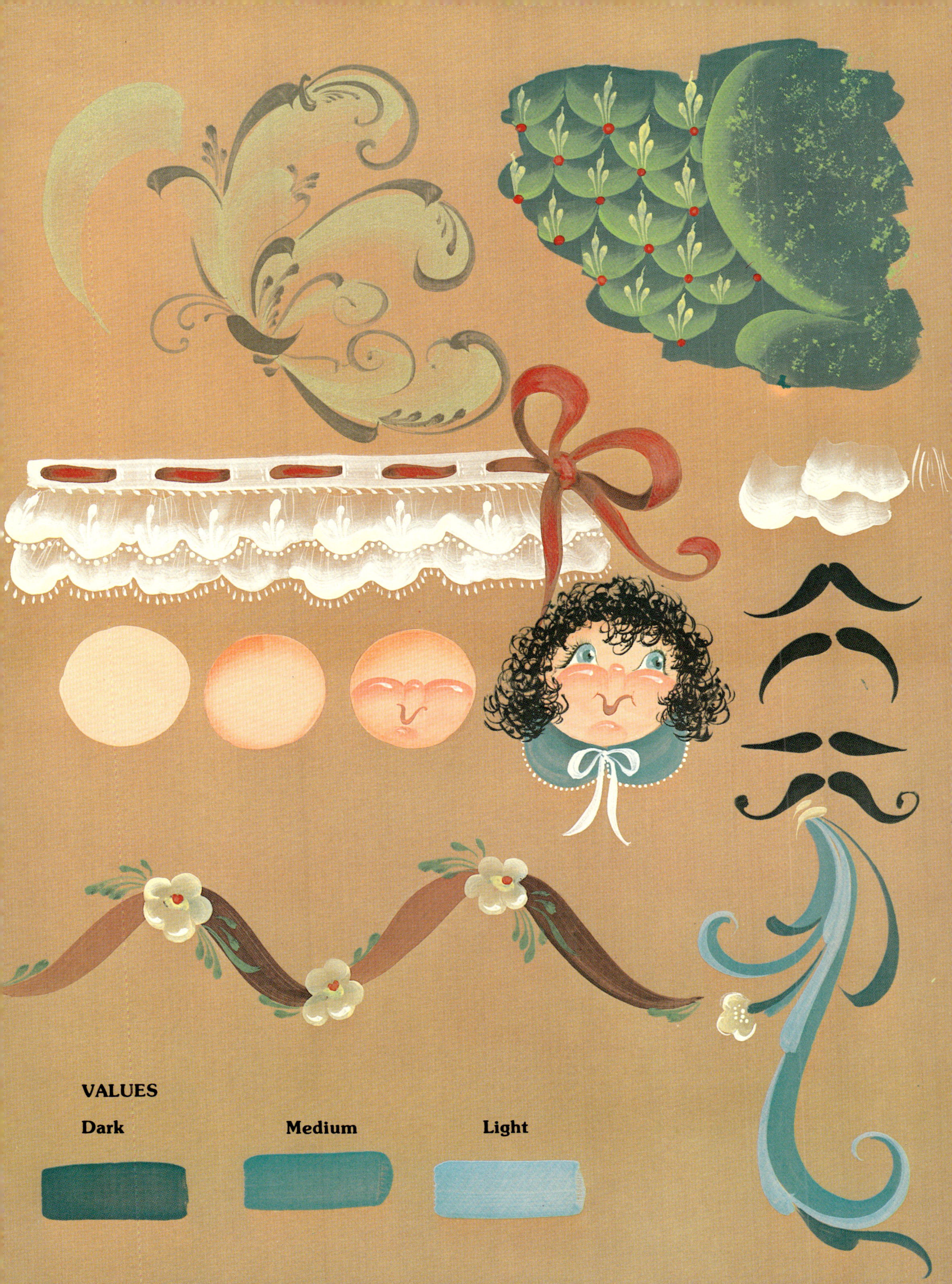
VALUES
Dark
Medium
Light

Adding white to **TINT** any color raises its value (lightness); adding black to **SHADE** reduces its value (darkness).

In mixing colors, always begin with the weaker or lighter color and gradually add the darker or stronger one to it.

COLOR SCHEMES:

MONOCHROMATIC - tints and shades of a single hue (i.e. blue).

ANALOGOUS - two to five colors which lie side by side on the color wheel (i.e. yellow, orange, red)

COMPLEMENTARY - two colors diametrically opposed on the color wheel (i.e. red, green)

SPLIT COMPLEMENTARY - three colors, including the key color and the two colors on either side of the key color's complement (i.e. yellow, red-violet, blue-violet)

TRIADIC - any three colors equidistant from one another on the color wheel (i.e. red, yellow, blue)

It has been quite apparent in teaching seminars across the country that one of the most troublesome areas to students in freehand designing is the selection of color schemes that work. Until such time as you have developed confidence in your understanding of color mixing and theory there are several aids which will help you over this hurdle:

1. Study wallpaper and upholstery sample books for color schemes which appeal to you. Borrow these books if possible and spend a day mixing color cards to match the samples. Keep these on file for future reference. You will be surprised at how great an inspiration the color cards will be.

2. Study catalogs, and fabric and linen departments. Save clippings of magazine ads and illustrations which have colors that please you.

3. Scrutinize your own wardrobe. What colors do you select to coordinate an outfit? You may know more about color theory than you give yourself credit for, even if you are unable to use all the proper terminology.

4. After basecoating a background, lay a piece of clear acetate over the project (plastic wrap or glass will do in a pinch). Test colors on the acetate to see how well they relate to the chosen background color.

5. In addition to basecoating the project, also paint a couple of pieces of light cardboard (from stockings, shirts, back of tablets, etc.) in the same color. Test your color scheme directly on the painted cardboard background.

6. Keep a notebook with photos of the projects you paint and a sample of the colors used.

7. When creating a color scheme, be sure that you repeat each color used in at least three places. This will prevent any one color from standing blatantly out from the others.

8. Spend more time familiarizing yourself with color values and intensities; worry less about color names. Once you are able to distinguish values (lights and darks) in paintings you will be much more adept at creating your own colorful interpretations. For instance, if you like the way a particular artist has rendered a bunch of purple grapes in a painting, but you actually prefer green grapes, you can learn to paint green grapes by concentrating on the placement of color values. Learn to study, also, the use of complementary colors in suggesting depth, transparency, reflections. Look for *all* the colors used in those purple grapes. *The whole secret to learning to paint with colors is learning first to **see** color.* Purple grapes are not just purple. Their color is affected by all the colors which surround them, the light in which they are seen, their varying degrees of ripeness, and so on. *Learn to look and see - not only that which you know, but that which is.*

The color schemes and combinations listed for each project are merely suggestions. Do not feel bound by them. Use them simply as starting points.

FREEHANDING - BUILDING UP ONE'S NERVE

If you have never painted, or if you have been accustomed only to painting with patterns, the very thought of freehanding can be unnerving. There are ways of tricking yourself into doing it.

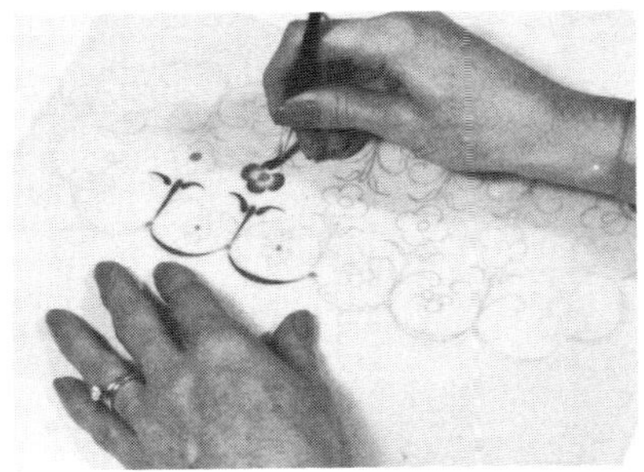

1. Practice repeatedly with paint on tracing paper which is initially placed over a design you would like to paint. Don't worry about staying precisely within, or completely filling, the pattern lines. Just concentrate on the type and placement of brush strokes. Later, practice the same design by merely *looking* at the pattern.

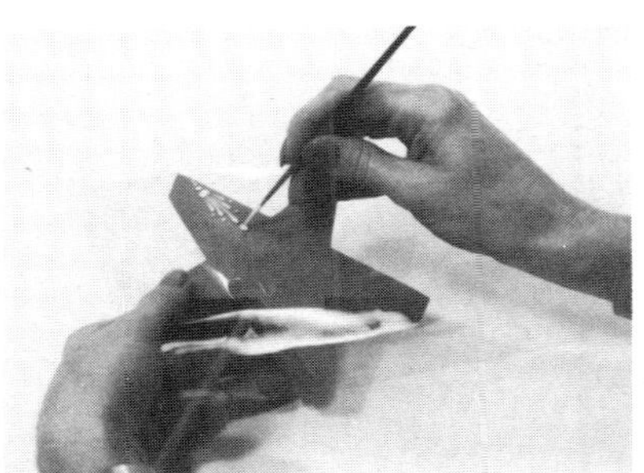

2. Place a piece of acetate on your project. Using paint, work out your designs on the acetate. This aid is ideal even for more advanced "freehanders," as it enables one to test out a color or element of design to see how it will fit into the design already in progress.

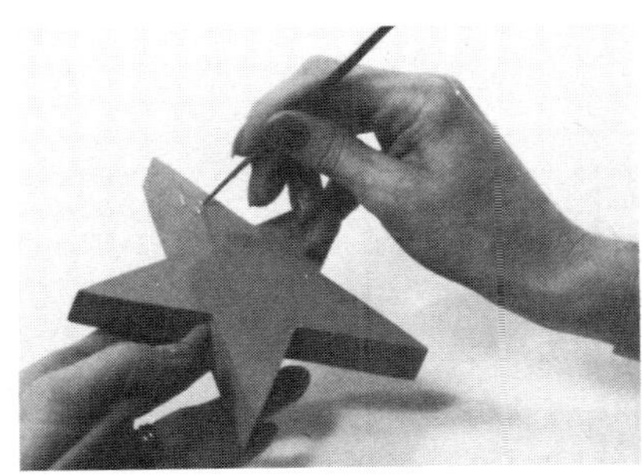

3. Practice with just plain water directly on the project. You will not be able to see the results of watered brush strokes for very long, but that is O.K. The purpose of this exercise is to give you the feel of working on the object. This is especially beneficial when you are contemplating (but dreading) painting a long scroll or doing liner work. Practice a few times with just water in your brush to build your confidence. Then without letting the worry centers of your brain know what you are up to, sneak a little paint in your brush and let loose. If you just will not worry about it, you will be surprised at how much easier it will be.

Some other tips which you might find helpful include:

Color combinations, patterns, and step-by-step painting procedures are given for each project. BUT - they are only suggestions. There are as many different ways of painting each toy as there are people who would paint them. Do not stifle your own potential creativity by rigidly following everything as laid out for you in the book. The ideas and techniques are presented to help you form a foundation on which to develop your own style.

Even if you do not plan to paint a particular project, scan the directions for ideas or techniques you might be able to adapt to other projects.

Keep tails and pull strings clean and unpainted by wrapping them with masking tape a couple of inches from the surface to be painted.

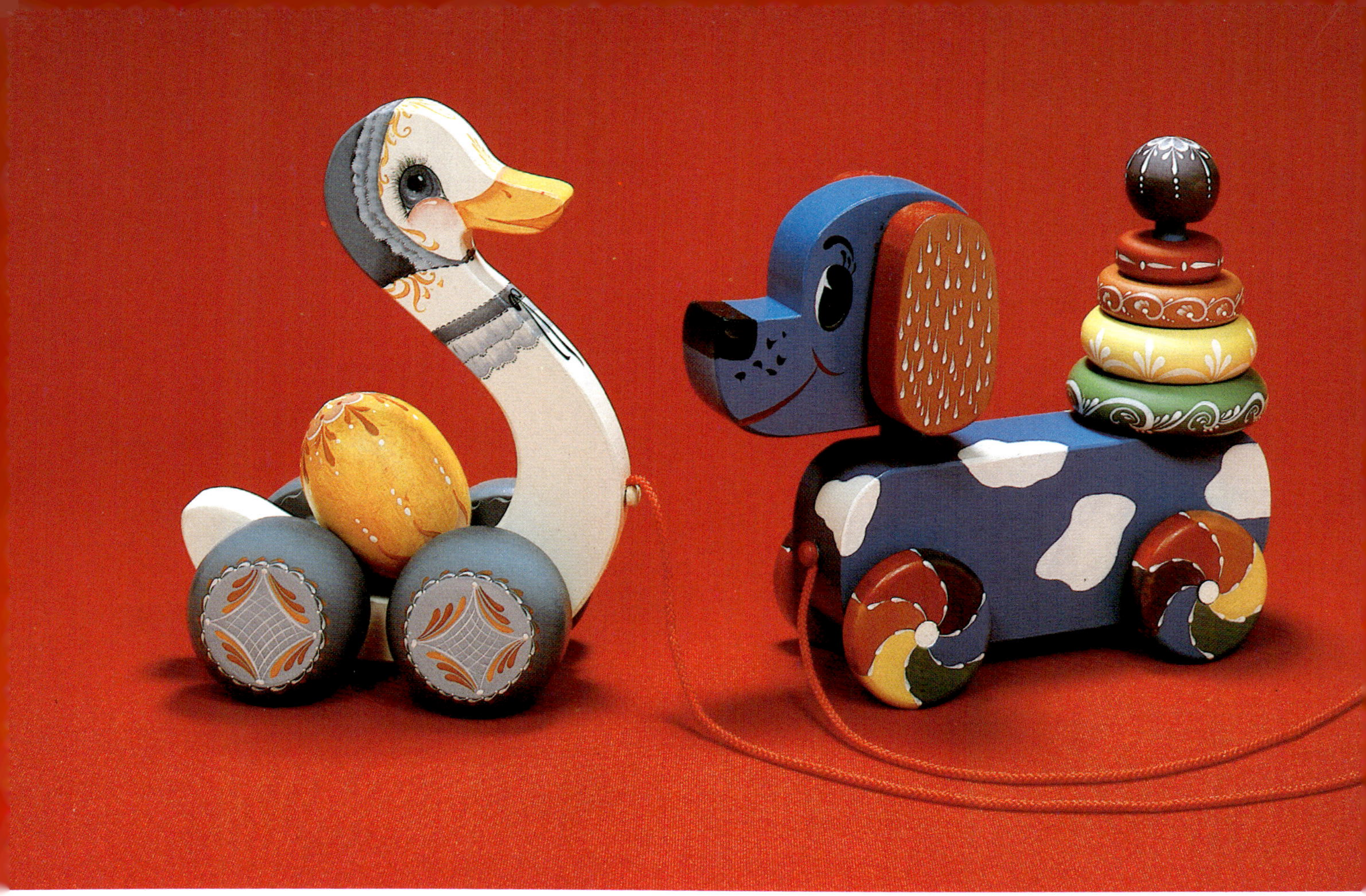

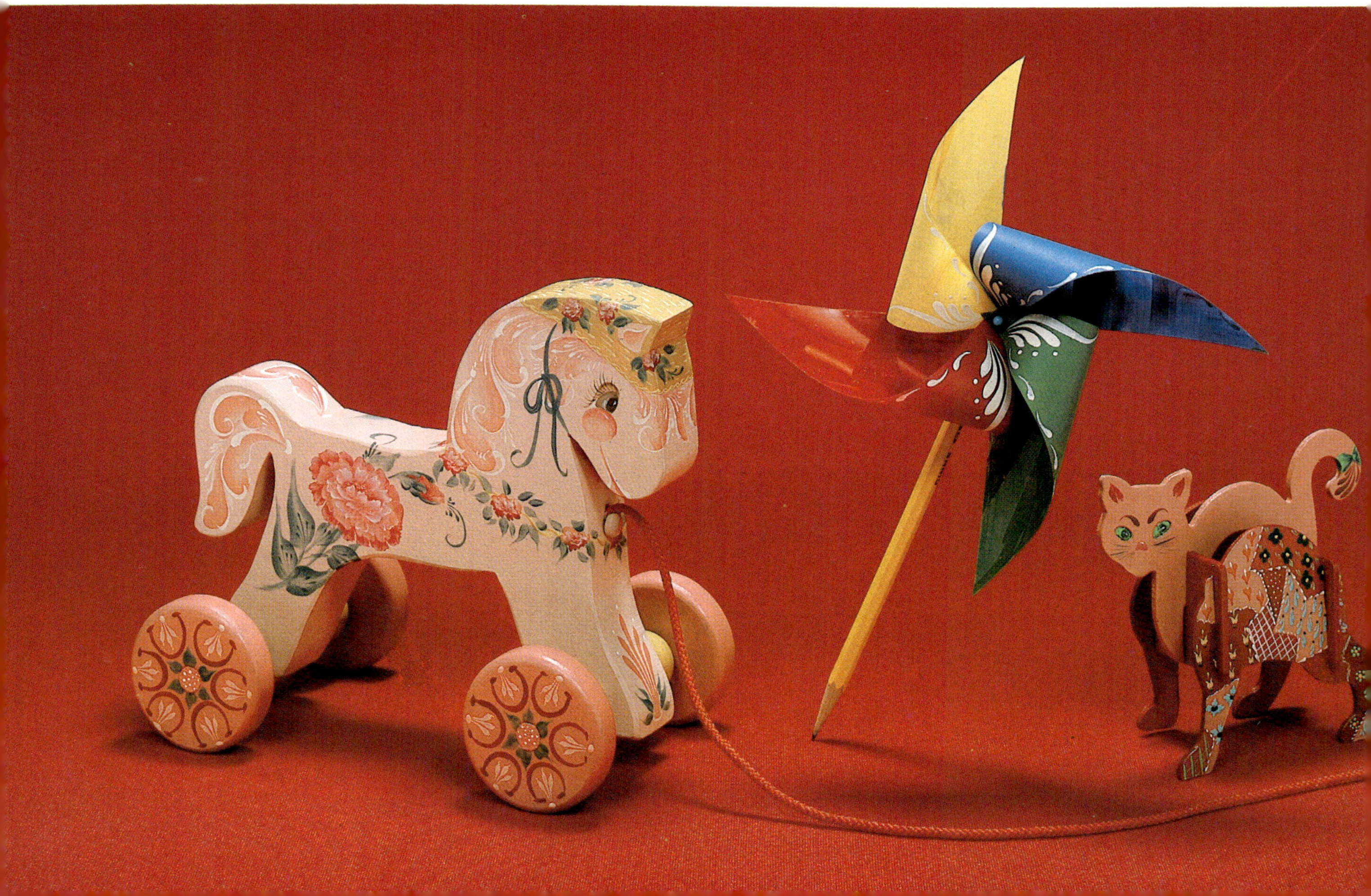

Do not feel thwarted by the size or complexity of a project. Concentrate on one element at a time (such as wheels, hat, clothing). Gradually the piece will emerge fully decorated. You can insure that its parts will relate as a total unit if you carry color theme and design elements throughout.

It is easiest to paint the toys unassembled (particularly for the basecoating). Before designing, however, be sure you know where one piece overlaps another (such as wheels on legs) so you do not end up with a vital portion of your design obscured by an overlapping piece.

Color mixtures are often used throughout this book. When you encounter something such as Norsk Blue + Lichen Grey + Old Parchment, the "+" tells you to mix everything together. The sequence of the colors listed in the paint combination tells you which color is predominant. In the blue mixture above, use more Norsk Blue, less Lichen Grey, and just a little Old Parchment. Had the combinations been listed in reverse order, the resulting mixture would have been a very light grey with just a hint of blue.

When you do mix colors and try to match them to the ones in the book, make yourself feel better by knowing that a perfect match is nearly impossible. Remember that you are three processes away from the original color sample: color photography, color separations, and color printing.

If you are using acrylic paints, keep in mind that as acrylic dries, it loses its glow or sheen. Life will return to your paint with a coat of varnish. To see just how much life is missing from the dried, unvarnished acrylic, brush water across it. The same brightness that is reflected through the water will return once the item is varnished.

Wear old clothes. Do not clutter your mind with worry about keeping you or your area clean while you work. That effort disrupts the creative flow. If you tend to be messy, spread newspapers, or a drop cloth. A disposable bed pad (similar to, but larger and thinner than, disposable diapers) makes an ideal lap cloth. It "protects" your old painting clothes and is great for always having a wipe cloth handy. (One of my art professors *required* that we wear old clothes to class so we could wipe dirty brushes and hands readily, without searching for a cloth, while in the broiling passion of creativity.)

Your creativity is limited only by your unwillingness to expand your horizons, to break out of safe patterns of behavior. Therefore:

BE CURIOUS; expand your awareness.

BE WARY of stalemating. Experiment with new methods and fresh viewpoints.

BE OBSERVANT; do not just look. Learn to *see*.

BE OPEN MINDED and receptive.

BE DARING; do not let fear of failure keep you locked in a safe, secure mold.

BE SELF-CONFIDENT; work with authority. Remember artistic license.

BE-GIN!

For an in-depth coverage of freehanding ideas, borders, flowers and leaves, and designing techniques, also refer to *Freehanding With Jackie,* ©1980, and *Rock 'N Tole,* ©1981.

SUE FLÉ (The Egg Scrambler)

COLORS

Ivory	Adobe
Cosmos Blue	Hallingdal Red
Midnight	Old Parchment
Butter Yellow	Black

PROCEDURE

Basecoat the entire body with Ivory, the centers of the wheels with a mixture of Cosmos Blue + Ivory, and the sides and backs of the wheels with Cosmos Blue.

Try sketching the following features on Sue Flé without resorting to tracing the pattern.

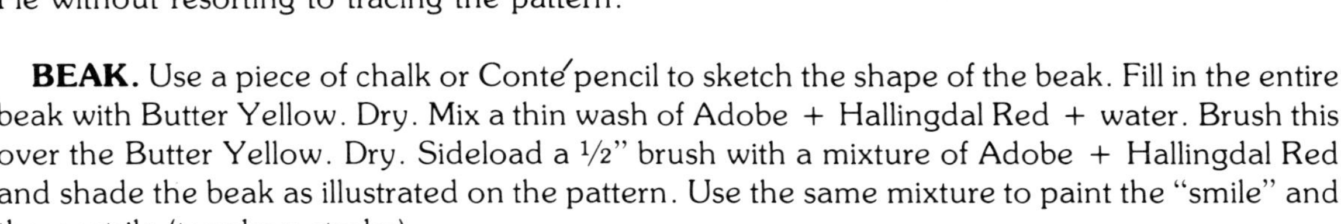

BEAK. Use a piece of chalk or Conté pencil to sketch the shape of the beak. Fill in the entire beak with Butter Yellow. Dry. Mix a thin wash of Adobe + Hallingdal Red + water. Brush this over the Butter Yellow. Dry. Sideload a ½" brush with a mixture of Adobe + Hallingdal Red and shade the beak as illustrated on the pattern. Use the same mixture to paint the "smile" and the nostrils (teardrop stroke).

CHEEK. Sideload a mixture of Adobe + Old Parchment into a #10 or #12 flat brush. Form a slightly rounded crescent stroke extending from the beak approximately ¾". Softly blend the bottom edge to fade out. Add an Ivory comma stroke or teardrop highlight.

EYE. With chalk, draw a horseshoe-shaped outline the width of the cheek and resting just above it. If you have basecoated your goose with Ivory, the eye area will already be white as needed. If you painted the goose any other color, fill in the horseshoe-shaped area with Ivory. Paint a large circle (the iris) in a medium value (Cosmos Blue). Paint a smaller circle (the pupil) in a dark value (Midnight). Paint thin lines radiating from the pupil across the iris a medium light value (Cosmos Blue + Old Parchment). Add a dark value wash (Midnight) above the iris, and a light value wash (Cosmos Blue + Old Parchment) below the iris. Make the eye sparkle by adding a strong highlight (Ivory) near the top of the pupil, and lesser highlights (Ivory thinned with water) near the bottom of the pupil and within the light wash area on the iris. Outline the eye and paint eyelashes with a dark value (Midnight or Black) and a #2 liner. See enlarged full color step-by-step illustration of painting of eye on page 56.

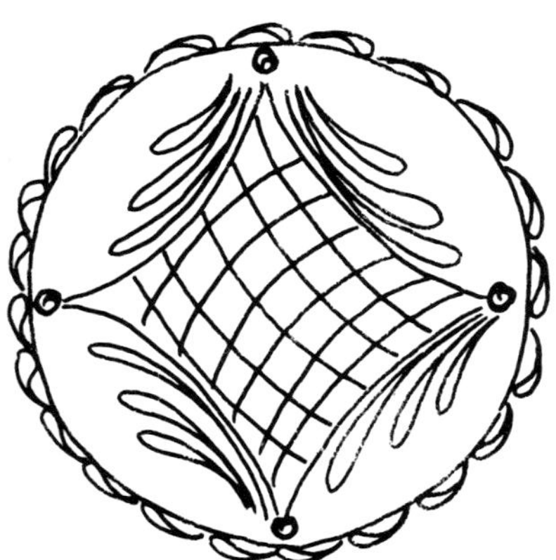

BONNET. Use a 1/2" flat brush to fashion a fancy bonnet for Sue Flé. There's no need to trace a pattern on. Just experiment a little with your brush and water. You may decide to give her a wide brimmed straw hat, a little tam with a feather, a pillbox with a veil, or perhaps just a big billowy bow. Whatever you decide, plunge in with confidence and paint it with authority. Besides, who has ever seen a goose parading with an egg on her back and bonnet on her beam? However your creation may turn out,

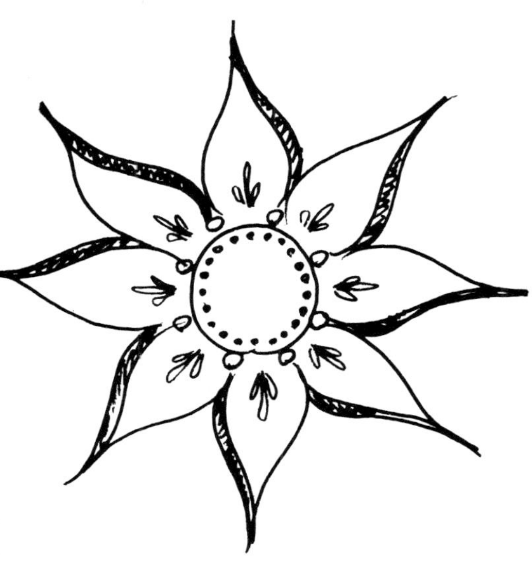

it will be a success because of its uniqueness. Once her bonnet is in place, your little goose will begin to radiate personality. Sou Flé's bonnet was painted Cosmos Blue with a 1½" brush. Midnight shading and stitching was added along the bottom. Two rows of lace (Cosmos Blue + Ivory) trim the bonnet. Small Ivory dots and gathering lines add interest to the lace. Delicate Midnight shading, done with a sideloaded wash in a #4 or #6 flat brush, helps add dimension. See full color illustration of painting lace on page 15.

HAIR. Sou Flé's wispy hair is styled with "C" and "S" curves and scrolls. And only her hair dresser knows for sure that her hair color is a mixture of Hallingdal Red + Butter Yellow. Another time, Sou Flé may decide to try bangs and a page boy, or ponytails or pigtails. And while she's at it, she may just become a brunette or a redhead. She's bold and loves to experiment - keeps life exciting that way. Since she's so willing, why don't you be as daring. As likely as not, you'll create a coiffure even more to her (and your) liking than her original hair dresser did. Be sure to add GOOSE FEATHERS above her beak and on her tail!

LACE COLLAR. Two layers of lace were painted with a ½" brush and a mixture of Cosmos Blue + Ivory. A Cosmos Blue band tops off the lace. Detail dots and teardrop strokes were added with a #2 liner and Cosmos Blue. A Midnight bow completes the collar. You might decide to replace the lace with a necklace, cameo, or victorian choker. Or how about a plaid muffler or a fringed shawl? *Let your imagination wander. Only wonderful things can happen.*

WHEELS. Embellish the wheels with a profusion of strokes using any of the colors already used in the decoration of the goose.

GOLDEN EGG. Here is another opportunity to let your creative impulses surge. First of all, do something fun to basecoat the egg - marbleizing, sponging, etc. Sou Flé's egg was basecoated with Butter Yellow. Then a thin wash of Hallingdal Red was applied. This step must be done with a large brush, thin paint, and quickly to avoid overlapping streaks. (Press a push pin into one end of the egg to provide a "handle.") Dry. Use chalk or Conté pencil to divide the egg into quarters lengthwise. You may also want to make some divisions crosswise. Now doodle, doodle, doodle. The colors used in decorating Sou Flé's egg were Hallingdal Red, Ivory, Adobe + Old Parchment.

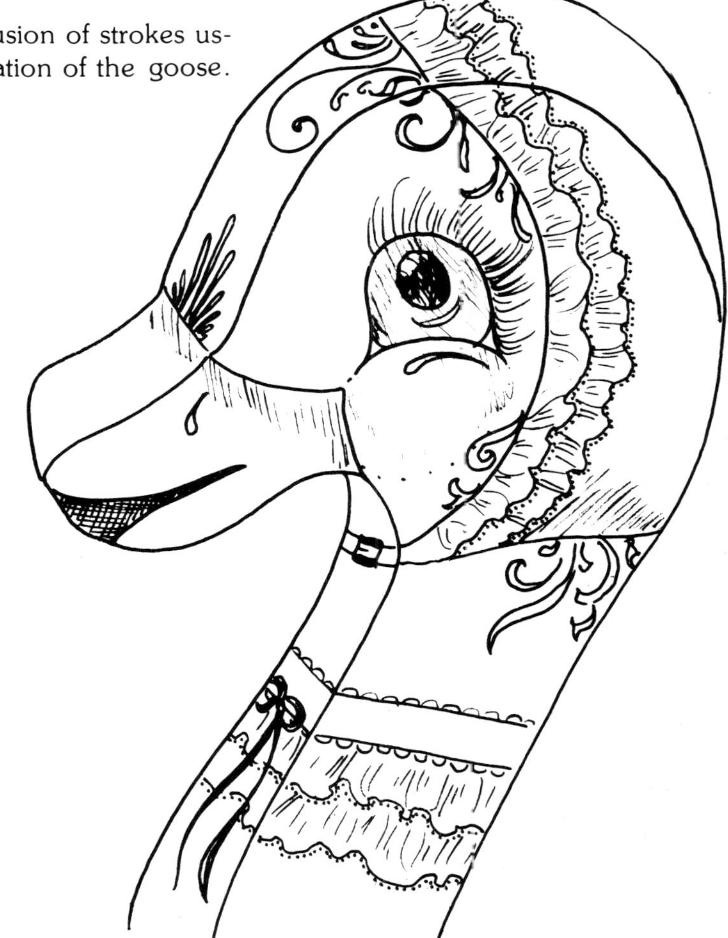

Place the egg on her back, pull her string, and presto! Instant scrambled wooden egg. (The wheels cause the egg to turn over and over as Sue Flé waddles along). She's waddled off to page 18 to appear in all her glory.

PAINTING THE LARGE PEONY

1. Draw an ellipse with chalk. Divide it into thirds. See facing page.

2. With short, choppy strokes, fill in the lower two-thirds of the ellipse with the *dark* value.

3. Use a #10 flat brush to paint *dark* value petals around the outside edge of the lower two-thirds.

4. With the same brush, paint *medium* value petals around the remaining one-third of the top of ellipse. Fill in the top of the ellipse with the medium value. Let all paint dry before proceeding.

5. Still using the #10 flat brush and the *medium* value, paint a second row of petals on the bottow two-thirds.

6. Lighten the medium value slightly (*light medium)* and add a second row of petals to the top one-third.

7. Using the same value from step #6, add a third row of petals to the lower two-thirds.

8. Use a *light* value now and switch to a #6 flat brush to paint the inner small petals.

9. Continue adding more small, *lighter* value petals to the center until the ellipse is filled. Permit a little of the dark basecoat to show through the center.

10. Sideload a #6 flat brush with the very lightest value and apply a very thin wash to the edges of most of the petals. Begin in the center to provide the sharpest highlight accents there. Permit the highlights to fade quite pale on the larger outside petals by adding more and more water.

11. Paint the large and small peony leaves by sideloading the brush (#12 flat for large leaves and #2 flat for small leaves) with a green of your choice. Each leaf consists of two strokes. See illustration.

PAINTING THE SMALL PEONY

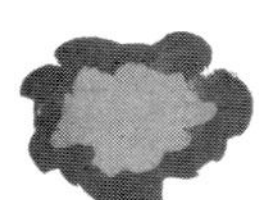

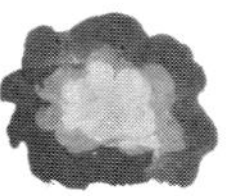

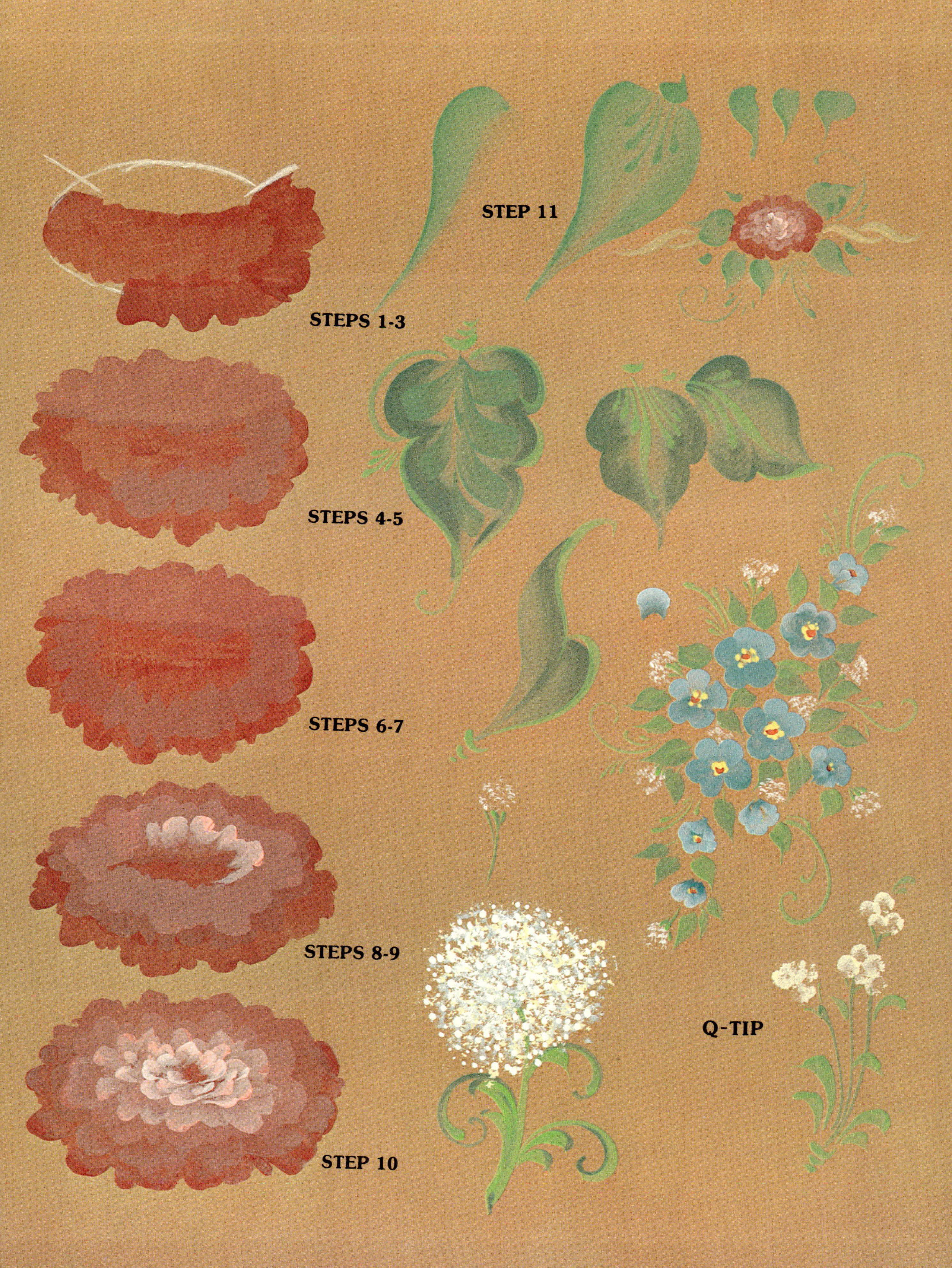
STEP 11
STEPS 1-3
STEPS 4-5
STEPS 6-7
STEPS 8-9
STEP 10
Q-TIP

P´Ony

COLORS

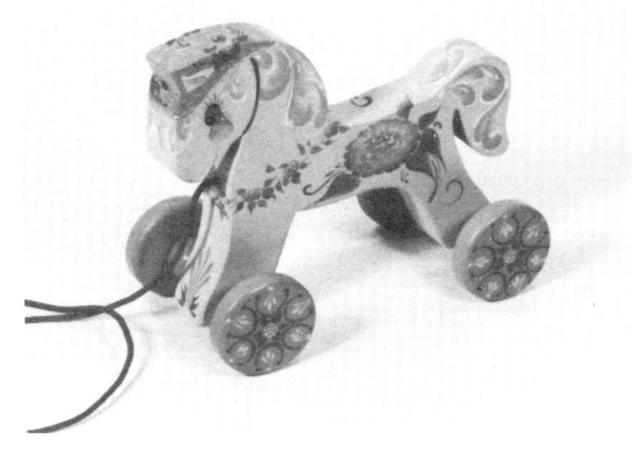

Pink Angel	Salem Green
Fiesta Pink	Tompte Red
Spice Tan	Autumn Brown
Maple Sugar	Burnt Umber
Pineapple	Ivory

PROCEDURE

Basecoat P´Ony as follows:

Pink Angel - body
Fiesta Pink - wheels
Spice Tan - spacers between wheels and body

As usual, paint the face first. It is much more fun to work on the toys when their grins and sparkling eyes beam approval at your every decorative effort.

CHEEKS. It is helpful to paint the cheeks first. This gives you a convenient place to put the eyes. Sideload a #6 flat brush with Fiesta Pink. Paint a circle, having the predominance of color at the top. Dry. Shade the top of the cheek with a thin wash of Tompte Red. Add an Ivory highlight.

EYES. With chalk, sketch a horseshoe shape above and just resting on the cheek. Fill in the area with Ivory. Paint the iris Autumn Brown, and the pupil Burnt Umber. Add Ivory highlights. To paint the eyelid, sideload a #2 flat brush with Burnt Umber. Begin at the top of the eye with the intense color to the top of the brush. Pull an "S" stroke down the back edge of the eye. Add Burnt Umber lashes with a #2 liner. (See illustration).

MOUTH. Paint a large (from cheek to cheek) grin in Fiesta Pink shaded with Tompte Red. Long thin Ivory comma strokes suggest P´Ony's lips.

MANE AND TAIL. If you plan to give your pony a hat, sketch its placement with chalk or Conté pencil before painting the mane. Sideload a #12 or ½" flat brush with Fiesta Pink. Paint scrolls on head, forehead, and tail. Outline and detail the scrolls with Ivory.

HAT. Paint the hat Spice Tan, being certain to leave holes for P´Ony's ears to poke through. Suggest a woven straw hat by filling in the area with teardrop strokes of Maple Sugar + Pineapple. Use this same mixture to paint an "S" braid around the bottom edge of the hat. Decorate the hat with random peonies of Fiesta Pink shaded with Tompte Red and highlighted with Ivory. Tie the hat on P´Ony's head with a Salem Green bow and #2 liner.

EARS. Paint inside the ear with Fiesta Pink and a #4 flat brush. Outline the top edge with an Ivory "S" stroke and a #2 liner.

NECKLACE. Paint a garland of "S" strokes with the Maple Sugar + Pineapple mixture. Shade with "S" strokes with Spice Tan. Scatter small peonies and leaves, like those painted on the hat, around the necklace.

LARGE PEONY. Follow step-by-step full color illustrations on pages 22 and 23. The colors used on P'Ony's peony were:

Dark Value - Tompte Red
Medium Value - Fiesta Pink
Medium Light Value - Fiesta Pink + Ivory
Light Value - Fiesta Pink + Ivory + more Ivory
Lighter Value - Ivory + very little Fiesta Pink
Lightest Value - Ivory

(Note: By using a scale of five to six values, you can easily change the colors of your peonies. You might, for instance, mix two colors (such as Tompte Red and Fiesta Pink or Midnight Blue and Norsk Blue) to arrive at your medium value. Then proceed to lighten this mixture to get the lighter values. Learn to think of the things you paint in terms of values rather than the color names and you will find it much easier to make creative changes to suit your own color preferences.)

WHEELS. Since horses tend to wear through a number of horseshoes in a lifetime, I decided to be sure that P'Ony was well heeled to start with. Each wheel was divided into 6 sections and Tompte Red horseshoes painted in each section. Little Salem Green leaves surround the hub of the wheel. Pink Angel strokes and dots complete the decoration.

HORSEFEATHERS. P'Ony rates two sets of these - on the front of her front legs and on the back of her hind legs.

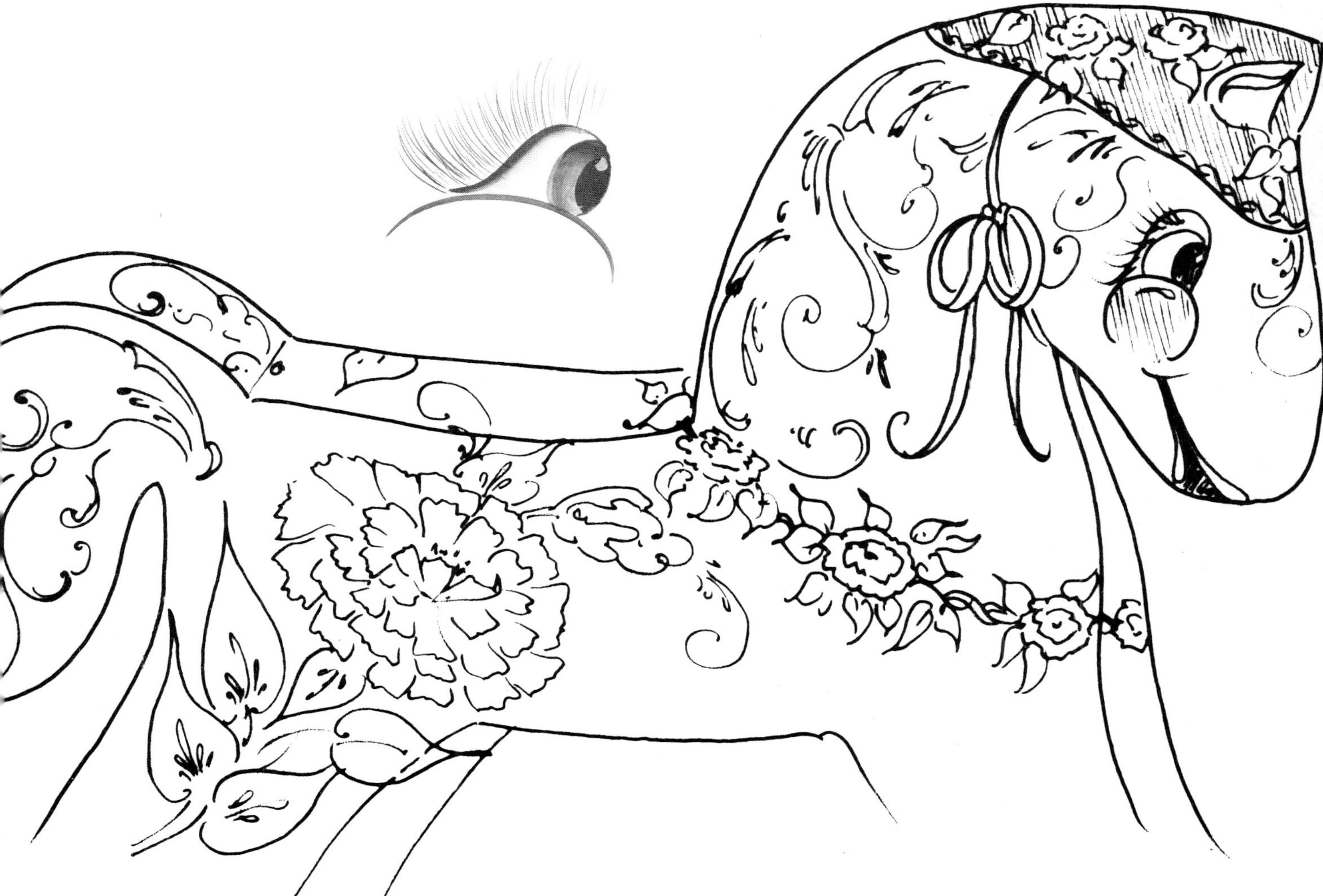

RAINBOW-WOW

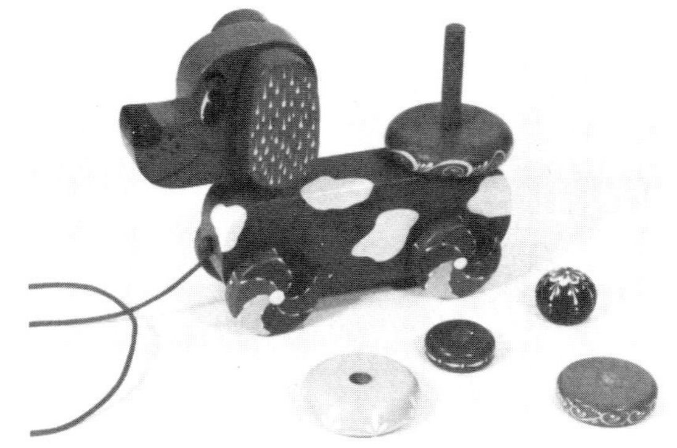

COLORS

Copen Blue
Georgia Clay
Tompte Red
Seminole
Butter Yellow
Antique White
Black

PROCEDURE

HEAD and BODY. Paint Rainbow-wow's head, neck, body and tail Copen Blue. Paint Antique White clouds (spots) at random on his body.

EARS. The ears are Georgia Clay edged with Tompte Red. Antique White teardrop strokes suggest falling raindrops (or hairy ears).

EYES. Draw large oval eyes with chalk. Follow the illustration to fill the eye in with Black and Antique White. Add Black comma stroke lashes and eyebrows.

NOSE. Paint a large Black nose, highlighted with a thin wash of Antique White, and several Black "chocolate chip" freckles. Give Rainbow-wow a big Tompte Red grin.

RINGS. The largest ring is Seminole, the next one Butter Yellow. Next is Georgia Clay, then Tompte Red, and finally, the knob on top is violet (a mixture of Copen Blue + Tompte Red). Now comes the fun part.

Load your #2 liner with Antique White and doodle a different border or design on each ring. The designs used on Rainbow-wow are illustrated here. Don't try to duplicate exactly the designs shown. That's too confusing and doesn't give your imagination opportunity to develop.

WHEELS. Use chalk to divide the circle into thirds and then into sixths (think of a clock). Begin at the base of one segment and draw a curved line to the top of the next segment. Continue adding curved lines to achieve a pinwheel effect. Paint the sections in a rainbow sequence using the same colors as used on the rings. Delineate each section with Antique White teardrop strokes.

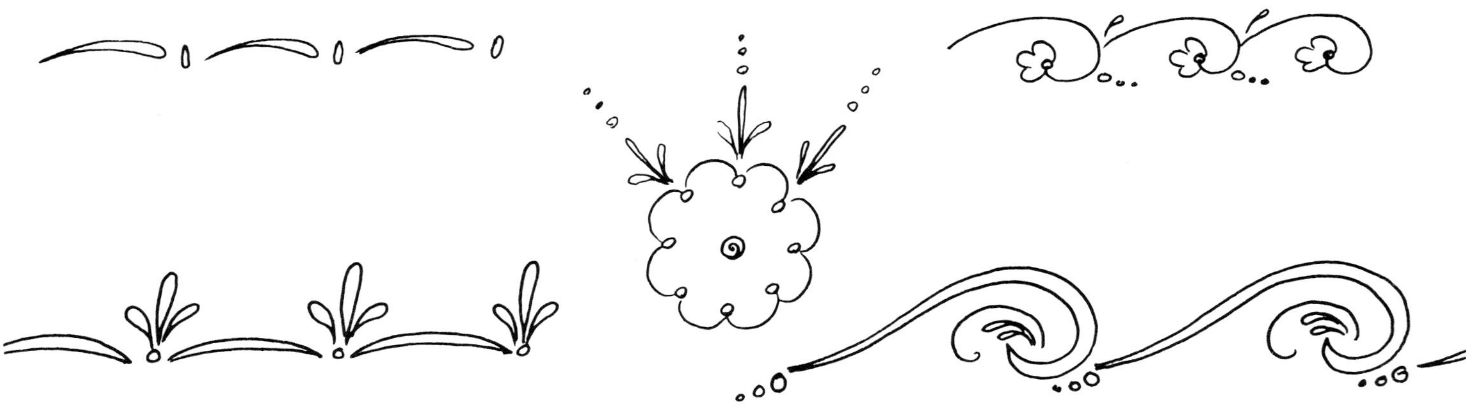

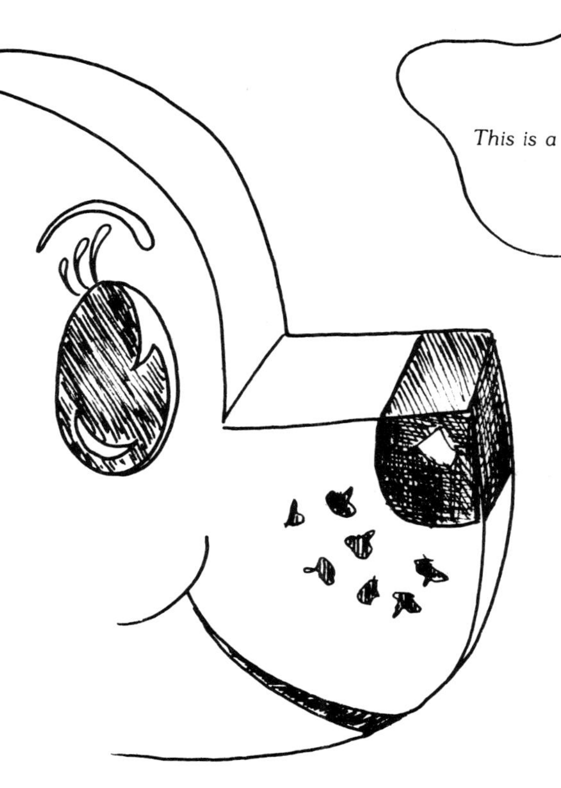

This is a typical cloud.

Rainbow-wow's ears "wobble to and fro" and the rings on his tail are removable. His bright colors were chosen to appeal to younger children. Use him for teaching color names and for counting (rings, wheels, ears, etc). Rainbow-wow can be spotted on page 18.

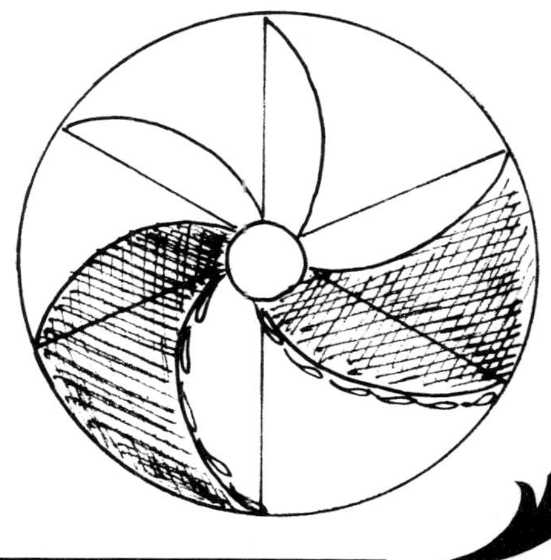

CAT ASTROPHY

COLORS

Fiesta Pink
Tompte Red
Maroon
Vivid Green
Dark Forest
Ivory
Assorted other colors

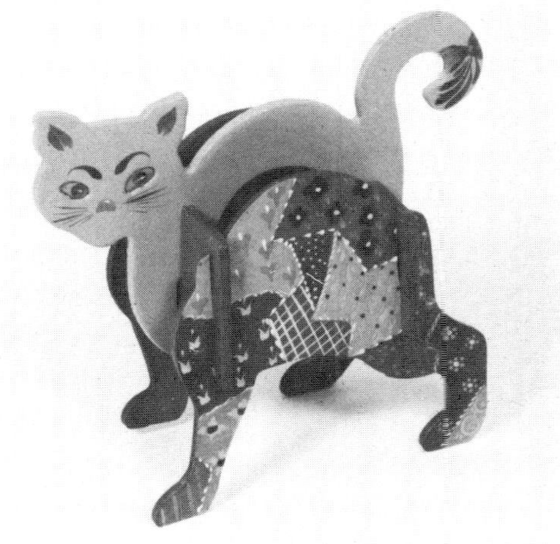

PROCEDURE

The center section is basecoated with Fiesta Pink. The remaining areas are patches of assorted reds. Each patch is decorated differently. The eyes and bow are Vivid Green, shaded with Dark Forest and highlighted with Ivory.

CAT FEATHERS appear on the tail. (Well, after all, one might expect a cat who is so fond of birds to have lots of feathers somewhere around her.)

Cat Astrophy has already lived through many of her 9 lives, and now she's held together with calico patches. She's a little container for hair barrettes, safety pins, rubber bands, dried flowers, or just a small child's tiny treasures.

This is an inexpensive, die-cut, easily assembled item -- ideal to give to little hands to decorate.

STILTS

COLORS

Butter Yellow	Black
Terra Cotta	Turquoise
Fiesta Pink	Fjord Blue
Adobe	Midnight
Ivory	and any other colors that suit your whimsy

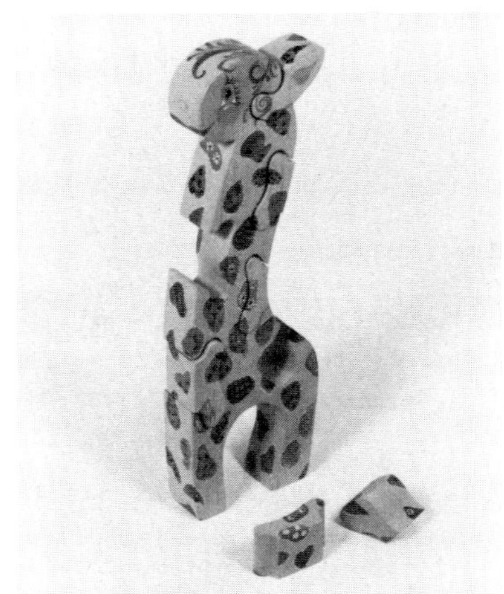

PROCEDURE

Basecoat all puzzle pieces with a thin wash of Butter Yellow.

SPOTS. Paint spots Terra Cotta. Wherever spots overlap puzzle pieces, carry the spot over the edge so that even the insides of the pieces are decorated. (Stilts has 62 spots on the outside pieces plus everything that wraps to the inside).

FACE. Paint the cheeks Fiesta Pink, highlighted with Ivory. Select light, medium and dark values of a blue, green or brown, and paint the eye according to the step-by-step color illustrations on page 56. (Detailed directions can also be found on pages 20 and 21 for Sou Fle's eyes). The colors used in Stilts' eyes are Turquoise, Fjord Blue, Midnight. A large Adobe grin and a Fiesta Pink nose finish off the face.

SPOTS. See how many different designs you can create. Be sure you are in stable condition before tackling this as it can drive you nuts! A good idea is to leave Stilts standing near your painting area. Whenever you complete a session of painting something else, use the left over paints to decorate a few spots. A better idea is to give your leftover paint and an old liner to a youngster and let her (or him) have a ball. Children's imagination is fantastic. And to have been allowed to have a hand in decorating one of their own toys makes that a very special toy indeed!

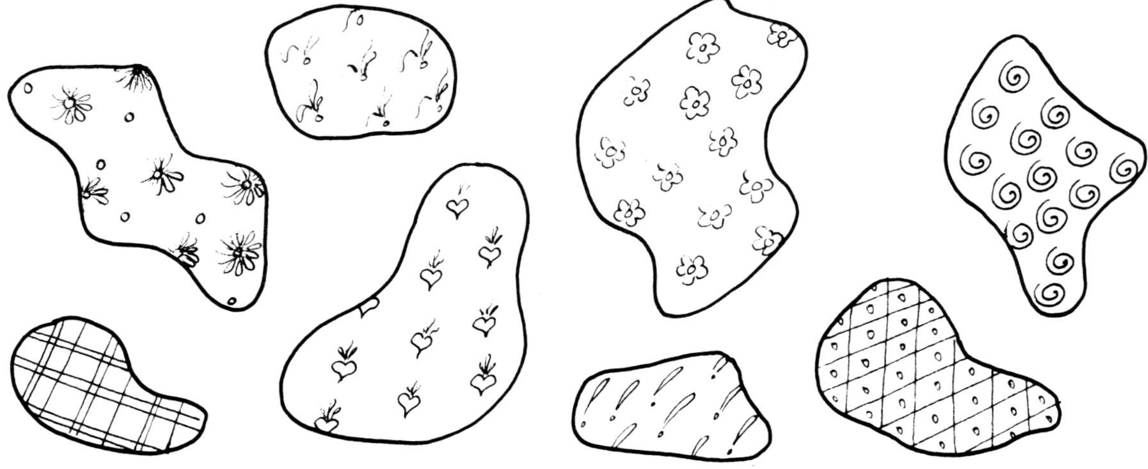

Hint: Think of what a colorful animal you would have if each spot were not only decorated differently but had a different color background.

SIR SHELLEY

COLORS

Maple Sugar	Ivory
Timberline	Dark Forest
Red Tile	Black Green
Old Parchment	Apple Green

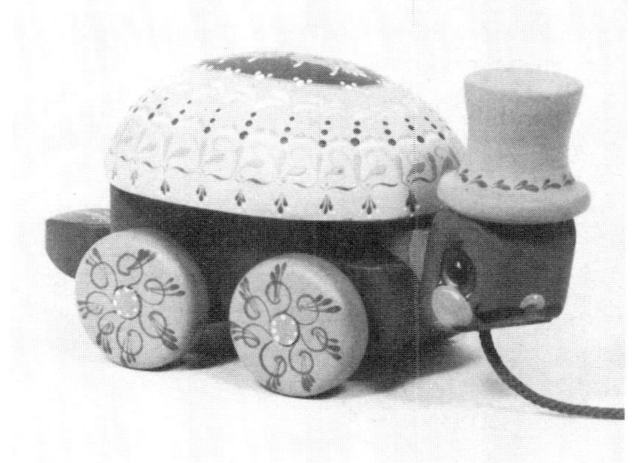

PROCEDURE:

Basecoat Sir Shelley's shell with Maple Sugar. His head and body are Timberline, and his top hat, wheels, and turtleneck (suggested by our 10-year old Jenny) are Red Tile + Old Parchment. Sir Shelley is suave and debonair in his turtleneck and top hat; and he's a real charmer once his face, complete with mustache, has been painted.

CHEEKS AND NOSE. Mix Red Tile + Old Parchment. Fully load a #10 flat brush with the mixture and paint round cheeks. Use a #2 flat brush to paint a nose. Highlight cheeks and nose with Ivory.

MUSTACHE. Use the #2 liner and Black Green to style a handsome mustache for Sir Shelley. See page 15 for a full color illustration of several styles. Begin the brush stroke at the base of the nose, applying pressure for greater thickness, and releasing pressure to taper off at the ends.

EYES. Sir Shelley's are a deep, rich green. Using chalk or Conté pencil, outline a horseshore shape the width of the cheek, and just above it. Fill in this area with Ivory. Paint a large Dark Forest iris (#6 flat) and a Black Green pupil. Paint thin lines of Apple Green radiating out from the pupil. With a #4 flat, shade above the pupil with a thin wash of Black Green. Highlight below the pupil with a thin wash of Apple Green. Add a strong Ivory highlight above the pupil, and lesser highlights below the pupil. Outline the eye with Black Green and provide abundant eyelashes. See page 56 for full color, step-by-step illustrations of painting an eye.

HAT. Add a band and a feather (or perhaps a medallion) in any of the colors already used on Sir Shelley.

SHELL. Sketch concentric rings on Sir Shelley's back with chalk or Conté pencil. These rings will serve as guides for a series of borders painted in Timberline, Red Tile + Old Parchment, and Ivory. Or, further divide the shell into segments and paint a different design in each section.

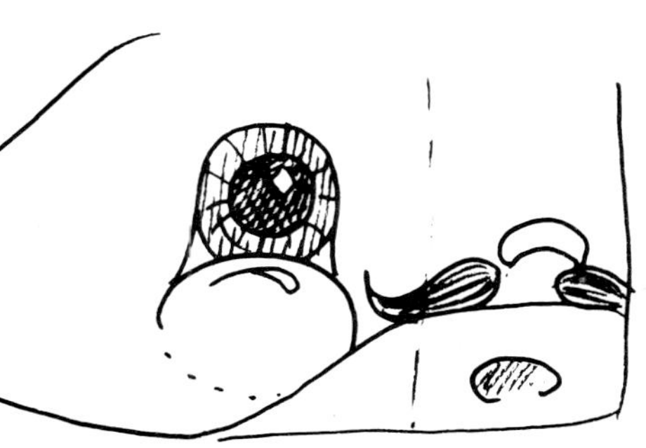

WHEELS. Here is a good place to *Dare to Doodle*. Dots, scrolls, and teardrops of Timberline decorate Sir Shelley's wheels, giving them the appearance of motion.

TURTLE FEATHERS of Red Tile + Old Parchment are on Sir Shelley's tail.

When his string is pulled, Sir Shelley moves out smartly, by turning his head from side to side looking to see who is looking to see him. You can see him, incidentally, on the back cover.

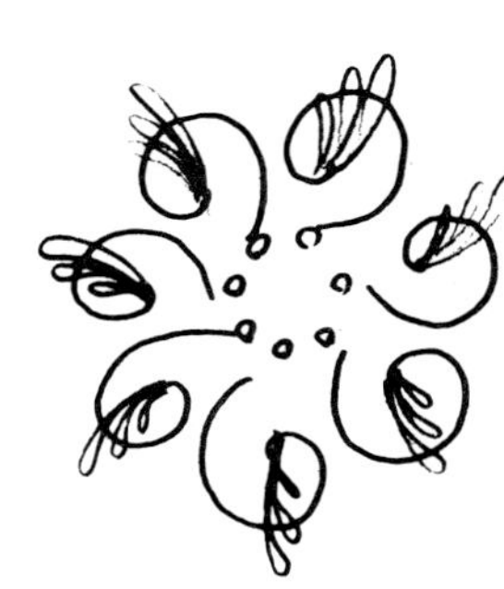

PINWHEEL

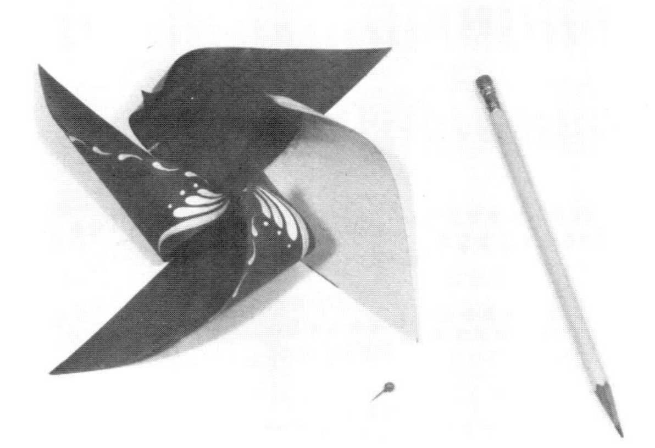

Here is a project which will keep little hands busy while *you* paint. The directions are written for your youngsters to read and understand. "Pinwheel" is excerpted from *You Can Do-Things By Yourself*, an easy reader. *Do-Things* features over 50 creative craft ideas involving common household items to entertain the 4-10 years olds so you can play!

You will need: paper
crayons
a pencil with an eraser
a straight pen
scissors

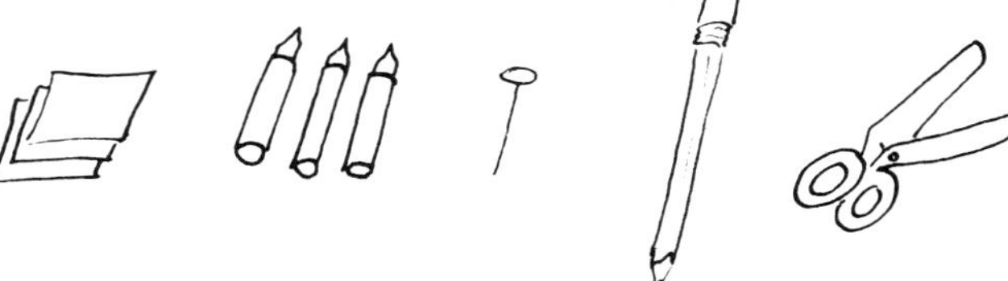

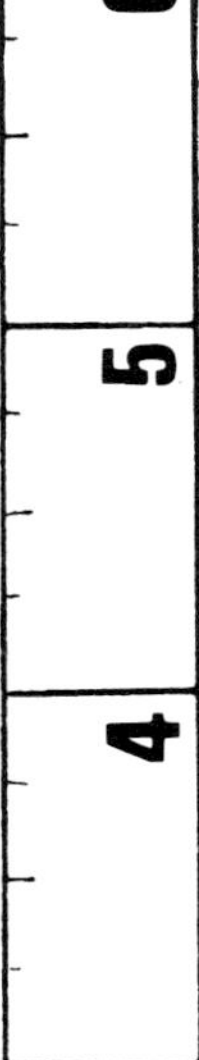

1. Make a 6-inch square.

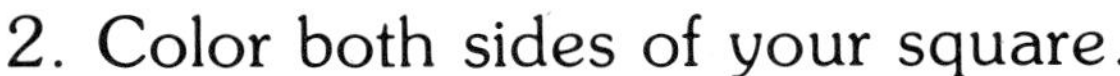

2. Color both sides of your square.

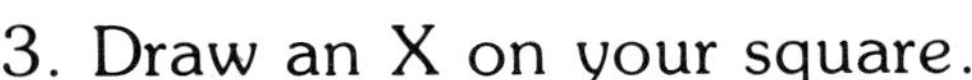

3. Draw an X on your square.

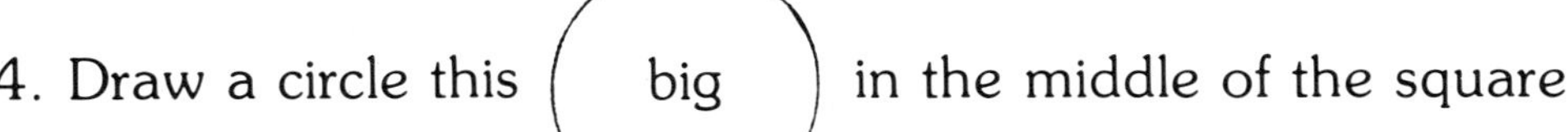

4. Draw a circle this big in the middle of the square.

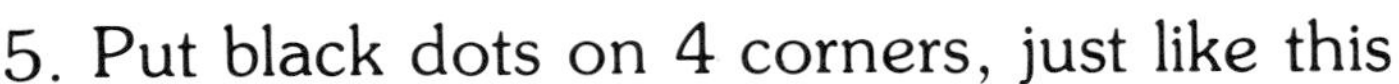

5. Put black dots on 4 corners, just like this.

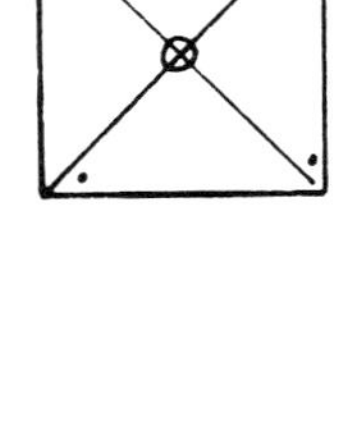

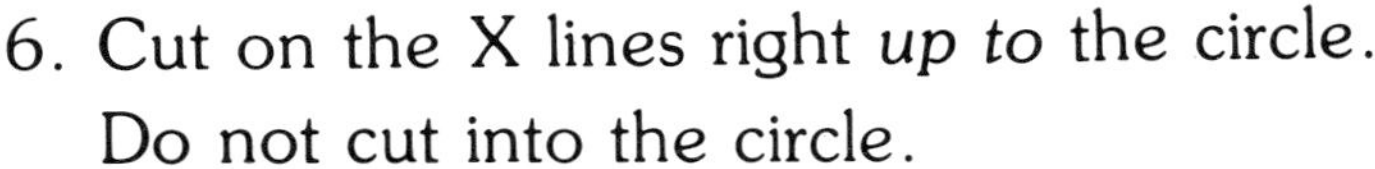

6. Cut on the X lines right *up to* the circle. Do not cut into the circle.

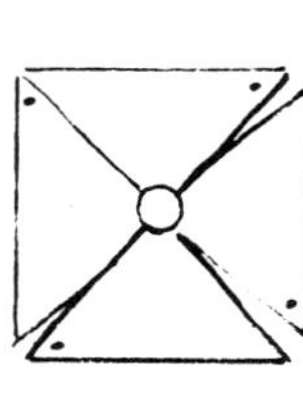

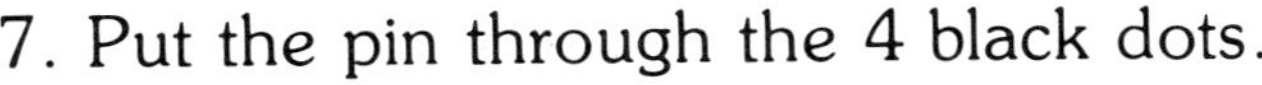

7. Put the pin through the 4 black dots.

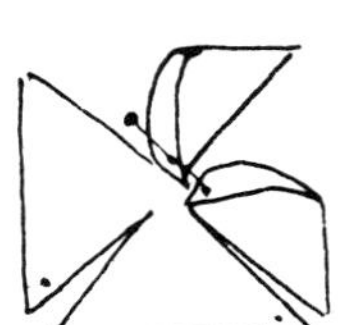

8. Push the pin into the eraser.

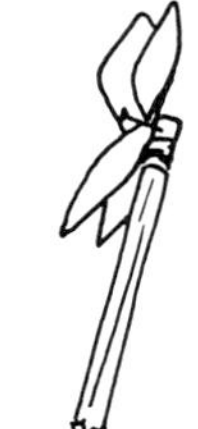

Acetate is an ideal "paper" to use - sturdy and durable. Any paper will work, however, except flimsy tracing paper. Encourage young hands to decorate the pinwheel using crayons, paints, or magic markers.

MENTAL BLOCK

COLORS

Bonnie Blue
Fjord Blue

PROCEDURE

Number the pieces. **Repeat: number the pieces!!** It is one thing to decorate this crazy cube; quite another to re-assemble it!

Select a color scheme to complement your own family room or living room. Then, once the cube is decorated, set it out within reach of a visitor you would like to drive nuts. Make it especially difficult by setting it out *unassembled* so that the unsuspecting victim will not have the advantage of seeing how it comes apart before attempting to put it together. To retain your own sanity, be sure to take notice of how the cube comes apart -- there is a secret.

To impress your friends (after they've spent hours in frustration) you can reassemble this infuriating block of wood easily if you'll work a marking system into your design for each piece. Sneaky, eh? Although I've painted strokes and dots on each of the six sides of the cube (as well as all over the insides) the dots on one of the sides are in sequence from one to nine (representing the nine separate pieces). Since the pieces are so busily decorated, no one even suspects the built-in clues.

Another idea. Call the cube a "Blockhead" and paint a different face on each of the 6 sides. (This, of course, makes it much easier to assemble because the clues are obvious.)

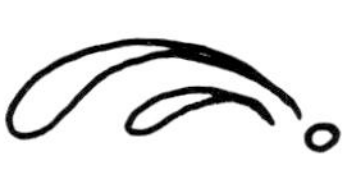

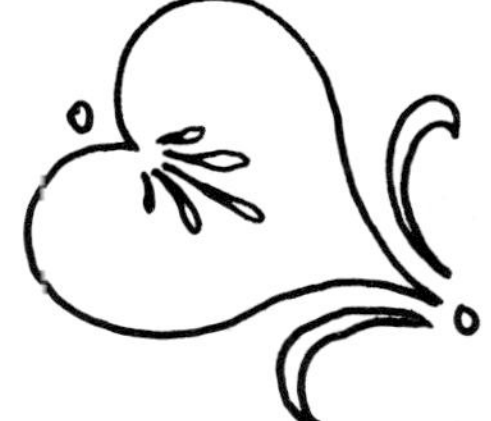

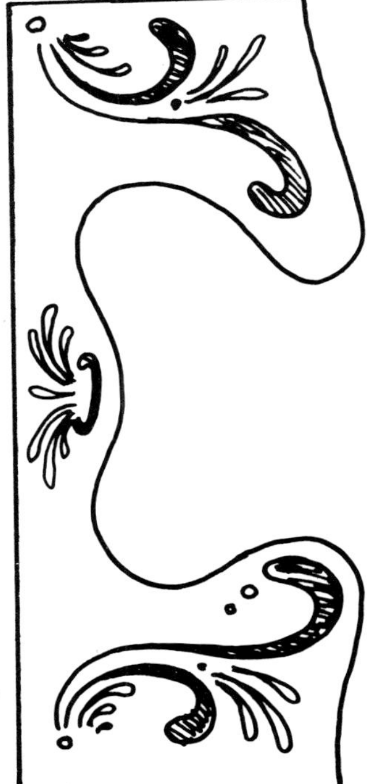

Clown (age 16) and Baby (age 10) have been in this position for days now. They seem to be making little progress overcoming their Mental Block.

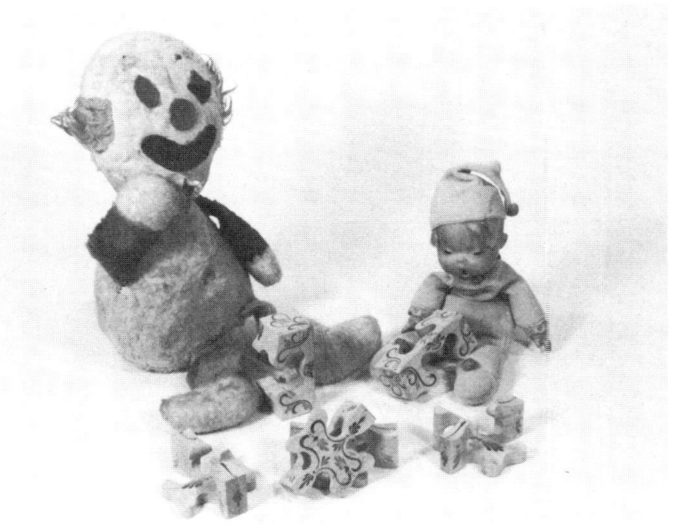

SPEEDY VAN

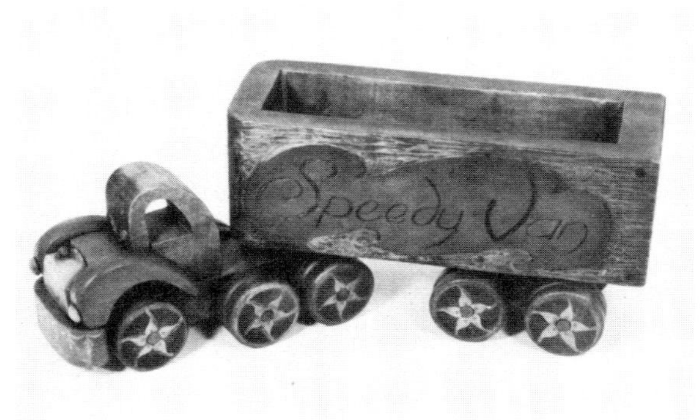

COLORS

Red Iron Oxide
Tangerine
Butter Yellow
Vivid Green

PROCEDURE

Speedy Van had such a nice, broad surface that it afforded an opportunity to make an even messier mess than was possible with only paints. If you have access to a couple of carving gouges, dig in! The bigger the mess you make, the more creative you'll feel, and creative people are always so nice.

CARVING – General Directions

You can do quite an interesting job of carving with only two tools -- a "U" gouge and a veiner. Just as good brushes are essential in painting, likewise good tools are important in woodcarving. And it is imperative that carving tools be kept sharp. Dull blades on soft woods leave torn cuts. The softer the wood, the sharper the tools must be. (It is sort of like cutting a really ripe tomato with a dull knife - everything just gets smashed and mushy.) Besides, you are much more likely to goof or injure yourself using dull tools since dull gouges and chisels resist the task at hand and require you to exert much more pressure. This pressure could result in slipping, and consequently in disastrous cuts - not only to your project, but also to yourself.

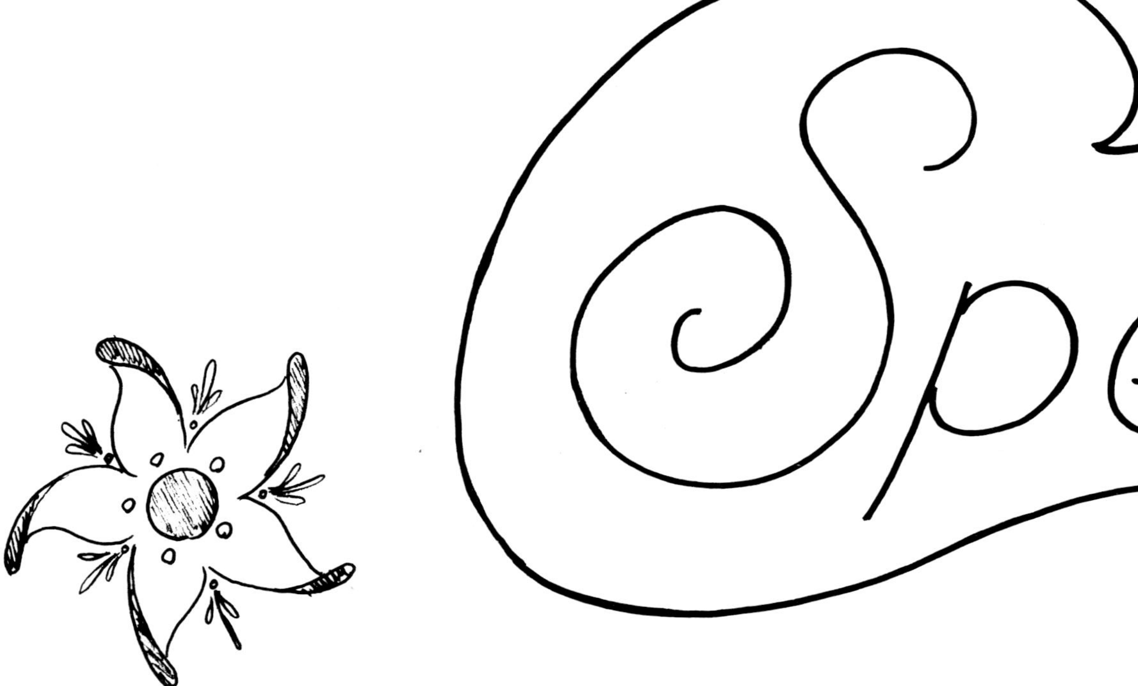

Personal injury is a clear-cut result of careless carving habits and can be totally avoided. 1. ALWAYS use sharp tools. 2. ALWAYS keep your "extra" hand out of harm's way by keeping it BEHIND the carving action. 3. ALWAYS push gouges AWAY from you when carving. 4. Use a "C" clamp to fasten a "stop" (a piece of 2x4 works nicely) to the work bench. Or nail the wooden stop in position. Place the object to be carved up against the stop. The stop acts as an extra hand and eliminates the urge to place your non-carving hand in the path of an errant gouge as you apply pressure towards the stop. When doing tight, close, detail work, I like to use my right hand as the force behind the handle and my left hand - a finger or two on the gouge itself - as a restraining and guiding force. Lacking a third hand to hold the project, the "stop" comes in *handy*.

TRANSFERING THE PATTERN. Transfer the pattern to the wood by your usual method. Transfer the pattern darkly (and heavily is O.K. too, since you will be gouging the lines). Before launching into an actual project, practice on scrap wood to get the feel of your tools.

OUTLINING. Outline the entire pattern with the veiner. The more parallel the gouges are held to the board, the shallower the grooves will be. For deeper grooves, hold the gouge up at a greater angle.

STOP-CUTTING. This technique helps prevent running "splits" from running where they shouldn't and serves to make a barrier for gouging recessed areas. For this technique, you would need another carving tool, a chisel (or a curved gouge on curved areas). "Stop-cut" around the design, instead of outlining, by slicing into the wood about 1/8" or however deep you plan to carve. Place the "stop-cuts" to the waste side of the pattern - the part which will be carved out - to provide an extra measure of margin for error and for pattern preservation. When gouging out waste, the "stop-cuts" will actually help stop the gouging action at the edge of the design.

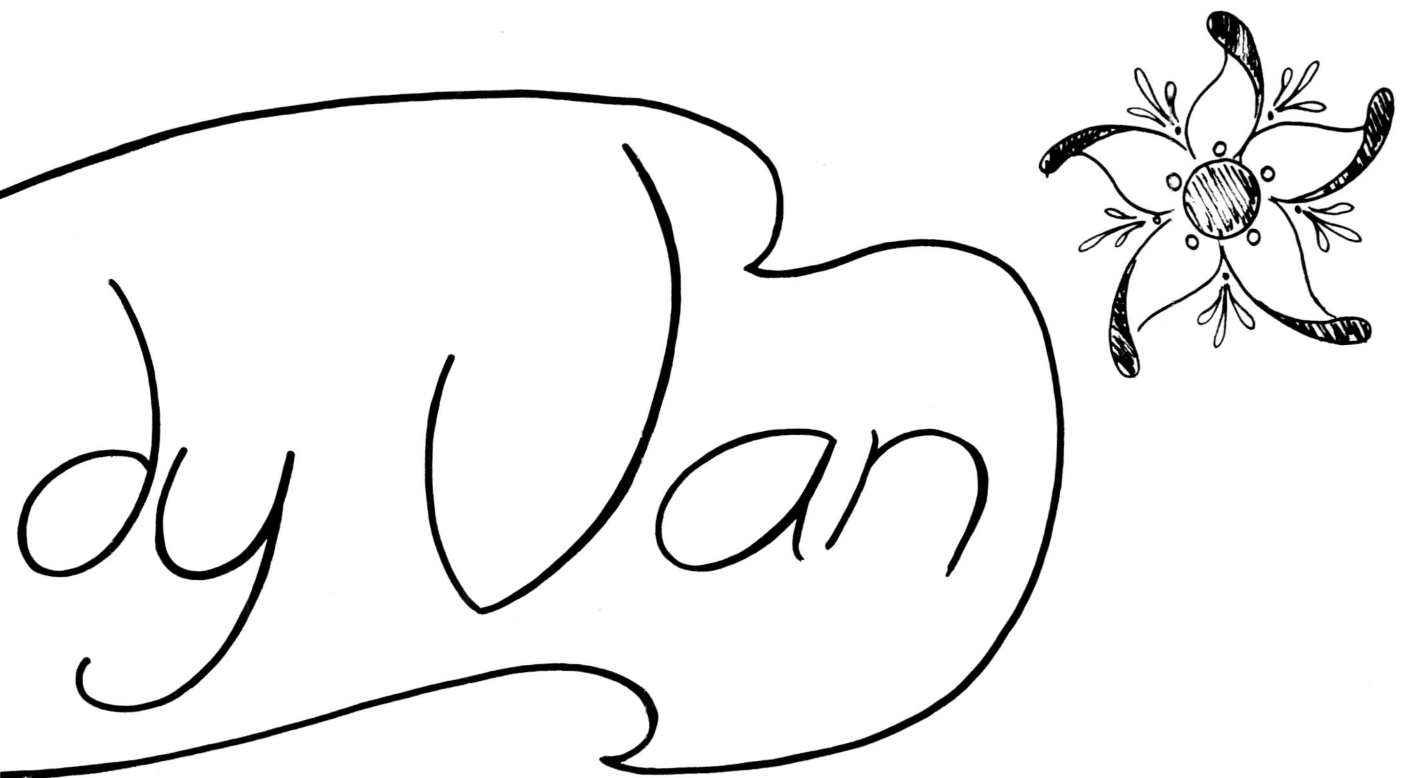

GOUGING. Different effects can be achieved on the same design depending upon whether (1) the background is gouged out leaving the design raised in relief or (2) the design is gouged out, recessing it down into the wood.

WHOOPS! If you goof, you may be able to patch it up: (1) A chipped off piece can be glued back into place with white glue. (2) A drastic, misplaced gouge-cut may be disguised with wood putty. (3) Minor ailments can sometimes be softened by sanding. (4) Attitude adjustment. If all else fails, remember: the final effect is going to be charming anyway. And that goof is nothing more than the sunny freckles on a smiley-faced little child - all personality and character. So jump in and have fun!

Carving instructions excerpted from *Tole Techniques and Decorative Arts, Session IV,* ©Jackie Shaw 1976.

Upon completion of the carving, decorate Speedy Van as your whim directs. On the van pictured on page 41, the red areas were scumbled in Red Iron Oxide and Tangerine. The highlights, grille, petal designs on the wheels, and other embellishing strokes were painted Butter Yellow. Vivid Green dots top off the strokes.

Speedy Van was antiqued with Burnt Umber oil paints after the decoration was completed. See instructions on pages 86, 87 for antiquing.

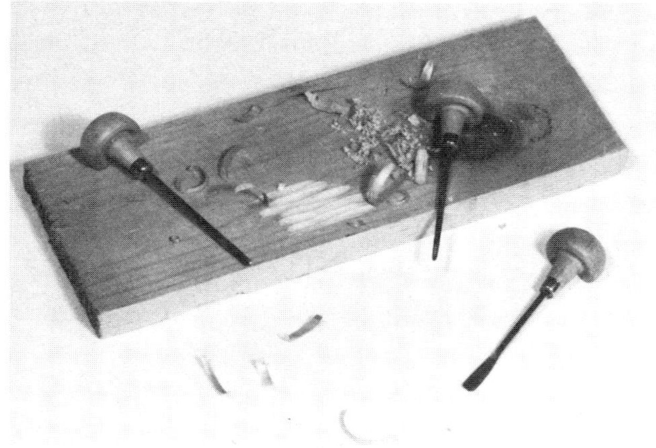

1. Always work with sharp tools.

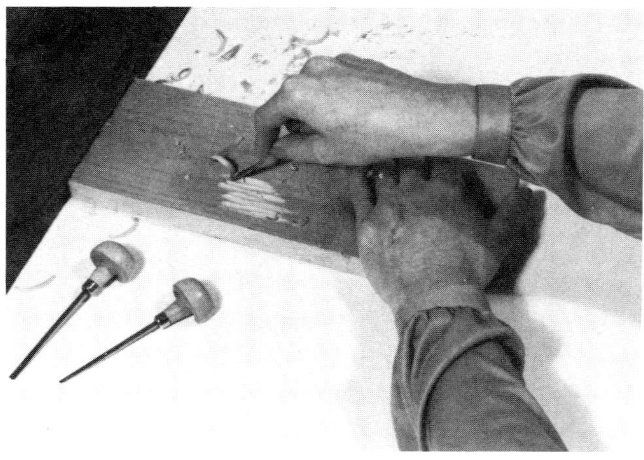

2. Keep your "extra" hand out of harm's way, behind the action. Push gouges away from you. Use a carving stop or another board fastened to your work table with a "C" clamp against which your carving rests.

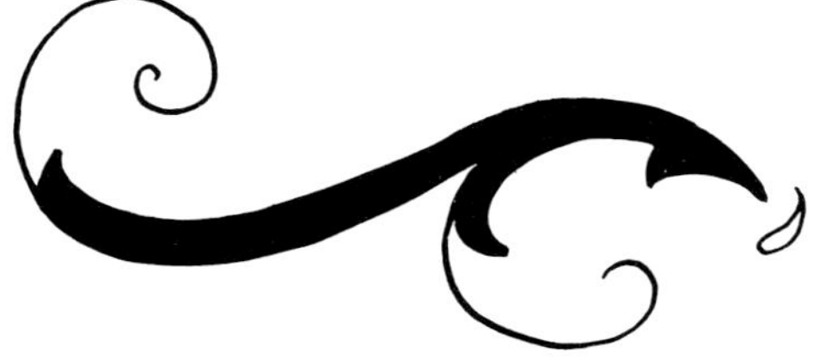

DEREK'S GUARDIAN ANGEL

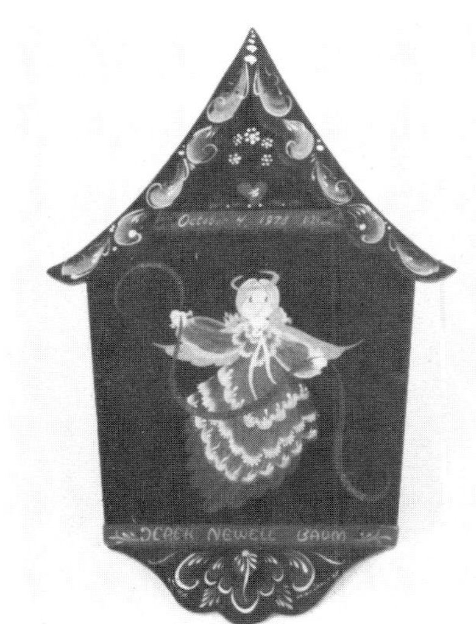

COLORS

- Old Parchment
- Georgia Clay
- Adobe
- Fjord Blue
- Red Iron Oxide
- Midnight Blue
- Bonnie Blue
- Burnt Umber
- Forest Green
- Ivory
- Golden Brown
- Butter Yellow
- Kim Gold

PROCEDURE

This little angel first appeared in *Pigments of Your Imagination, Vol. 3,* as a Christmas angel. Full directions for painting her are shared in that book. She is presented here just to give you another idea for using her, and another project idea for commemorating an important birth. Derek's Guardian Angel was painted for our good friends George and Julie Baum's oldest son, Derek.

Without her halo, the little angel also makes a fine tooth fairy. Paint her on a piece of fabric which is then stitched on 3 sides to a pillowcase to form a lost tooth pocket. If you're really ambitious, decorate the whole pillowcase. The tooth fairy pillowcase makes the tooth fairy's job a whole lot easier. Of course the tooth fairy can no longer use the excuse, "The tooth must have gotten lost," when she forgets to leave a coin.

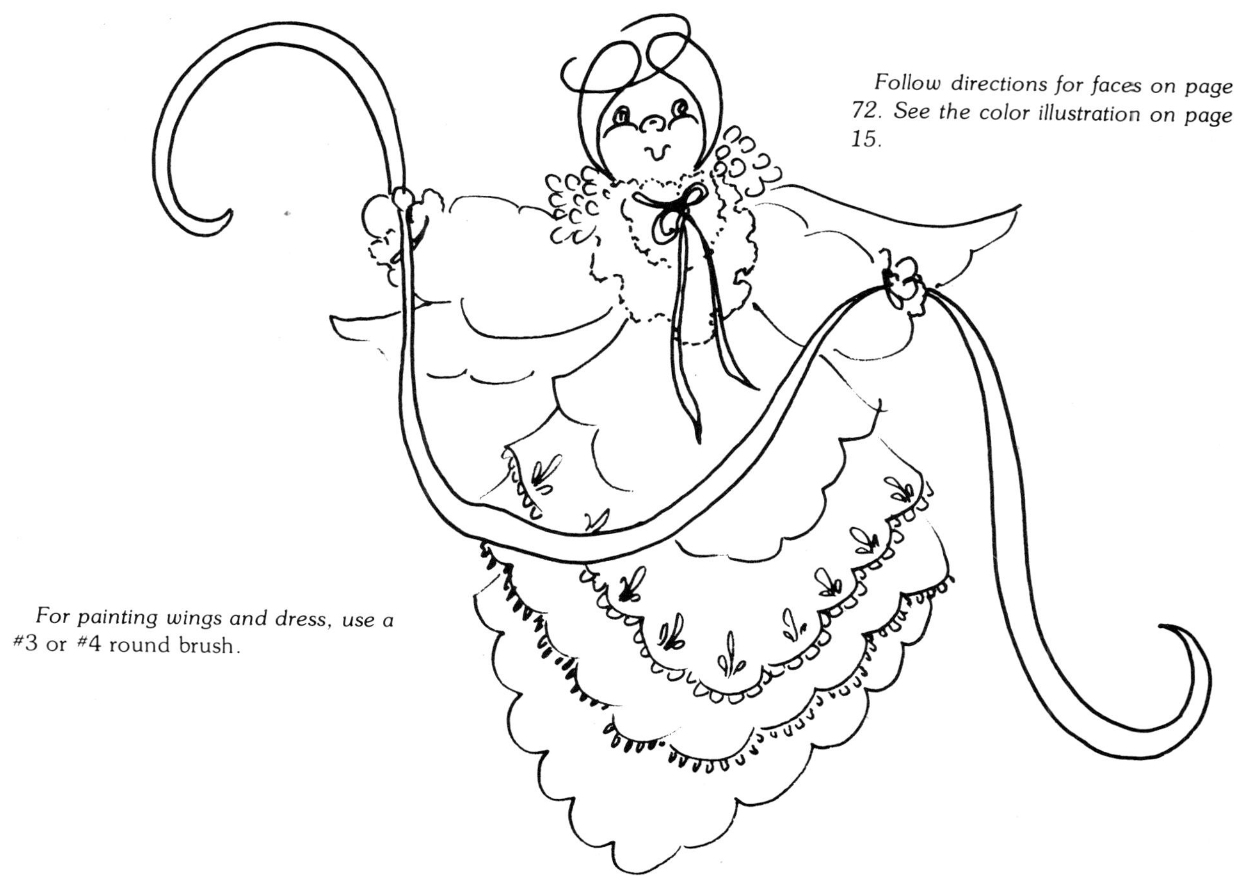

Follow directions for faces on page 72. See the color illustration on page 15.

For painting wings and dress, use a #3 or #4 round brush.

CHOPPER

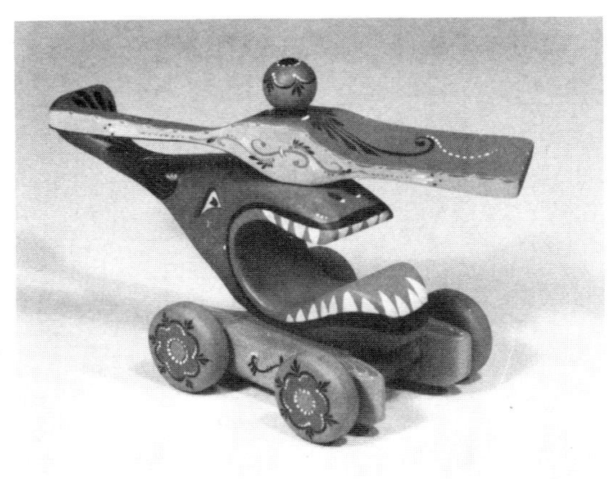

COLORS

Colonial Blue
Marshmallow
Fiesta Pink
Blue Spruce

PROCEDURE

Basecoat as follows:

Colonial Blue - body, top and bottom of propeller (aviators call it a rotor blade - but what do they know)

Colonial Blue + Marshmallow - sides of propeller, base

Fiesta Pink - inside mouth, wheels, knob on top

EYE. Fill in with Marshmallow. Outline, and paint eyelashes with Blue Spruce. Add a Blue Spruce "chocolate chip" eyeball.

PROPELLOR. Paint a swirly, twirly design on the propeller to suggest motion. Use all the colors listed above.

MOUTH. Outline in Blue Spruce. Add ferocious teeth in Marshmallow, and mark his hungry gullet with a Tompte Red epiglottis.

WHEELS. Embellish the wheels, base and body with strokes. And, if you look in your dictionary, along with such things as helicopters, heliports, helicoids, and heliclines, you will surely find HELIFEATHERS! Chopper has them on his tail.

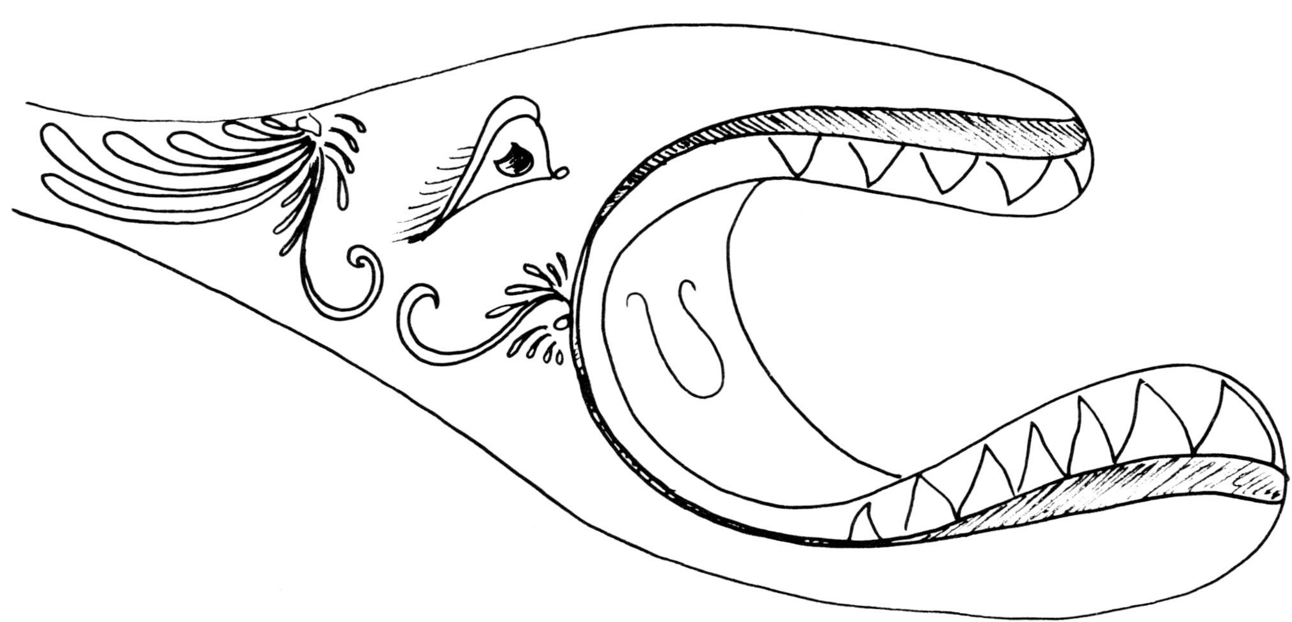

While watching Chopper emerge from my palette and take on his whimsical personality, I was reminded of Herbie, one of my first grade students in Butzbach, Germany about 18 years ago. Herbie was the most colorful, imaginative, uninhibited artist I've ever known, and also the noisiest.

Heavily influenced by living among the military with constant maneuvers, training, convoys, etc., Herbie's favorite artistic theme dealt with ground wars and mighty sea battles. When Herbie drew a picture, it was a 3-D, surround-a-sound, ever-progressing production. Ships and soldiers moved back and forth across his paper. Bombs sailed through the air, complete with sound effects and hand movements, landing on a previously drawn target, and totally obliterating that target in a fury of crayon marks. When drawing time was over, one look at Herbie's artwork was proof positive that a battle had occurred. But unless you were standing nearby and saw all the action you could not fully appreciate this young master's effort. If only we all had a little bit of Herbie's different drumbeat in us.

ADAM

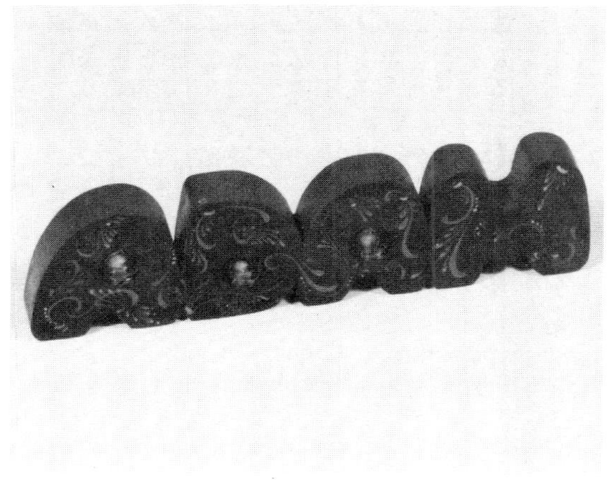

COLORS

Midnight Blue
Red Iron Oxide
Antique Gold

PROCEDURE

Basecoat the front in Midnight and the edges in Red Iron Oxide. Doodle all over with Antique Gold.

OPTIONAL IDEAS. 1. Decorate individual letters with a calico pattern design. 2. Basecoat each letter a different color, and paint a special design on each letter. 3. Paint the name to match the decor or wallpaper in a child's bedroom. Hang on the door. 4. For an older child, paint the name a solid color. Let friends autograph it for a keepsake.

Wooden name shapes are appreciated gifts and popular items to sell at craft shows and fairs. They are easily cut out at home if you have a jig saw. Keep the lettering style simple (clean, uncluttered lines) for easier cutting. Suggest open inside areas, as in "o", "a", "p", by indenting the area very slightly with a chisel or large drill bit.

CHARLIE-CHARLIE-TANGO

COLORS

Norsk Blue	Red Tile
Lichen Grey	Ivory
Old Parchment	Forest Green

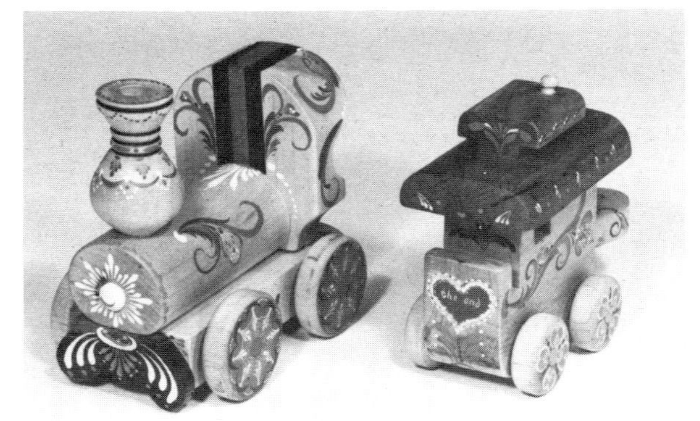

PROCEDURE

You will probably not want to hide the beautiful hardwoods used in constructing this toy, so instead of basecoating the pieces with color, just use a clear sealer. You can paint the scrolls, strokes and flowers directly on the sealed surface. Execute the designs in light and dark values of three color mixtures (listed below), and accent with Ivory. Control the values by adjusting the proportions of colors mixed.

Blue mixture = Norsk Blue + Lichen Grey + Old Parchment
Orange mixture = Red Tile + Old Parchment
Green mixture = Forest Green + Lichen Grey

Although sample scrolls and design elements are illustrated here for you, for goodness sake don't attempt to trace them onto your project. You inhibit your own creative development by doing so. Study the designs. Visually pull them apart to learn how they were put together. Place tracing paper over the designs and paint them several times for practice. However, do not try to follow my brush strokes exactly. That is too confining. As your courage increases, load your brush with water and practice designing directly on the project. It is only water, so if you goof, you have not spoiled a thing. You cannot decorate with this "invisible paint" forever, however. Sooner or later you must proceed, headstrong, and set down your brushstrokes with authority!!

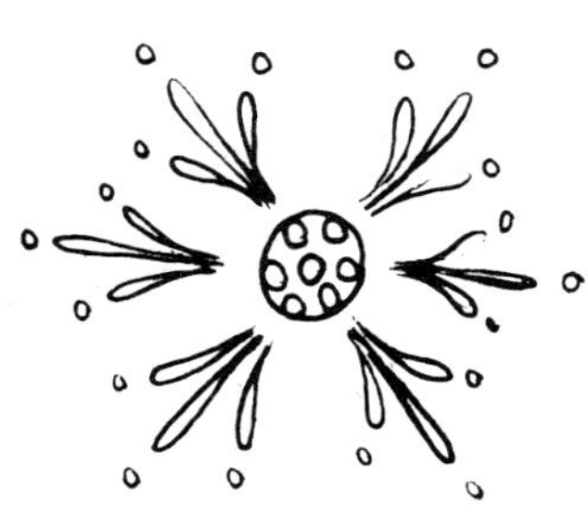

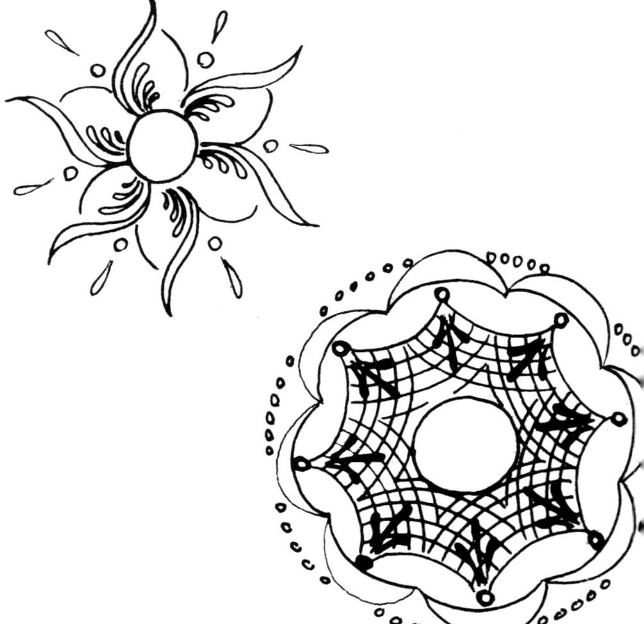

"Charlie Charlie Tango" may seem like a strange name for a train. But to us, and our three children, **C**hoo **C**hoo **T**rains *have always been* **C**harlie **C**harlie **T**angos. *It has something to do with raising a family under the influence of the military's "phonetic" alphabet. This alphabet has a clearly pronouncable word representing each letter. It is used to make sure that messages are clearly understood, even through static. Soldiers can get pretty creative in its use. Just don't ask me why grown men call a train a Choo Choo Train in the first place!*

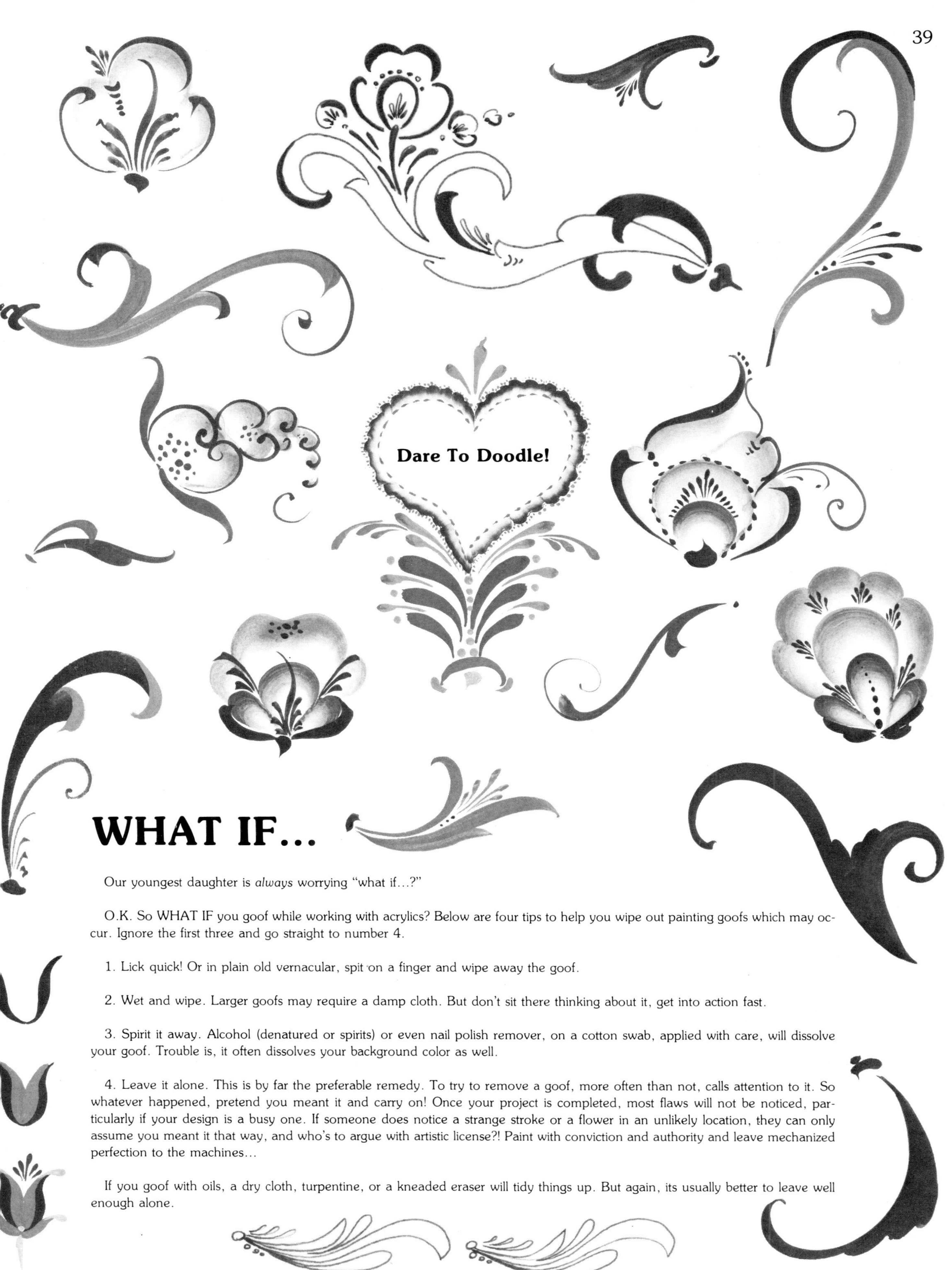

WHAT IF...

Our youngest daughter is *always* worrying "what if...?"

O.K. So WHAT IF you goof while working with acrylics? Below are four tips to help you wipe out painting goofs which may occur. Ignore the first three and go straight to number 4.

1. Lick quick! Or in plain old vernacular, spit on a finger and wipe away the goof.

2. Wet and wipe. Larger goofs may require a damp cloth. But don't sit there thinking about it, get into action fast.

3. Spirit it away. Alcohol (denatured or spirits) or even nail polish remover, on a cotton swab, applied with care, will dissolve your goof. Trouble is, it often dissolves your background color as well.

4. Leave it alone. This is by far the preferable remedy. To try to remove a goof, more often than not, calls attention to it. So whatever happened, pretend you meant it and carry on! Once your project is completed, most flaws will not be noticed, particularly if your design is a busy one. If someone does notice a strange stroke or a flower in an unlikely location, they can only assume you meant it that way, and who's to argue with artistic license?! Paint with conviction and authority and leave mechanized perfection to the machines...

If you goof with oils, a dry cloth, turpentine, or a kneaded eraser will tidy things up. But again, its usually better to leave well enough alone.

HAPPY LITTLE YELLOW CAR

COLORS

Butter Yellow
Leaf Green
Thalo Blue
Cosmos Blue
Old Parchment
Fiesta Pink

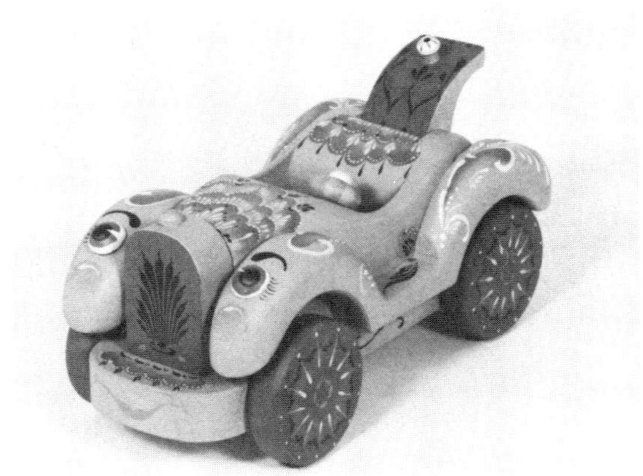

PROCEDURE

Basecoat as follows:
- Leaf Green - wheels, trunk, grille
- Old Parchment - headlights
- Cosmos Blue - hub caps
- Butter Yellow - remainder of car

EYES. On each headlight, leave a partial ring of Old Parchment showing under a big Thalo iris. Add Black pupils and comma stroke eyebrows.

CHEEKS. Both front *and* back! Large Fiesta Pink circles highlighted with Old Parchment give our little car a rosy feeling.

MOUTH. A big Fiesta Pink smile is sure proof it is a happy car.

Now all that remains is to doodle away your creative inhibitions. Obviously, since the car now has eyes, cheeks, and a big grin, it is going to be unlike any car anyone has ever seen. So nothing you do to it now can possibly harm it. And since it is not exactly modeled after any specific Detroit or import car, there are no set precedences against which your decorations could be compared unfavorably. So with nothing to lose, there is nothing to do but to do it. And have fun!

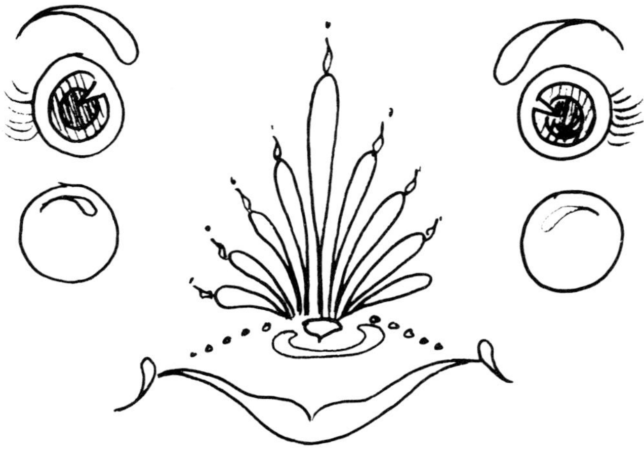

A few years ago, our family loved our "Happy Little Yellow Car" - a Kharmann Ghia convertible. It carried us on many delightful forays under the blue sky, through the green forest, and into the bright yellow sunlight. It added a rosy dimension to our lives. It was a sad day when we faced the fact that the little car wasn't growing as our three daughters were - and had to be replaced since it no longer fit.

This little toy car embodies all the happy colors and feelings we associated with our "Happy Little Yellow Car."

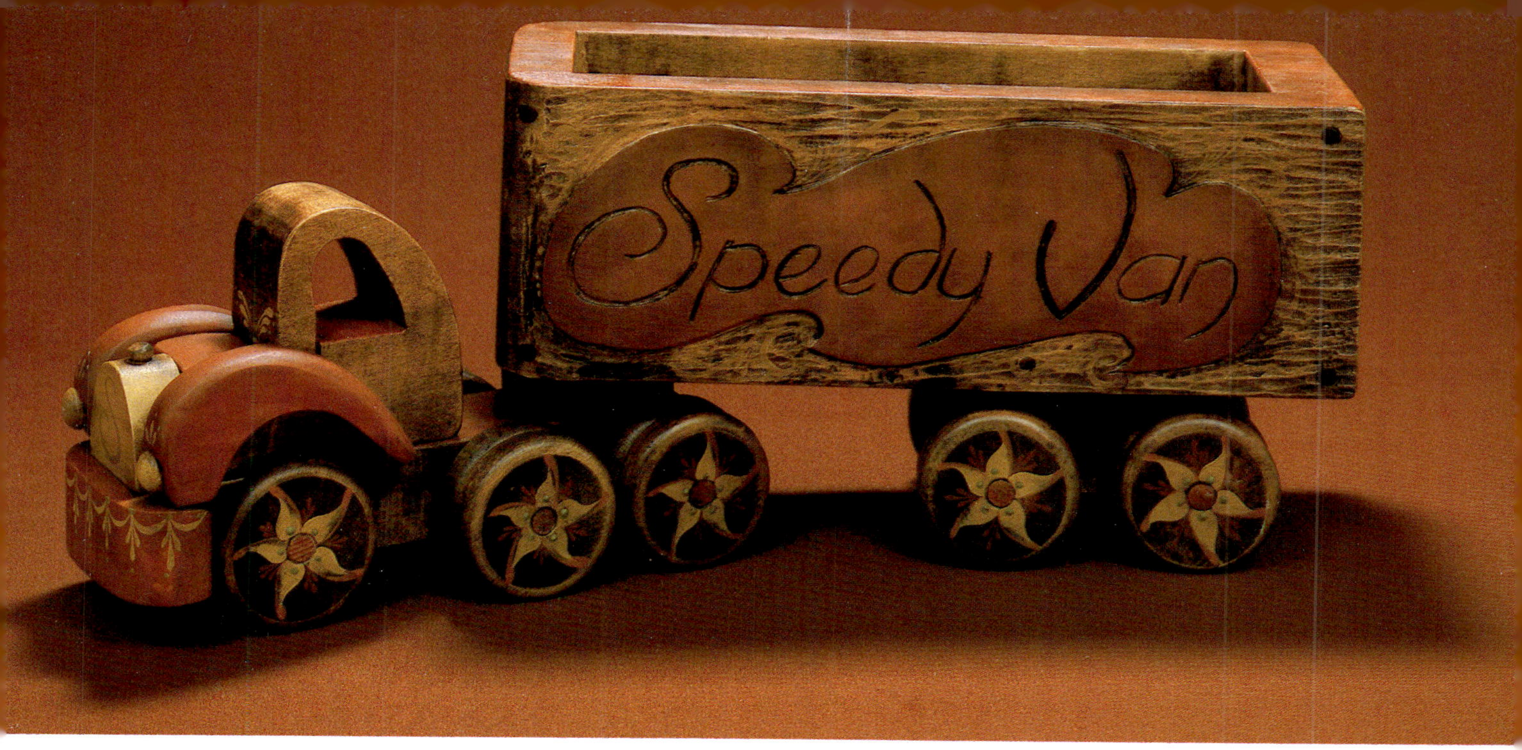

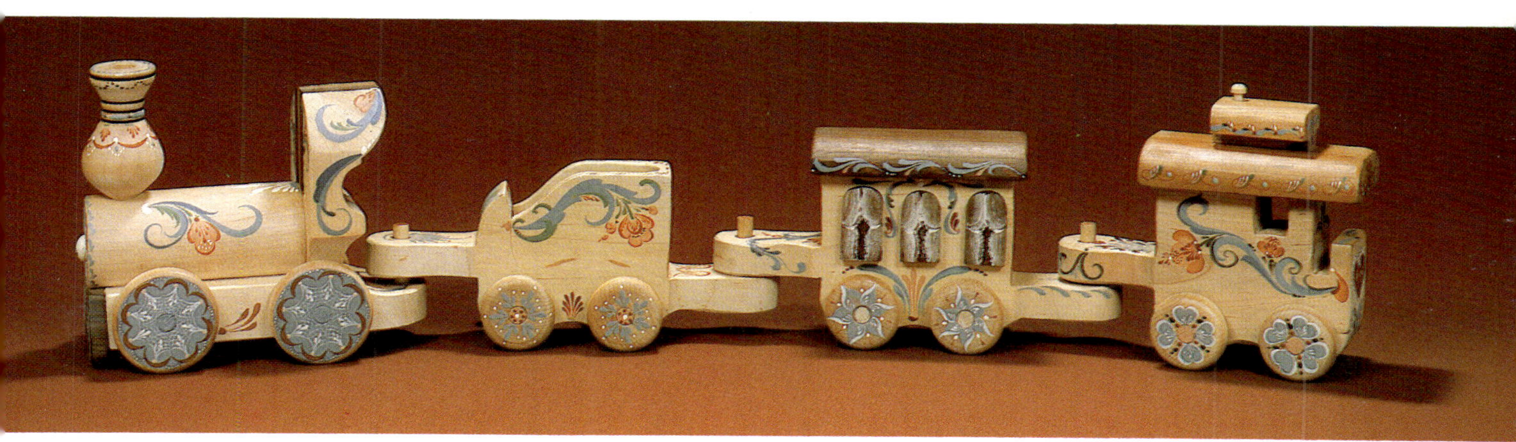

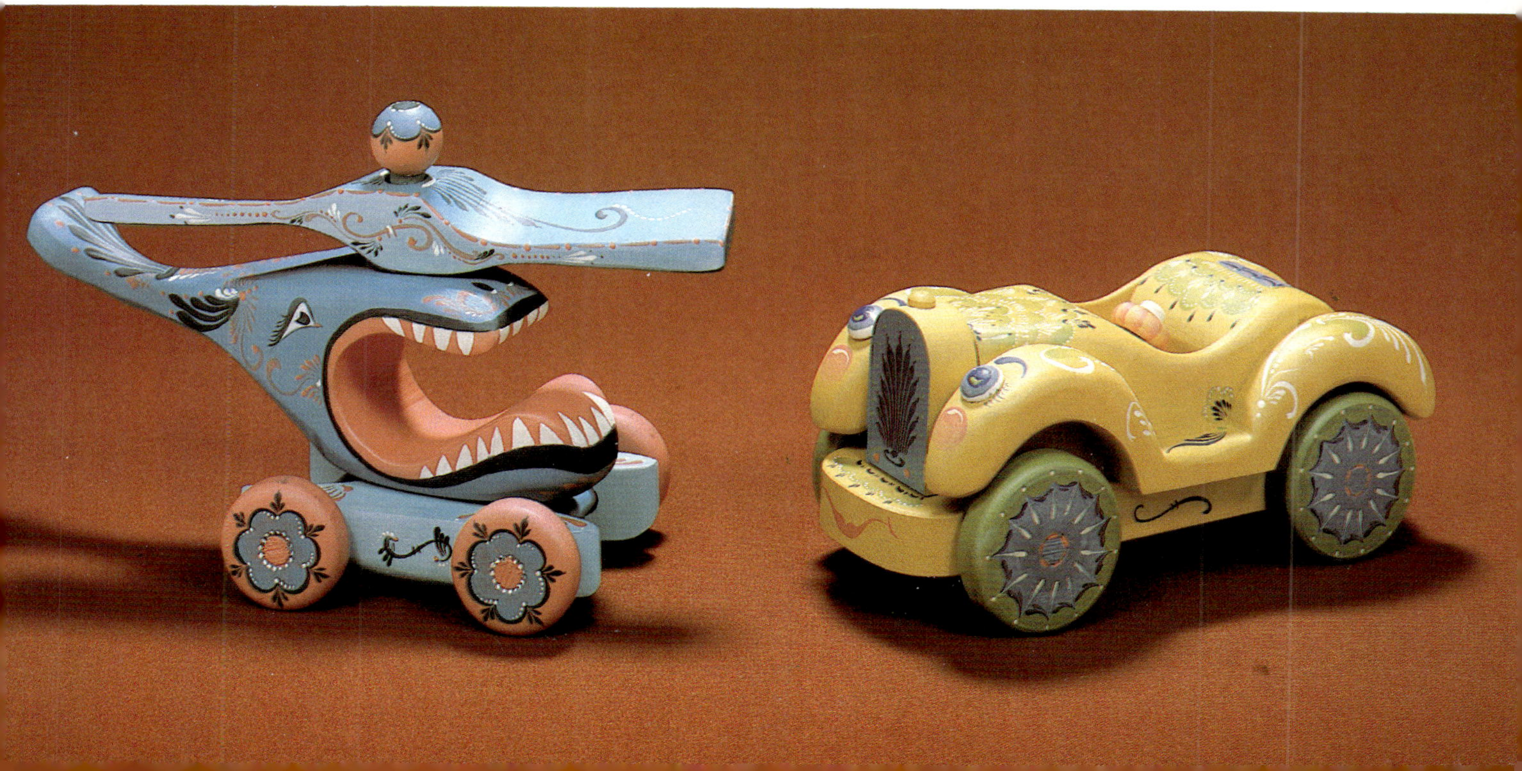

SNORT, THE CRAYONASAURUS

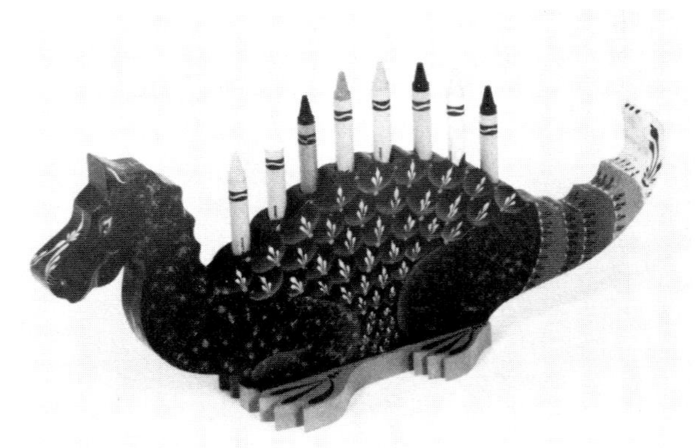

COLORS

Blue Spruce	Tompte Red
Vivid Green	Hallingdal Red
Norsk Blue	Butter Yellow
Grape	Orange

PROCEDURE

Basecoat all except Snort's tail and feet with Blue Spruce. Basecoat the feet with Vivid Green. Paint stripes on the tail in Norsk Blue, Grape, Tompte Red, Hallingdal Red, and Butter Yellow (on the tip).

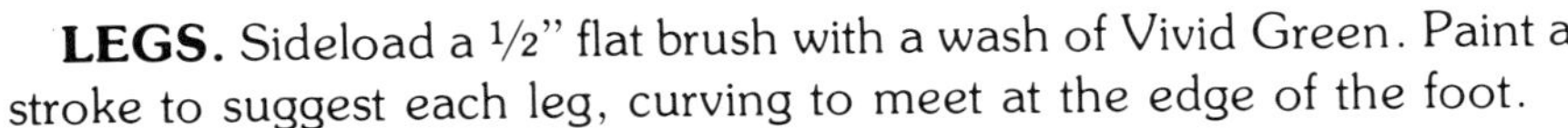

LEGS. Sideload a 1/2" flat brush with a wash of Vivid Green. Paint a stroke to suggest each leg, curving to meet at the edge of the foot.

SCALES. Working across the top of Snort's back from the base of his neck to the beginning of his tail, paint sideloaded crescent strokes of Vivid Green. Continue building down from this row in brick layer fashion, gradually decreasing the size of the scales in each layer. Embellish each of the scales with strokes and dots. Here's a nice place to doodle. A few variations are illustrated to help get your creative cogs in gear. Study them for ideas, then doodle your own designs on the empty scales.

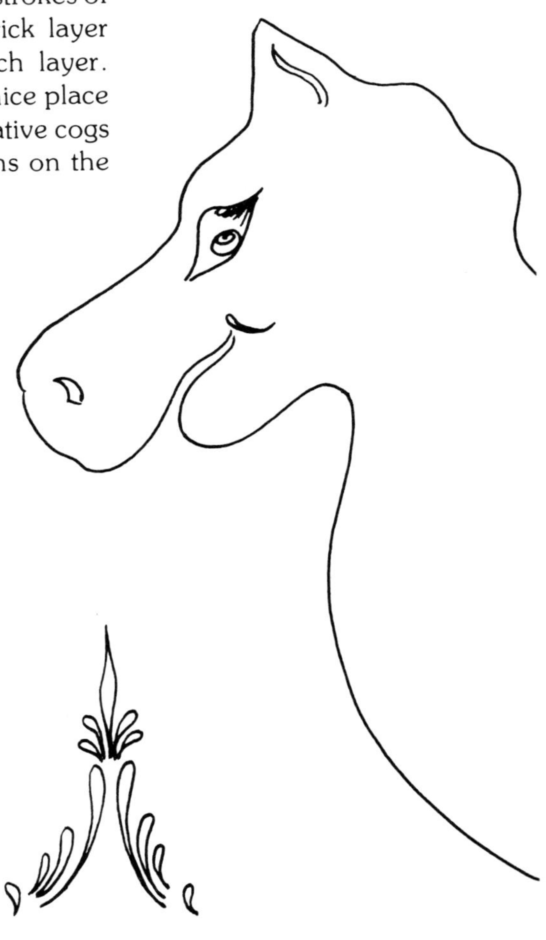

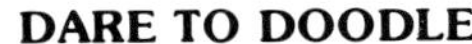

DARE TO DOODLE

Here are some other suggestions for embellishing the scales. You doodle your own ideas on the blank scales.

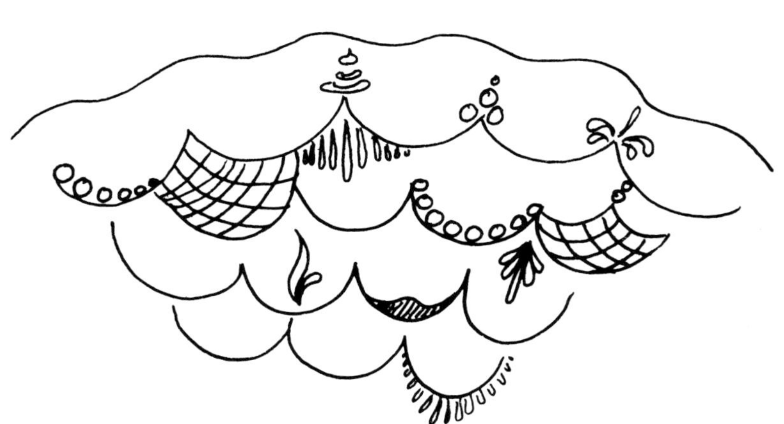

EYES. Outline a pointed eye with two Vivid Green "S" strokes. Fill in the back part of the eye with Butter Yellow. Add an Orange iris and a Tompte Red pupil. Highlight with Butter Yellow.

MOUTH. Outline the mouth and cheek line with Orange. Add a Tompte Red tongue.

NOSTRILS. Two little oval dabs of Orange provide a nice place from which Butter Yellow "smoke" strokes can emerge.

EARS. Paint a Vivid Green "S" stroke with a #4 flat. Outline that stroke with a Butter Yellow "S" stroke using the #2 liner.

FEET. Give old Snort three large Blue Spruce toes (comma strokes) on each foot.

TAIL. Decorate each colored segment of the tail with Blue Spruce strokes and dots.

SPECIAL EFFECTS. Give Snort an almost ethereal effect by lightly sponging Vivid Green over the tail, legs, and neck. See color illustration on page 15. Leave the scales and face unsponged for contrast.

CRAYONASAURUS FEATHERS bedeck Snort's chest. Orange "S" and comma strokes finished off by chocolate chips make a striking contrast against the Blue Spruce body.

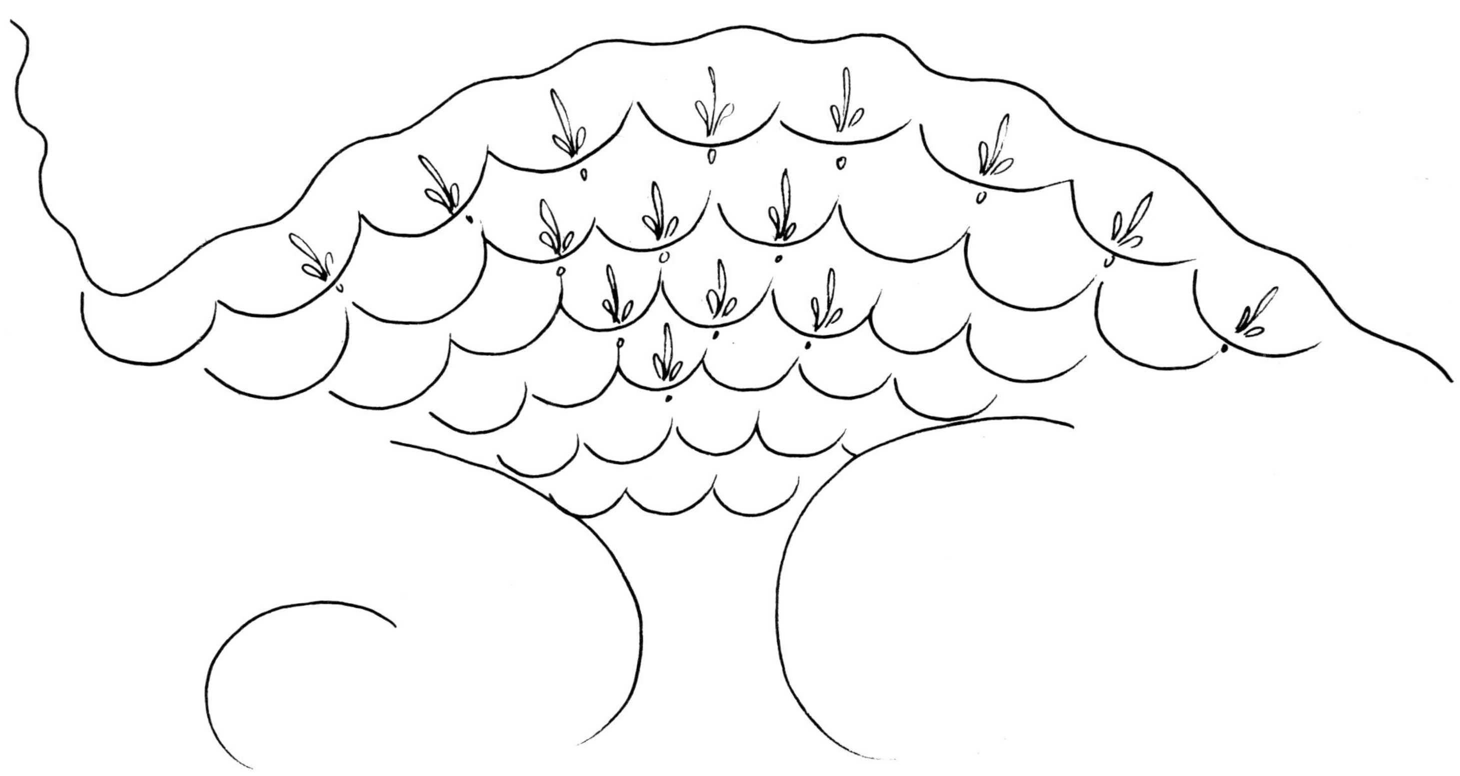

MAGIC FAIRY WAND

COLORS

Norsk Blue
Wedgewood Green
Metallic Silver
Aluminum Bronzing Powder
Adobe

PROCEDURE

This is a good little project on which to experiment with different color schemes. To simply duplicate the wand as pictured and to follow the accompanying directions to the letter would be most unadventuresome of you. The directions are shared with you only to help get you started. You say you have never seen a real fairy wand and therefore do not know how they should look? Well that's great! No one else knows either. So keep your little secret and just paint it as if you had been born with one. As long as you paint it like you mean it and have fun doing so, it will be a magical success.

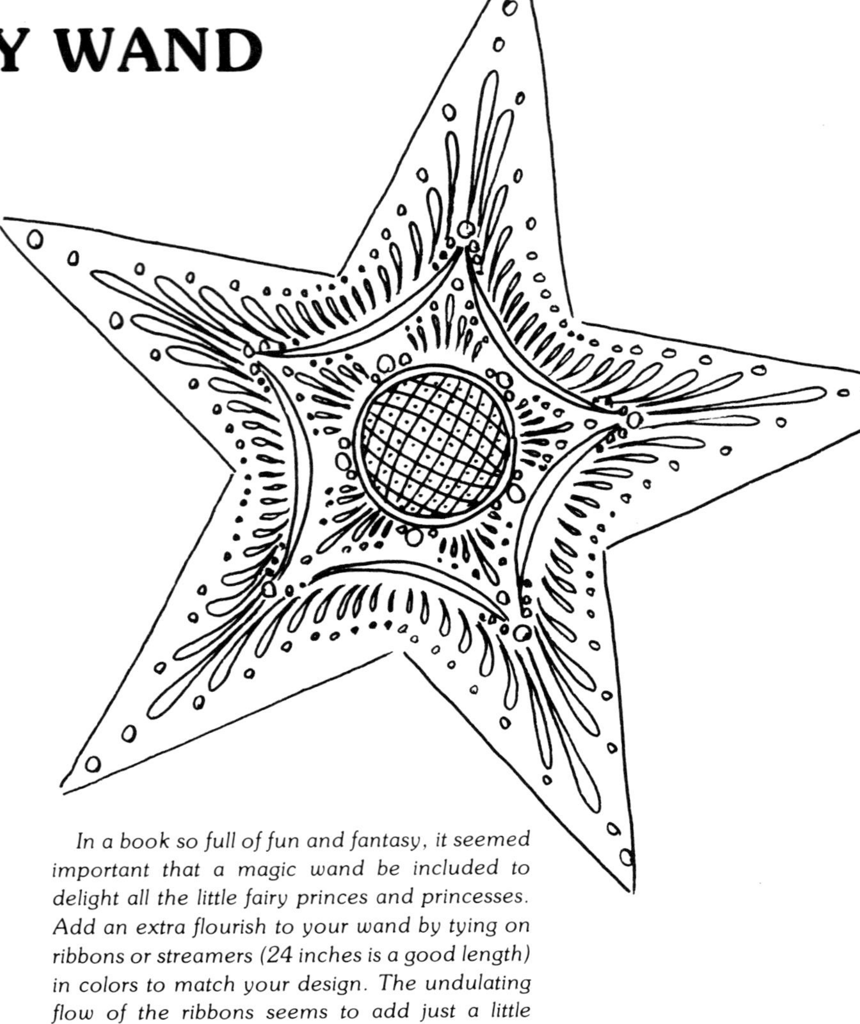

In a book so full of fun and fantasy, it seemed important that a magic wand be included to delight all the little fairy princes and princesses. Add an extra flourish to your wand by tying on ribbons or streamers (24 inches is a good length) in colors to match your design. The undulating flow of the ribbons seems to add just a little more mystery to the magic.

The handle is first basecoated with Wedgewood Green. Dry thoroughly. Wrap narrow masking tape in a spiral around the handle. Press the tape to seal the edges tightly. Paint the exposed areas Norsk Blue. Dry. Carefully peel up the tape. Mix the Metallic Silver acrylic with a little Aluminum Bronzing Powder to create a richer silver. Paint delicate strokes to edge the spiral.

Basecoat the front and back of the star with Norsk Blue, and the edges with Wedgewood Green. Then, let your imagination fly and decorate the front, back, and edges of the star with a brilliant burst of strokes, a bunch of flowers, a whimsical face or whatever suits your fancy. You can spend as little as a few minutes decorating the wand or lose yourself for several hours in intricate detailing. Either way, the finished product will surely delight a little one.

And just think what an ideal craft bazaar item this could be.

P.S. I have it straight from the paint brush genie that a hand decorated Magic Fairy Wand in the vicinity of your painting area will radiate magic energy to all your freehanding brushes. Now that you know the secret of the magic brushes, shouldn't you get busy and paint a wand.

MR. ALLEY GATOR

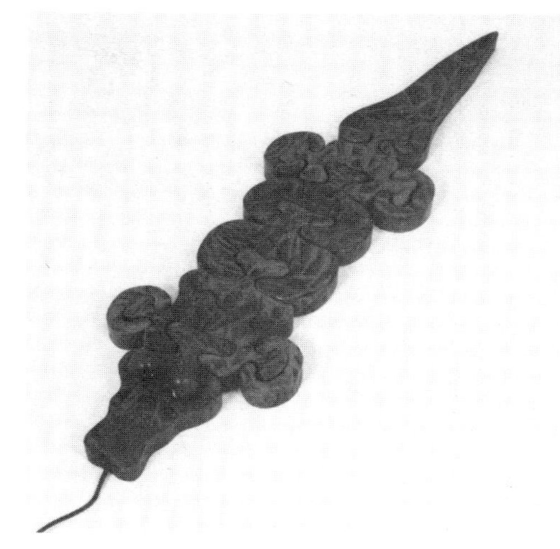

COLORS

Vivid Green
Dark Forest
Ivory
Cardinal Red
Black Green

PROCEDURE:

Basecoat the puzzle with Vivid Green. (If the puzzle is intended for a very young child, basecoat the underneath side in a different color to make it easier to assemble.) When the basecoat is dry, spread a thin wash of Dark Forest on the top and sides of one puzzle piece at a time. Quickly place a piece of plastic wrap on the wet wash. Marbleize each section as described on page 11.

An optional procedure is to assemble Alley Gator and marbleize the entire top as a unit. Then it will be necessary to marbleize the sides separately. The advantage to this method is that the top is uniformly marbleized. The disadvantage lies in the possibility of the wash dripping down the sides and drying in streaks before you are able to wash and marbleize them.

EYES. Paint the two round knobs Cardinal Red. Follow the directions and full color illustrations on page 56 for painting Alley Gator's eyes.

MOUTH. Paint a large grin in Cardinal Red.

ALLEY FEATHERS fit quite nicely on Alley's snout.

One of the songs I used to enjoy teaching my kindergarten and first grade students admonished them to "never smile at a crocodile, never tip your hat and stop to chat awhile." And though I'm sure the warning would hold true for all such fearsome reptiles, surely an exception could be made for our Mr. Alley Gator.

Once Alley is assembled, he can be pulled along by his string and all his pieces remain assembled. He is a very "together gator" who can be found in color on page 48.

SNAP DRAGON

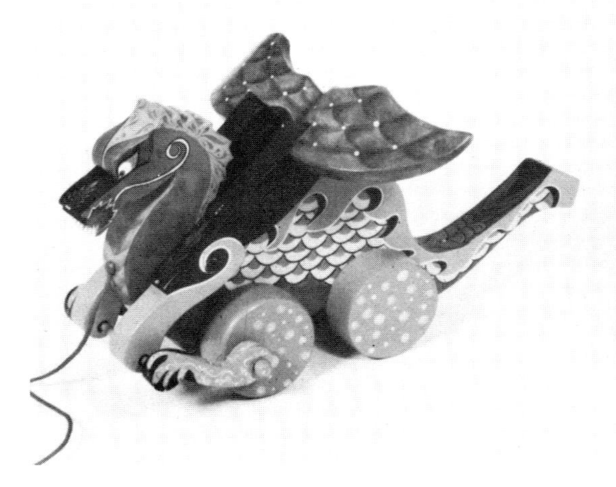

COLORS

- Vivid Green
- Forest Green
- Yellow
- Antique Gold
- Tompte Red
- Orange
- Norsk Blue
- Turquoise
- Old Parchment
- Thalo Blue
- Grape
- Black
- Queen Anne's Lace
- Walnut

PROCEDURE

Use chalk to divide Snap Dragon's body into areas (mane, scales, "waves"). Paint the face, body, and wings with a scumbling effect, using Vivid Green and Forest Green and a ½" brush. (See pages 10 and 11 for scumbling tips.)

Paint the dragon's eye with a mixture of Walnut + Old Parchment. Outline it with Black. Paint a Queen Anne's Lace egg-shaped eye with a dab of Tompte Red and a spot of Black for the pupil. Paint several thin lines of Forest Green surrounding the eyes.

The wheels, mane, and the area under the chin, belly, and tail are Orange + Tompte Red. Sideload a #12 flat brush with Tompte Red and paint wide "V's" on the dragon's chest. The forearms, lower section of wing supports, and "waves" on the back are Norsk Blue + Turquoise + Old Parchment. Give Snap Dragon "hairy" forearms by painting tiny scrolls, strokes and swirls in Queen Anne's Lace. Add Tompte Red fingernails (or are they toes?). Paint the

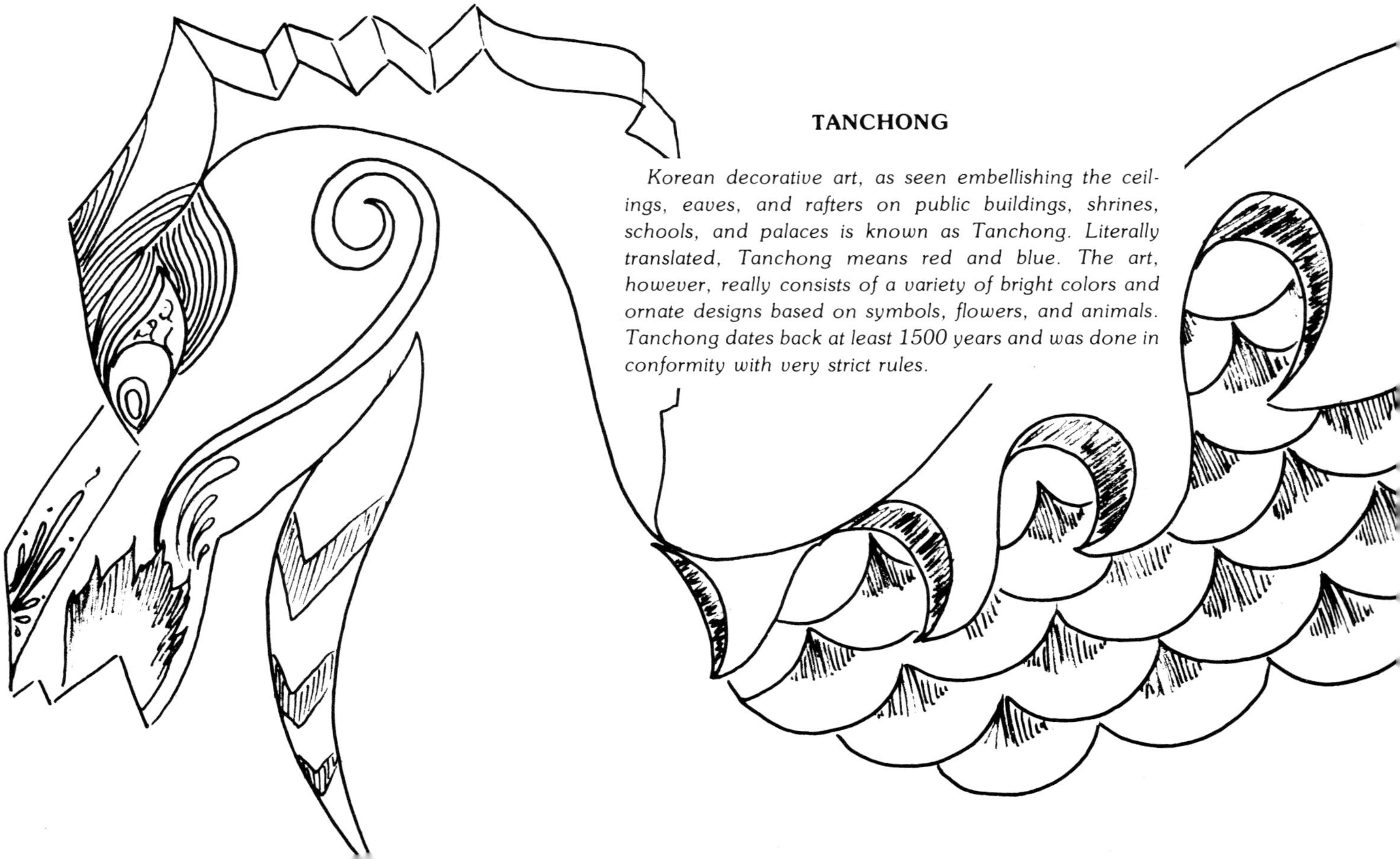

TANCHONG

Korean decorative art, as seen embellishing the ceilings, eaves, and rafters on public buildings, shrines, schools, and palaces is known as Tanchong. Literally translated, Tanchong means red and blue. The art, however, really consists of a variety of bright colors and ornate designs based on symbols, flowers, and animals. Tanchong dates back at least 1500 years and was done in conformity with very strict rules.

scales Yellow + Antique Gold. Use this same mixture and the handle end of a large brush to swirl large and small dots on the wheels. Accent the scales with the Orange + Tompte Red mixture. Use a #4 flat brush. Outline each scale with a thin, even width Black line using the #2 liner brush.

Mix Thalo + Grape + Tompte Red to a deep, royal blue violet. Paint the dragon's back, the upper part of the wing support, the spaces around the "toes" on the forearms, and accents on the "waves." Outline the "waves" with Queen Anne's Lace. Embellish his back, above the tail, with Vivid Green + Forest Green leaflike formations outlined in Black and accented with Tompte Red strokes. Divide the wings into squares with a crosshatch effect using Orange + Tompte Red. Shade two sides of each square with Forest Green. Place a Butter Yellow + Antique Gold dot at each intersection.

Paint the dragon's eye with a mixture of Walnut + Old Parchment. Outline it with Black. Paint a Queen Anne's Lace egg-shaped eye with a dab of Tompte Red and a spot of Black for the pupil. Paint several thin lines of Forest Green surrounding the eyes.

Around the mouth, paint a jagged-edged wash of the Thalo + Grape + Tompte Red mixture. Outline this with Queen Anne's Lace. Paint a long curly mustache in Queen Anne's Lace. Outline the mustache with Black. Add a few Tompte Red teardrop strokes below the mustache. Place ferocious Queen Anne's Lace teeth and a Tompte Red tongue in Snap Dragon's mouth.

Paint Tompte Red strokes on the mane. Use Tompte Red on the upper wing supports, and on the snout, to give Snap Dragon three sets of DRAGON FEATHERS for good luck!

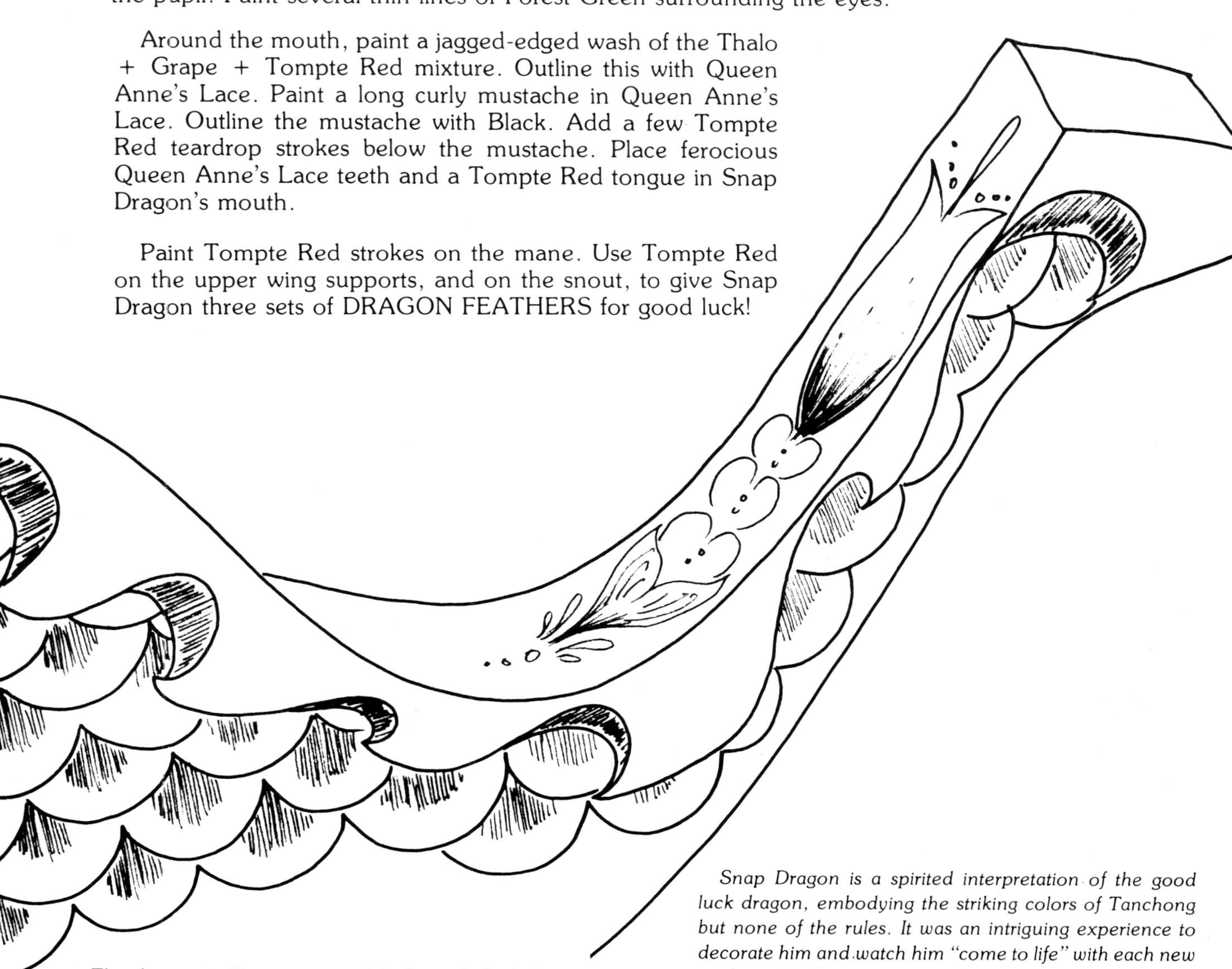

Snap Dragon is a spirited interpretation of the good luck dragon, embodying the striking colors of Tanchong but none of the rules. It was an intriguing experience to decorate him and watch him "come to life" with each new stroke and color experimented with. Snap Dragon's construction is genuinely clever. When pulled by his string, the wheels rotate moving his front forearms, and causing his massive wings to "flap." He is one of our favorite toys.

The dragon in Korea is a good luck symbol which is credited with guarding the good fortunes of the home. In particular, paintings of a blue dragon are often affixed to the front doors.

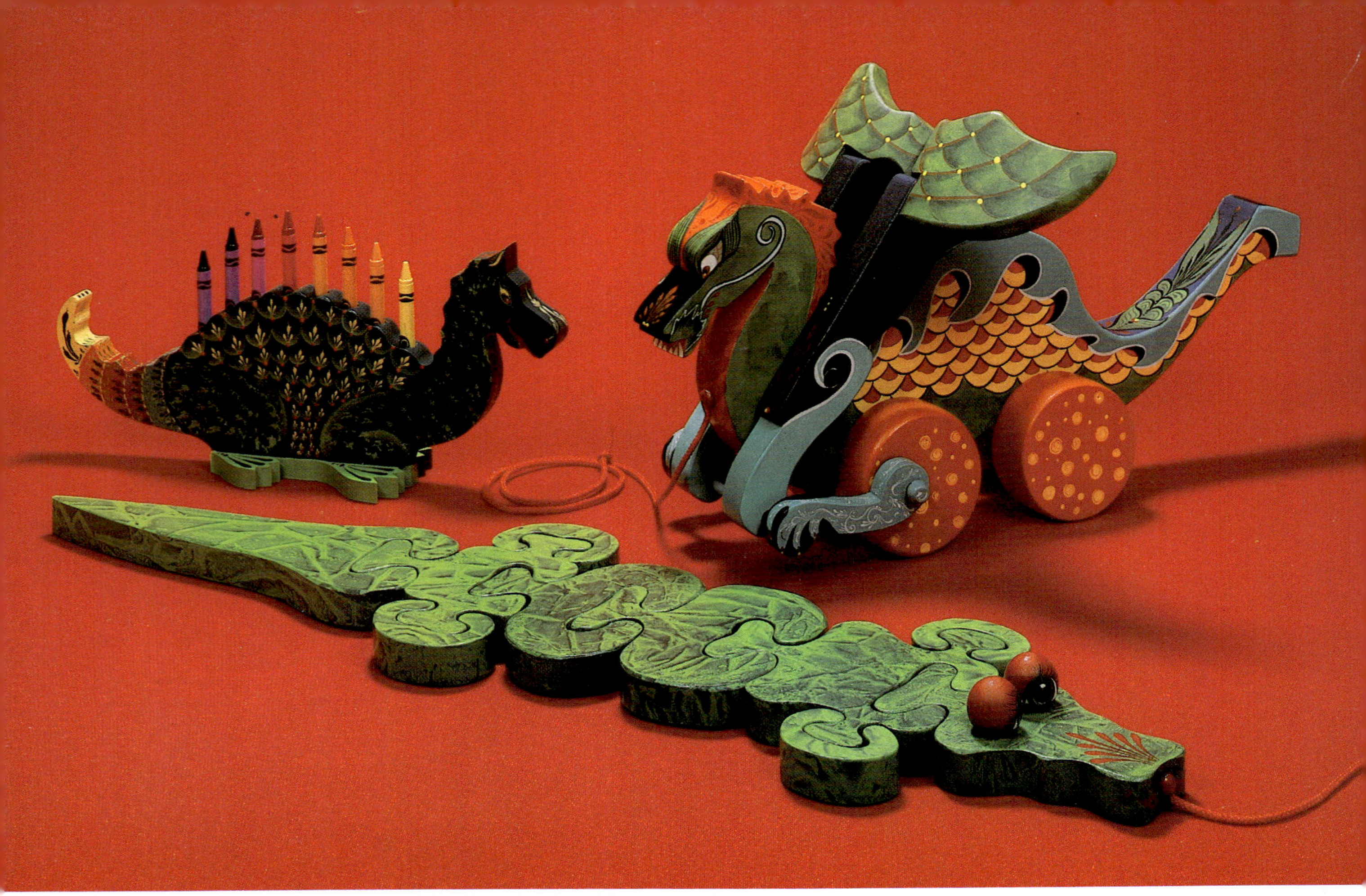

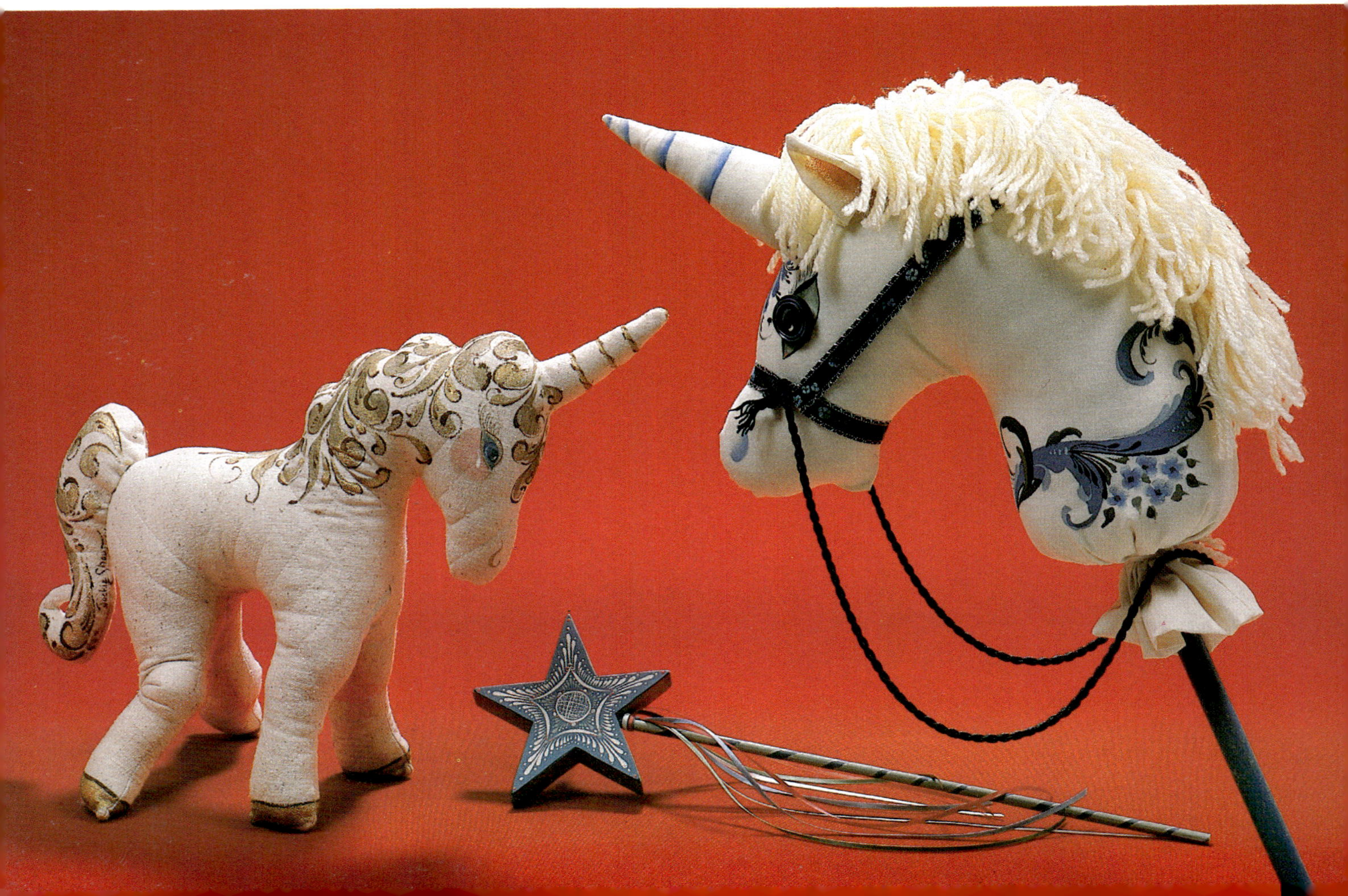

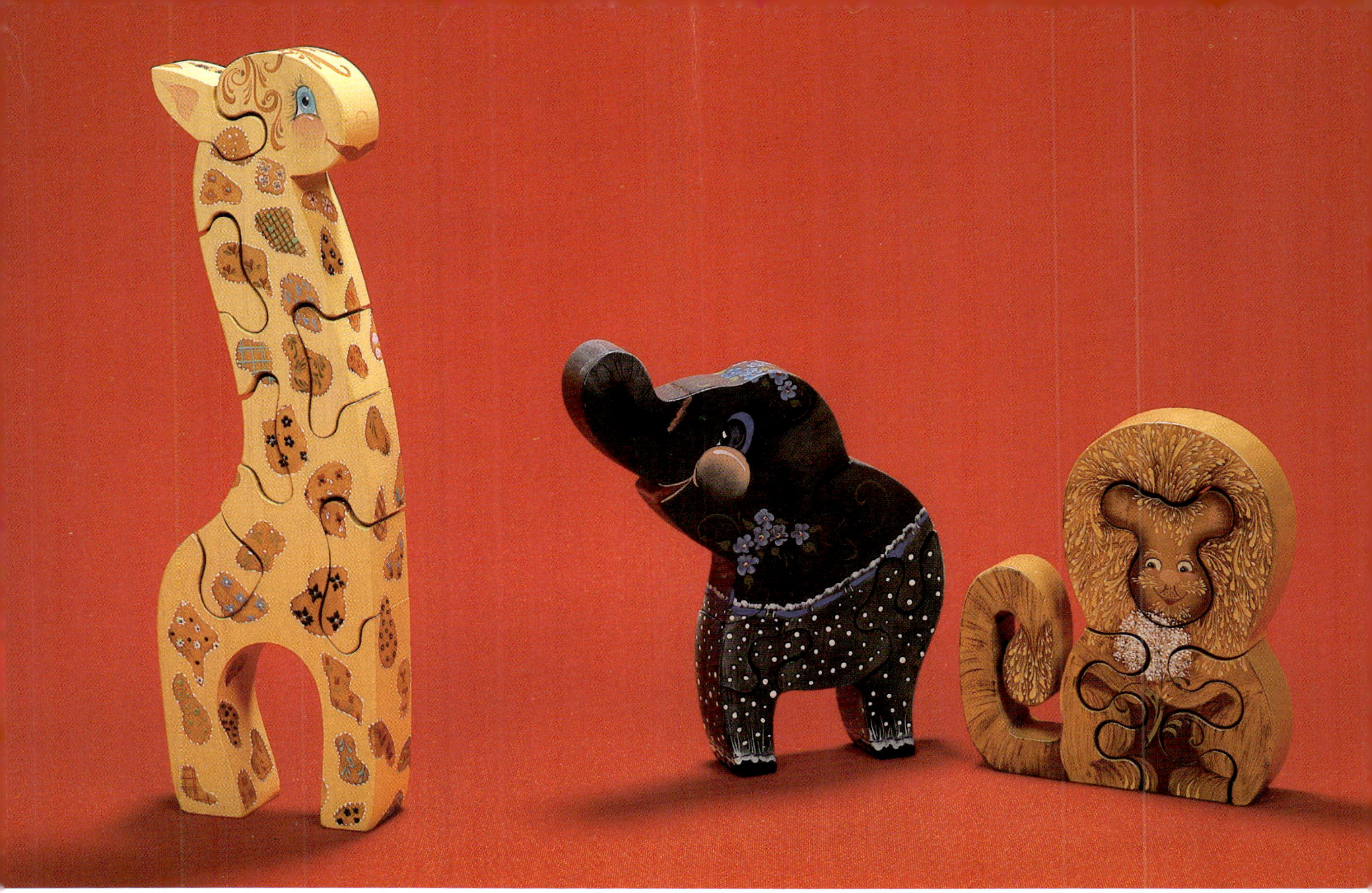

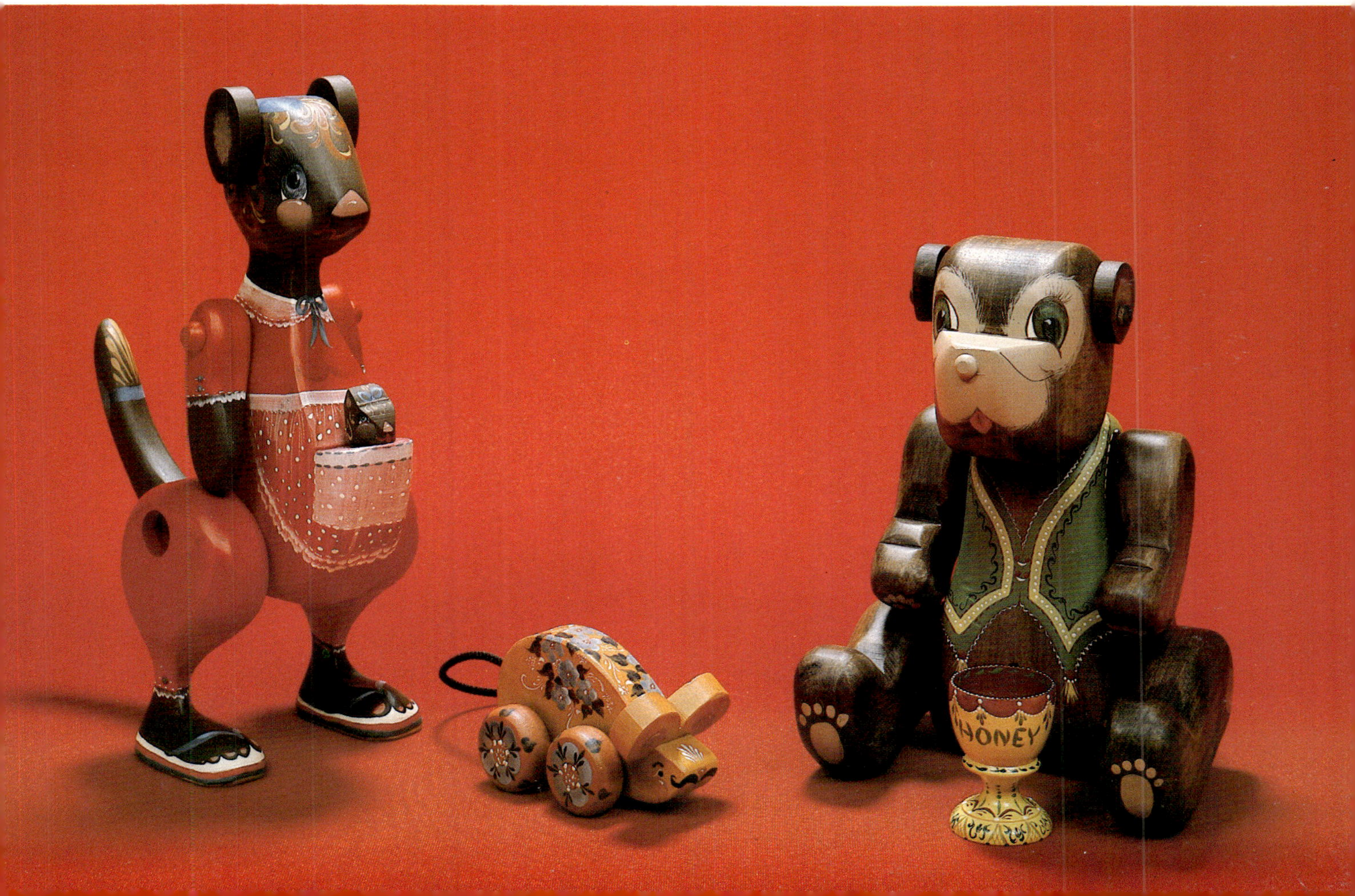

UNI-STICK UNICORN

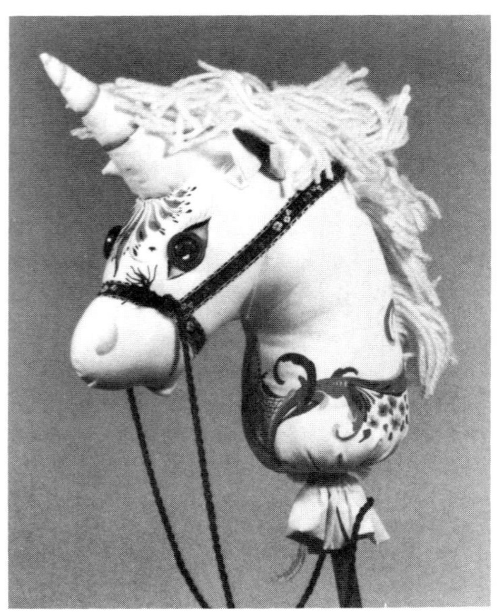

COLORS

- Fiesta Pink
- Copen Blue
- Salem Green
- Old Parchment
- Ivory
- Forest Green
- Chrome Green Light
- Wedgewood Green
- Black

PROCEDURE

EYE. Use a Conté pencil to sketch an eye shape approximately 2¼" long by 1" wide. Fill in the area with Wedgewood Green. Outline with Black, and add Black lashes. Place a Fiesta Pink dab in the inside corner of the eye. Sew a colorful, large button on each eye. Paint a Black pupil and an Ivory highlight on each button.

NOSE. Sideload a #12 flat brush with a mixture of Copen Blue + Salem Green + Old Parchment. Paint a short scroll stroke.

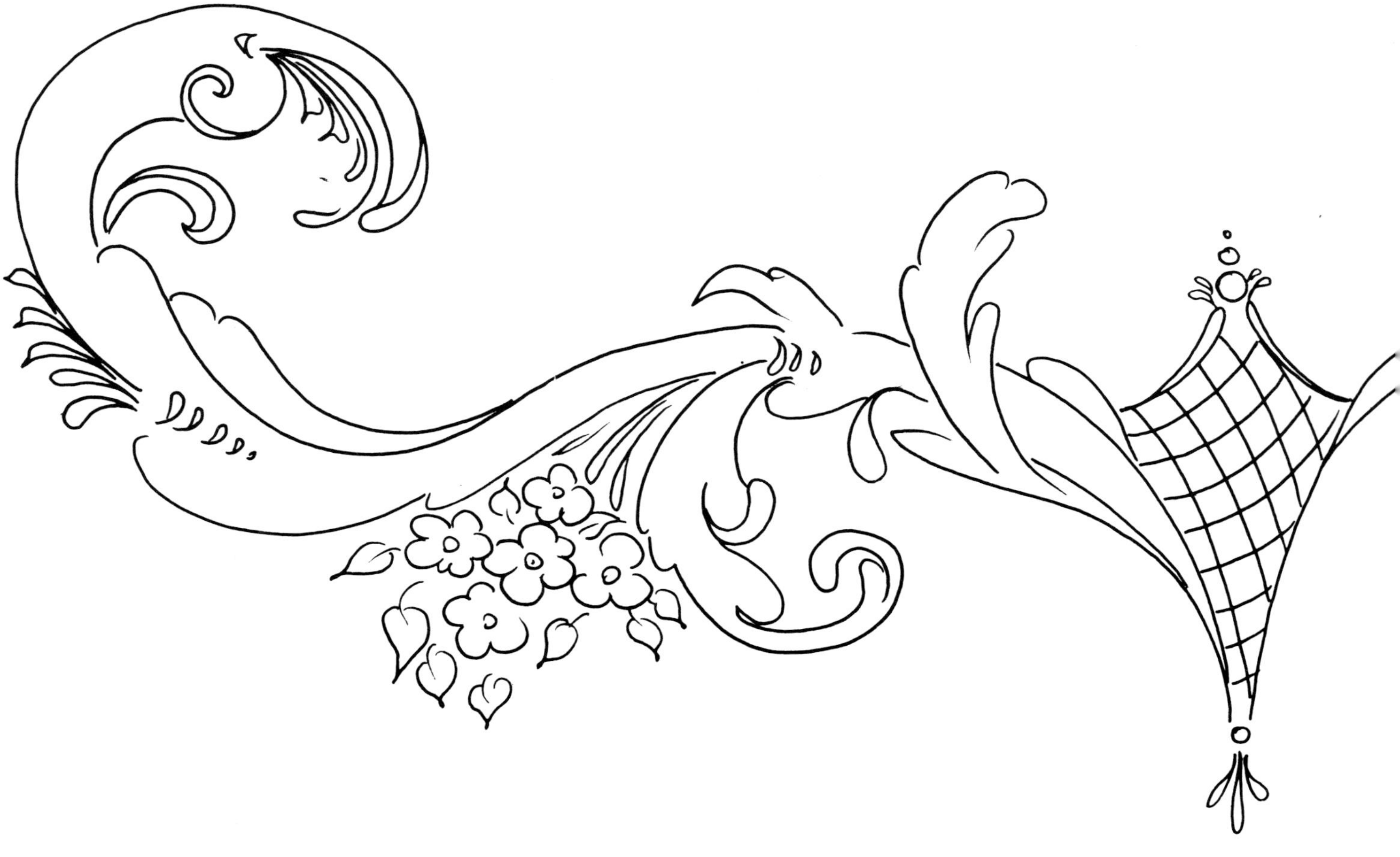

HORN. Using the Copen Blue mixture from above, sideloaded into a ½" brush, paint a spiral on the horn. The spiral is a wide stroke at the base decreasing to a narrower width as it progresses to the tip.

EARS. Basecoat inside ears with Ivory. Several coats will help provide stiffness to the ears. While the Ivory is still wet, brush Fiesta Pink in the centers and blend, fading at the edges.

SCROLLS. Use a #8 round brush. The large scrolls are a mixture of Copen Blue + Salem Green + Old Parchment. The scrolls are tipped and detailed with the Copen Blue mixture plus Ivory. The green scrolls are Forest Green, tipped and detailed with Chrome Green Light. Detail strokes in Black were painted with the #2 liner.

UNI-FEATHERS. Large comma strokes flanking a large "S" stroke radiate from the horn onto the forehead. Black detail strokes and dots are added with the #2 liner.

STICK. Use a natural sponge to apply Copen Blue and Wedgewood Green in a splotchy, mottled effect. See sponging, pages 10 and 11.

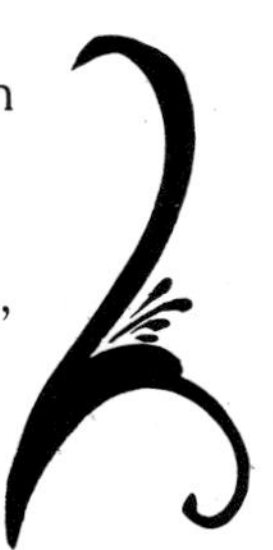

KATHY'S NOTE PAD

COLORS

Fjord Blue	Fiesta Pink
Colonial Blue	Tompte Red
Autumn Brown	Black
Golden Brown	Ivory

PROCEDURE

The background is basecoated with Fjord Blue. Lettering and stroke trim are Colonial Blue. The bear is Golden Brown, shaded with Autumn Brown. Fiesta Pink defines the cheeks, ears and nose. The eyes are Ivory, Colonial Blue, Fjord Blue, and Black. The necktie is painted Colonial Blue.

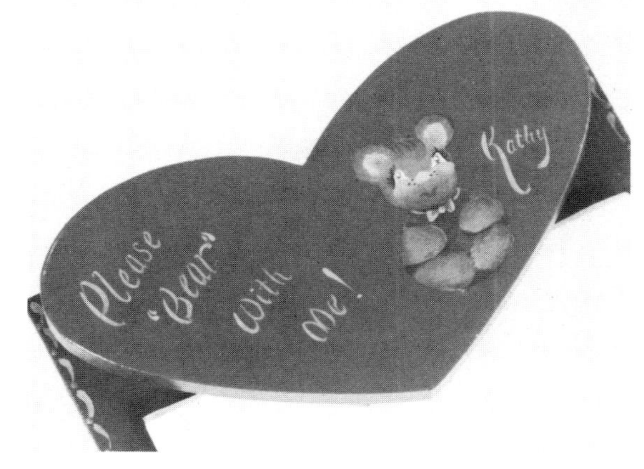

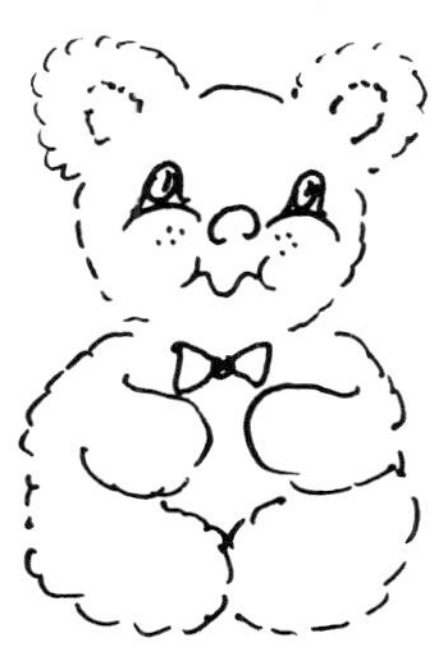

Another bear for Kathy's collection! Although the entreaty "Please bear with me" is most appropriate for teenage years, there couldn't be a better teen than Kathy.

DANDY LION

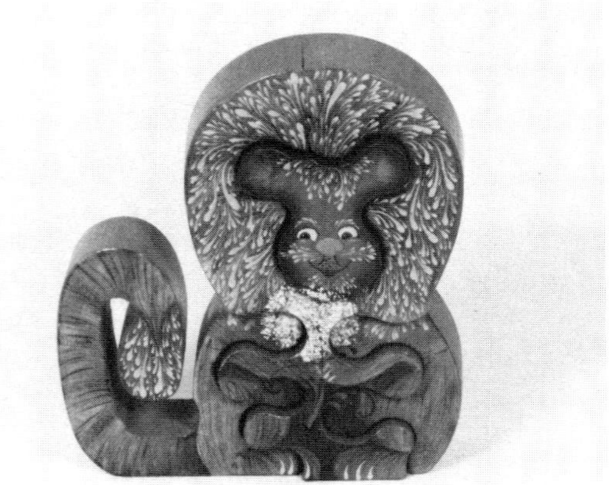

COLORS

Dark Brown
Autumn Brown
Golden Brown
Butter Yellow
Old Parchment
Fiesta Pink
Red Tile
Norsk Blue
Midnight
Tompte Red
Silver
White
Leaf Green
Dark Forest

PROCEDURE

Use chalk or Conté pencil to sketch paws and legs. Paint the area at the base of the tail, around the edge of the face, and behind the paws and legs Dark Brown or Autumn Brown. Paint all remaining areas Golden Brown. Blend the Golden Brown into the Dark or Autumn Brown on the face and tail by double loading the brush with the two values of brown. Coverage on the body may be a bit choppy, but do try to get a smooth gradual blend on the face. Use a dry brush and Dark Brown to shade the mane area near the face. Also dry brush the body with Autumn Brown. See dry brushing, below. Indicate hair on body and tail by painting thousands of *thin* lines using a liner and Autumn Brown, Butter Yellow, and Dark Brown, each thinned with water.

FACE. Paint Dandy's nose first. That gives you a nice starting point from which to determine the placement of all the other things necessary to a face. The nose is a mixture of Red Tile + Old Parchment, painted with a #2 flat brush. Next paint Fiesta Pink cheeks with a sideloaded #4 flat brush. Highlight cheeks and nose with Old Parchment. Use the #2 liner and Red Tile to paint wispy lines in the ears. Overstroke with Fiesta Pink. The eyes are based in with Old Parchment. Add Norsk Blue irises and Midnight pupils. Highlight with Old Parchment. Outline the eyes with Dark Brown and add a few comma stroke lashes. Paint a Tompte Red smile.

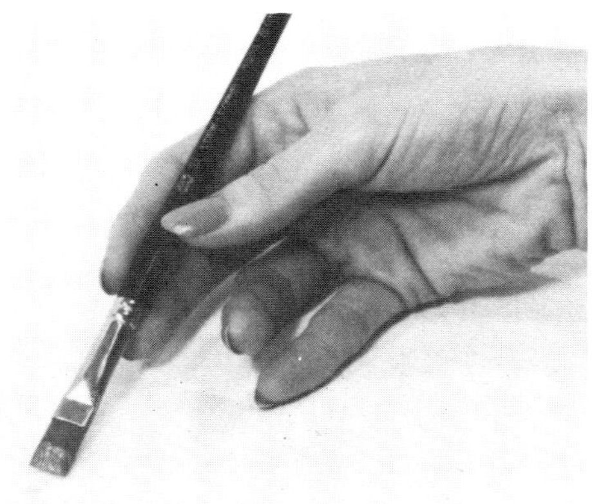

Dry Brushing. *Blot all water out of the flat brush. Pick up a very little paint on the hairs. Blot paint on a paper towel. Hold the brush loosely in your hand as pictured. Lightly skim the hairs across the surface, laying down very little paint.*

Dry Brush Stroke.

MANE, TAIL, MUSTACHE, ETC. Bet you never knew that a lion's mane was not hair but rather teardrops, thousands of them, painted in wild profusion. Use a #2 liner and Butter Yellow, and paint 6,034 (well, almost that many) teardrop strokes. Just when you're certain you cannot add another stroke, load the brush with Old Parchment mixed with a little Butter Yellow and paint another several thousand teardrops. Paint Dandy's tail, bangs, mustache, goatee, and eyebrows the same way.

TOENAILS. Paint three Butter Yellow teardrop strokes on each paw.

DANDELION. Use the #2 liner to paint the stem and leaves Leaf Green. Accent with Dark Forest. Paint "spokes" of Old Parchment radiating from the center of the flower. Sponge on Silver. Dry. Sponge on a very little Ivory. Dry. Add tiny White dots. See color illustration on page 23.

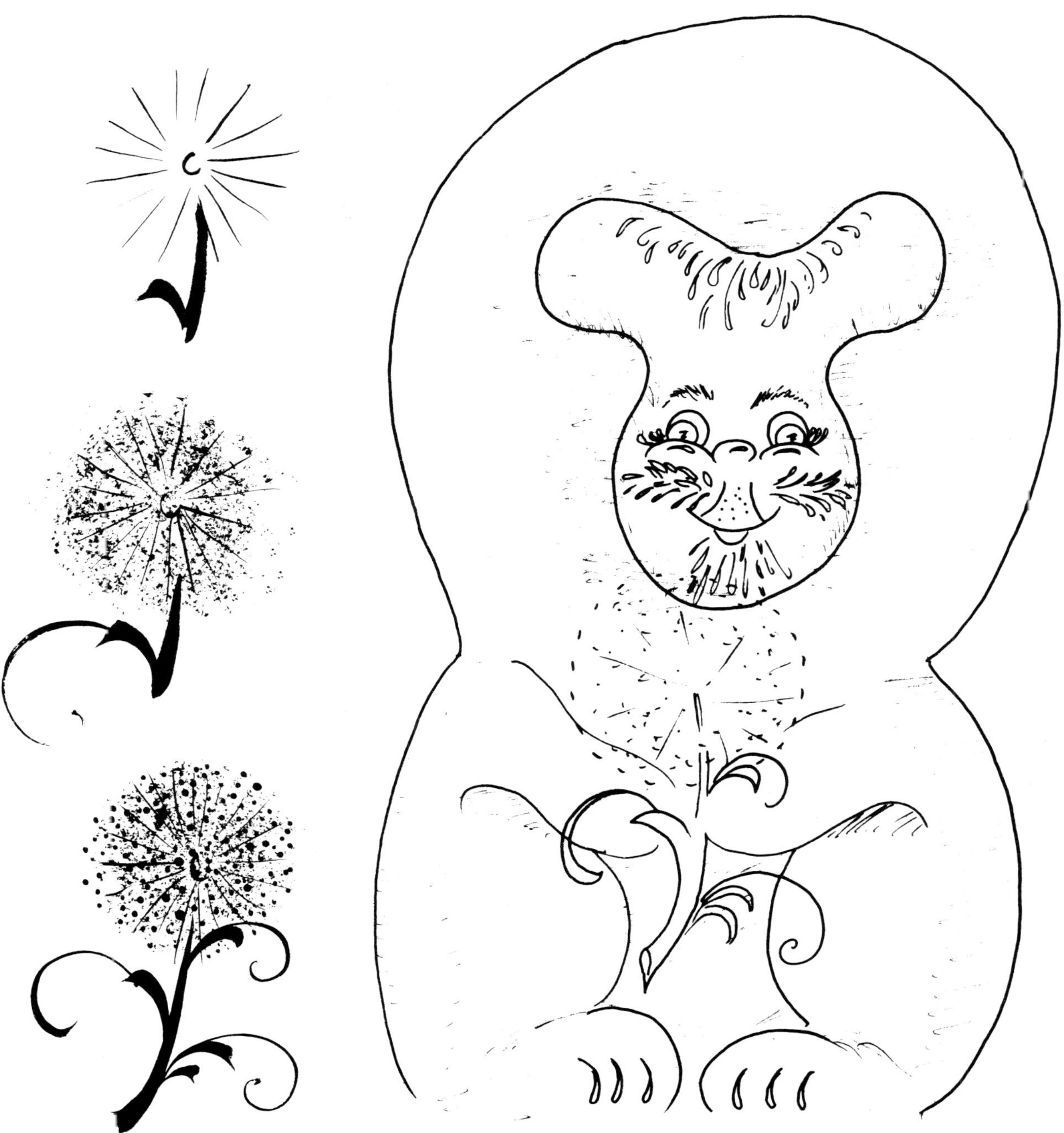

UNIQUE ORN

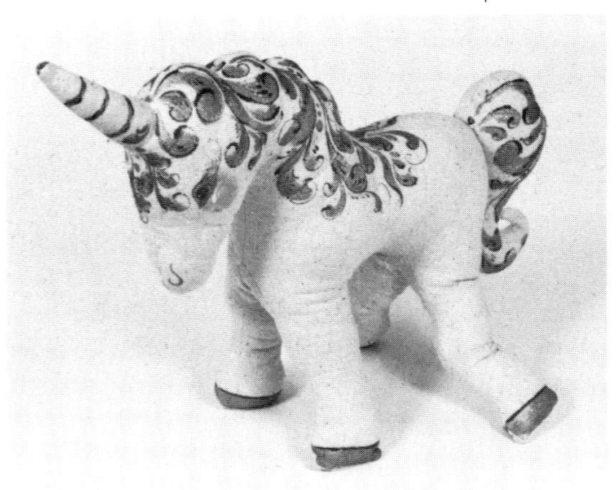

COLORS

Kim Gold	Wedgewood Green
Dark Brown	Copen Blue
Fiesta Pink	Midnight
Ivory	Gold Bronzing Powder

PROCEDURE

Although the colors suggested are acrylics, you may prefer to use dyes, especially if you want to paint a soft, cuddly animal for a younger child.

CHEEKS. Paint large Fiesta Pink + Ivory cheeks. Highlight with Ivory.

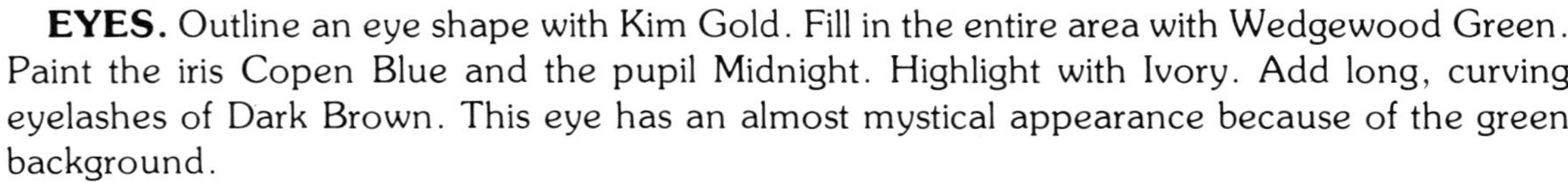

EYES. Outline an eye shape with Kim Gold. Fill in the entire area with Wedgewood Green. Paint the iris Copen Blue and the pupil Midnight. Highlight with Ivory. Add long, curving eyelashes of Dark Brown. This eye has an almost mystical appearance because of the green background.

NOSE. Two curved gold strokes suggest nostrils.

MANE AND TAIL. Mix Kim Gold with Gold Bronzing Powder to give additional lustre. Load a 1/2" flat brush with the gold mixture. Paint scrolls and strokes all over the mane and tail. Outline the scrolls and add details with Dark Brown in a #2 liner. (See color illustration on page 15.)

HORN. Paint a spiral, or rings of gold accented with Dark Brown on the horn.

FEET. Tip the feet with gold. Trim with Dark Brown.

Unique-Orn is pictured in color on page 48.

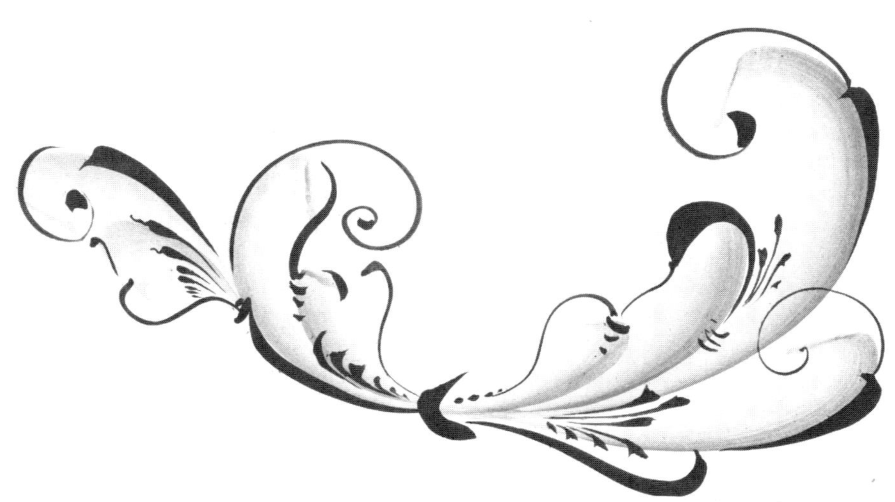

This toy came about because of our 13-year old Laurie's fascination with unicorns for the past year. Unable to find a stuffed one to decorate for her, I decided to design patterns for one myself. My sister, Bonnie, agreed to sew it together. She has since made more unicorns than she had ever imagined. If you are unable to find unicorns in your area suitable for painting, write or have your craft store contact Bonnie. Her address is in the back of this book.

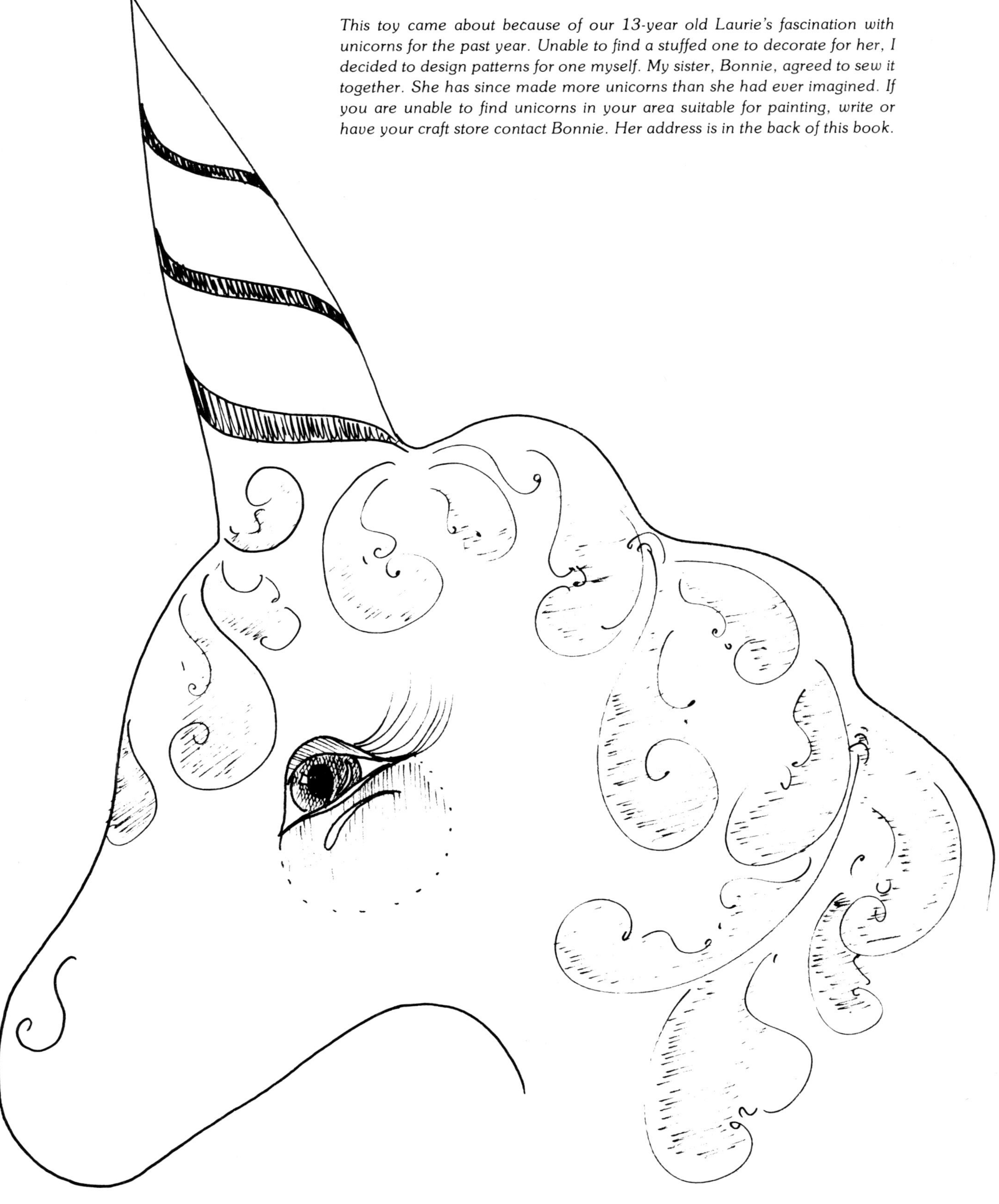

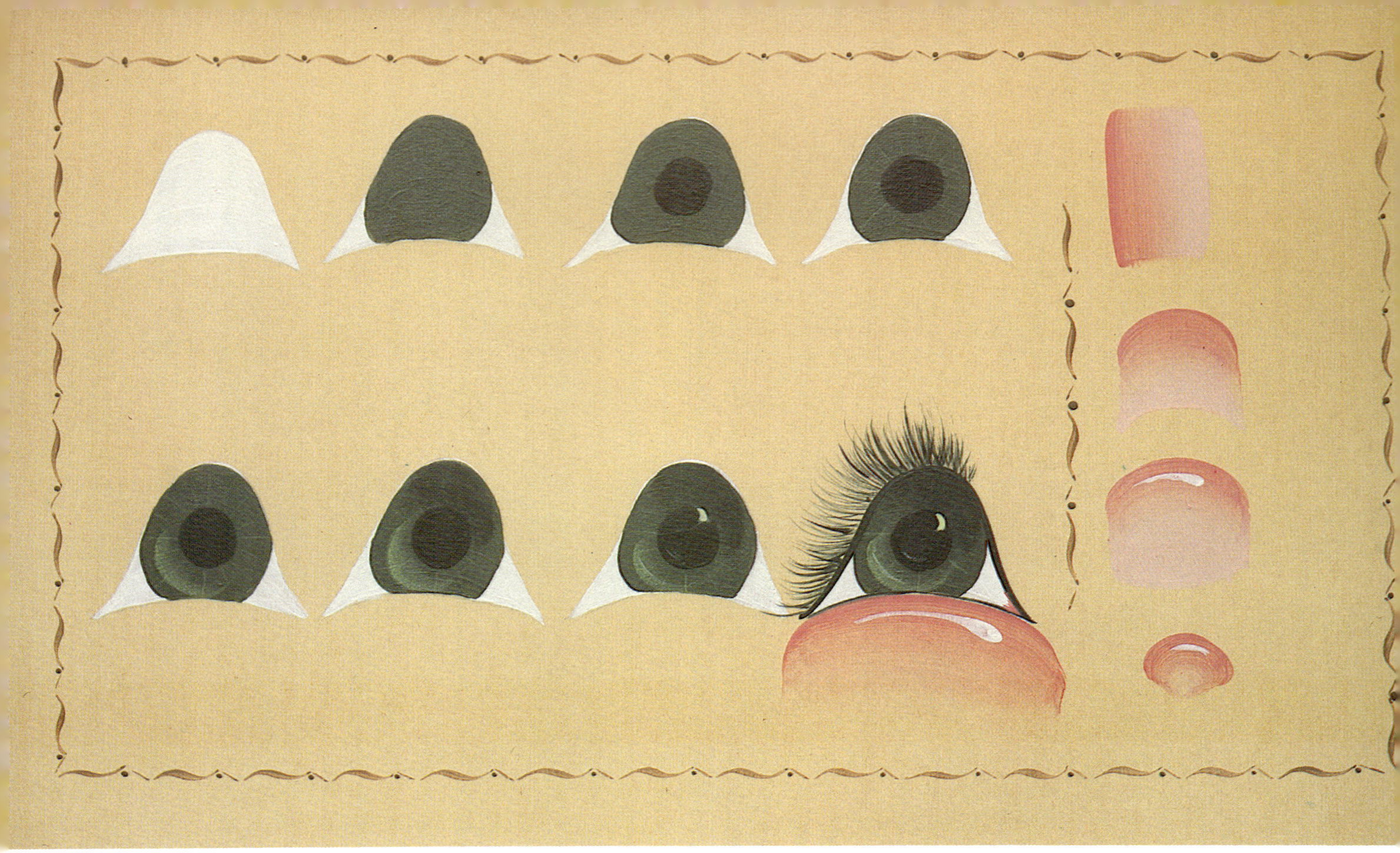

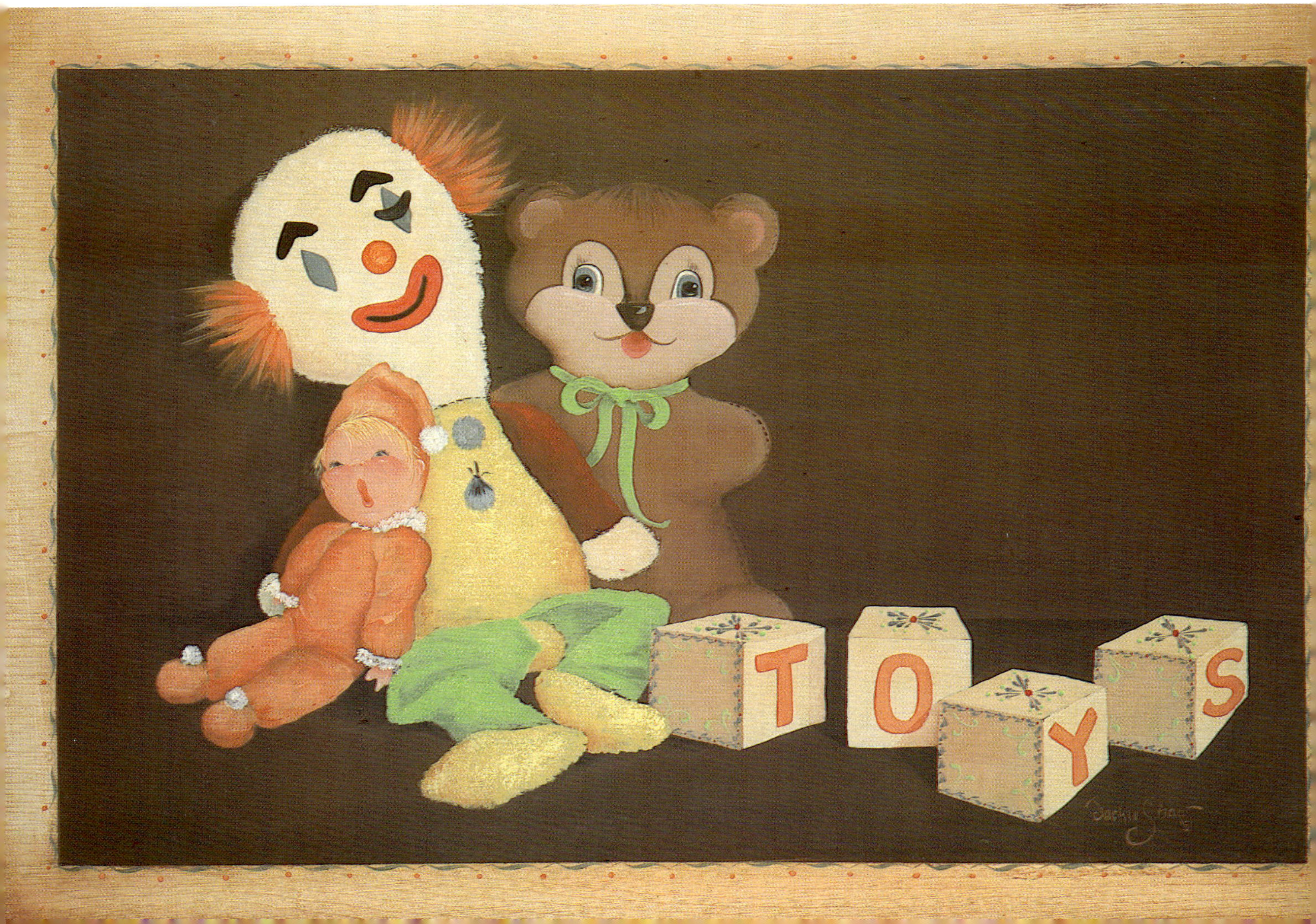

TOYBOX

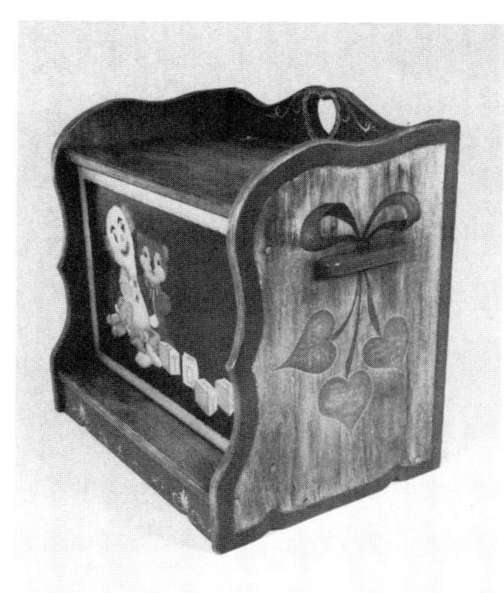

COLORS

Burnt Umber	Pineapple
Norsk Blue	Mocha
Old Parchment	Pink Angel
Adobe	Ivory
Tangerine	CF Native Flesh
Fiesta Pink	Lime Green
Red Iron Oxide	Dark Forest
White	Blaze
Midnight	Black
Butter Yellow	Marshmallow
Light Chocolate	Autumn Brown

PROCEDURE

BORDERS. Using 1" wide masking tape, mask the area which will become the light border around the brown background on the front of the toybox. Press the edges of the tape to seal tightly. Paint the background Burnt Umber. Refer to the front cover to see placement of other background trim colors. The blue trim is Norsk Blue, the red edges are a scumbled combination (see pages 10, 11) of Red Iron Oxide, Blaze, and CF Native Flesh. The remainder of the toybox is left unbasecoated. Peel up the masking tape and paint the border around the Burnt Umber background with Old Parchment.

SHADOWS. Before painting the blocks and childhood toys, lay in Dark Chocolate shadows, letting them fade softly into the background. Use a large sideloaded flat brush. Intensify the depth of the shadows up close to the trio of loved ones and blocks by laying a wash of Walnut over the dry Dark Chocolate. Painting the shadows on the Burnt Umber background will be a little tricky since water in your brush will make the Burnt Umber appear darker. Just have faith and confidence, and charge ahead. When the wash dries, you can tell if you were successful. If not, try again.

BEAR. Bear is just a little 2-piece, printed fabric, hand sewn animal. Paint him first. Basecoat his face with Light Chocolate and his body with Autumn Brown. Use Burnt Umber sideloaded on a #12 flat brush to shade the area to the left, next to Clown. A little shading should also be added to the other side to help suggest dimension. The light source is from the right, so place a sideloaded wash of Light Chocolate + Autumn Brown on the right, to the inside of the lightly shaded area. Paint cheeks in Pink Angel, highlighted with White. Eyes are Ivory, with Norsk Blue irises and Midnight pupils. The nose is Burnt Umber, the mouth is Fiesta Pink. Double load a #8 flat brush with Autumn Brown and Fiesta Pink to paint the ears. Finish Bear by adding Burnt Umber stitching with the #2 liner, and a Lime bow, shaded with Dark Forest.

CLOWN. Clown is a fuzzy, plush, stuffed toy whose plush is now quite worn, and whose stuffings have been re-stuffed several times. Basecoat Clown's hands and head Old Parchment. When dry, use cheesecloth to barely pat on Ivory. Dip the cheesecloth into Ivory, then pat several times on a paper towel to remove most of the paint. (See pages 10, 11.) Dry. Shade left side softly with Light Chocolate sideloaded in a large flat brush.

Basecoat his body and feet with Butter Yellow. Dry. Use cheesecloth to pat on Pineapple highlights. Dry. Shade the left side with Mocha + Butter Yellow sideloaded in a large flat brush.

Basecoat the legs with Lime. Dry. Use cheesecloth to pat on Lime + Pineapple. Dry. Shade with Lime + Dark Forest sideloaded in a large flat brush.

Dab on Blaze for the arms. Blaze is transparent, so use that feature to advantage. The background showing through the transparent Blaze will suggest shading. Areas to appear more intensely red and highlighted simply need more and more coats of the Blaze. Continue *dabbing* on new layers over dried areas until you achieve a brilliant red in the highlight areas.

The hair is brushed on wildly with a #8 flat brush and Tangerine. Slide the brush sideways, along the knife edge, beginning at the head and pulling outwards. Add some highlight touches with CF Native Flesh.

The felt eyes (at least what's left of them) are Norsk Blue with a Black overlapping piece.

The mouth is Blaze with a Black smile.

The tassels are Norsk blue, highlighted with Norsk Blue + Old Parchment, and shaded with Midnight. One of the tassels is about to follow the lead of a third tassel long since missing. Paint the threads which are barely holding it Midnight.

BABY. Paint Baby's face and hands a mixture of Adobe + Old Parchment. Shade with Tangerine + Fiesta Pink. For the cheeks, doubleload a small flat brush with Fiesta Pink and the mixture of Adobe + Old Parchment. Paint the mouth Fiesta Pink with a touch of Red Iron Oxide inside. The eyes are White with Norsk Blue irises and Midnight pupils. Outline the eyes in Midnight with a #0 liner. The hair is Butter Yellow, Pineapple, and Mocha - each color painted separately with a #2 liner and thinned paint. Highlights on the nose and chin are Pink Angel + Ivory.

The baby's clothing is made of a thin velour on which the lights create interesting highlights. First of all, block in the dark values with Tangerine. Fill in all remaining areas with a medium value mixture of Tangerine + CF Native Flesh. Do not worry about blending at this stage, just establish the values. Now, have at hand a wet paper towel for blotting or wiping the flat brush, and the dark and medium values you were just using. This time, you will lay in the colors again, in the same way as before, only you will just work on one section at a time (i.e. a leg, a foot, etc.). Use short, choppy, patting brush strokes. Work quickly. Lay in the dark value and while it is wet wipe the brush on the wet paper towel and double load it with both the dark and medium values. Blend these onto the edge of the shadow (dark) area. Quickly wipe the brush on the wet paper towel and pick up CF Native Flesh mixed with a little Tangerine (light value) and blend this in. Dry. To deepen any shadows and wrinkles, add a sideloaded wash of Red Iron Oxide + Tangerine. As a final touch, add the brightest highlights with CF Native Flesh. Pick up just a little of this color on the flat brush. Blot it on a dry paper towel to remove excess paint. Lay the brush in your hand very loosely (as pictured on page 52). Lightly skim the dry brush across the highlight areas, applying just a thin trace of the paint. Pompoms on the feet and hat are Ivory. The lace is also Ivory, painted with a #2 flat brush, sideloaded. Use a stylus to paint the dots on the lace.

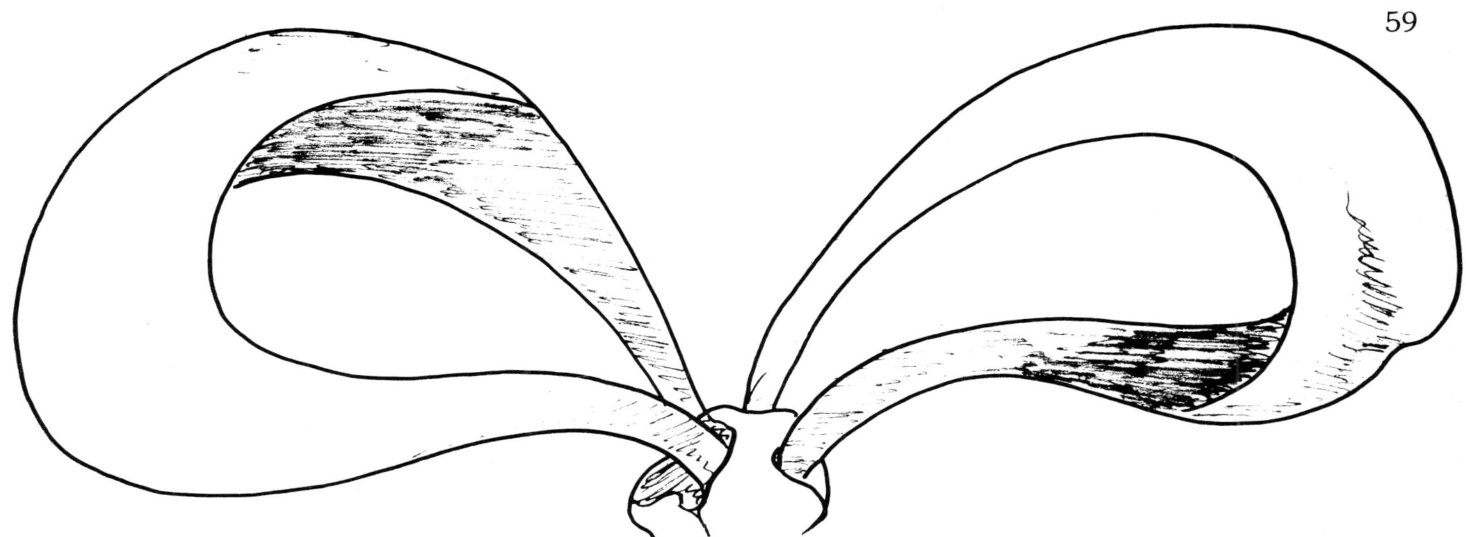

BLOCKS. The three visible sides of the blocks are each painted in a different value. The sides receiving the strongest light (on your right) are Old Parchment. The tops are Maple Sugar, and the shadow sides are Light Chocolate. Paint the letters Tangerine, and the decorative trim Norsk Blue and Lime Green.

BORDER. Surrounding the Burnt Umber background is a delicate "S" stroke border of Norsk Blue accented with Tangerine dots.

LACE. Lace around the heart is Old Parchment.

SCROLL. The scroll patterns on the lid are Norsk Blue. Mother's and Father's names and wedding year are also Norsk Blue.

BOWS AND HEARTS. On the sides, the large bows are Norsk Blue shaded with Midnight and highlighted with Norsk Blue + Old Parchment. The hearts are scumbled in the same colors which were used to trim the edges of the toy box.

ANTIQUING. Mix Burnt Umber oil paint with antiquing glaze. Follow directions on pages 86 and 87. Glaze one side at a time, applying the glaze heavily for thorough coverage. Wipe away excess with cheesecloth.

Name
Birth Date
Time

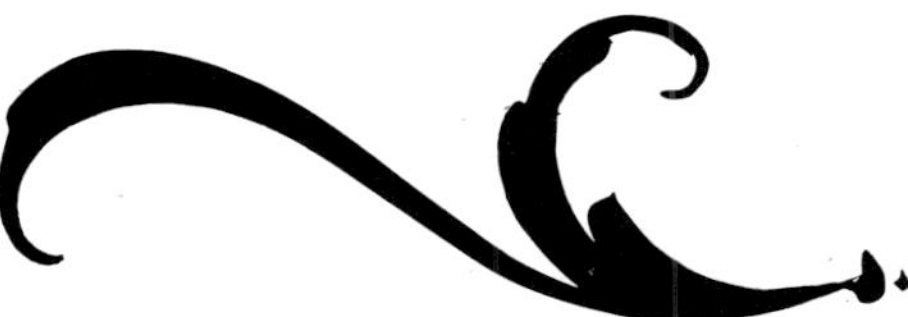

This is a very special toybox, which hopefully someday will be a "grandparents' toybox." Made for us by Jerry and Karen Hover of Treasures, it is now preserving puzzles and, appropriately, treasures from our three daughters' early childhood to be saved for our grandchildren. Its most cherished contents are portrayed on the front: Kathy's 16-year old, well worn, beloved Clown, Laurie's Bear, now 13, and Jenny's Baby, now 10. Clown and Baby, originally pictured in Tole Techniques and Decorative Arts, Vol. 3, *were taken from a portrait I had drawn of them in 1973. On the right side of the toybox is a large bow attached to three hearts, one for each child. The hearts contain birth date, place, time, weight, and length of each child. On the other side, a large bow is attached to nine smaller hearts. Pertinent birth information on our grandchildren will be added when the time comes.*

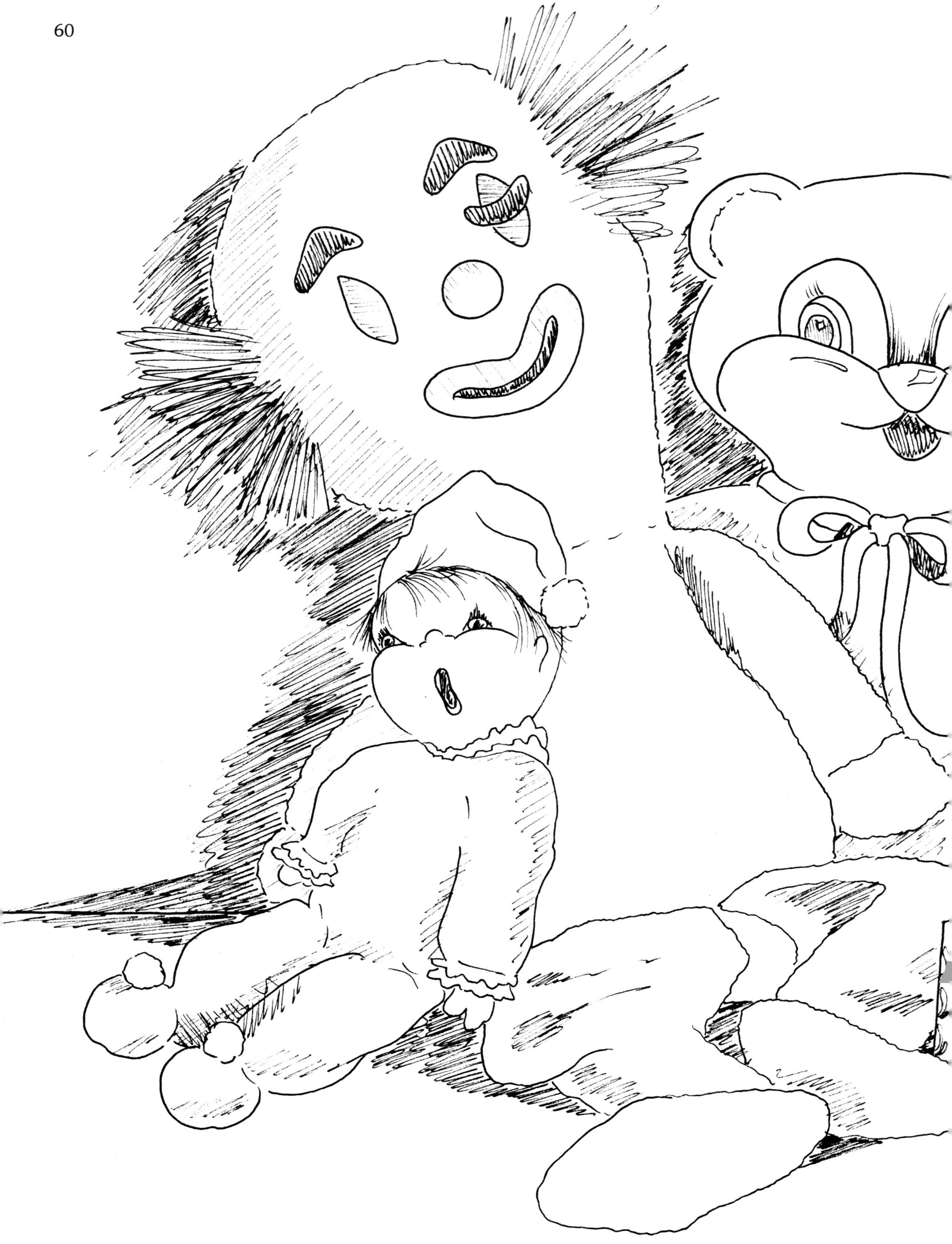

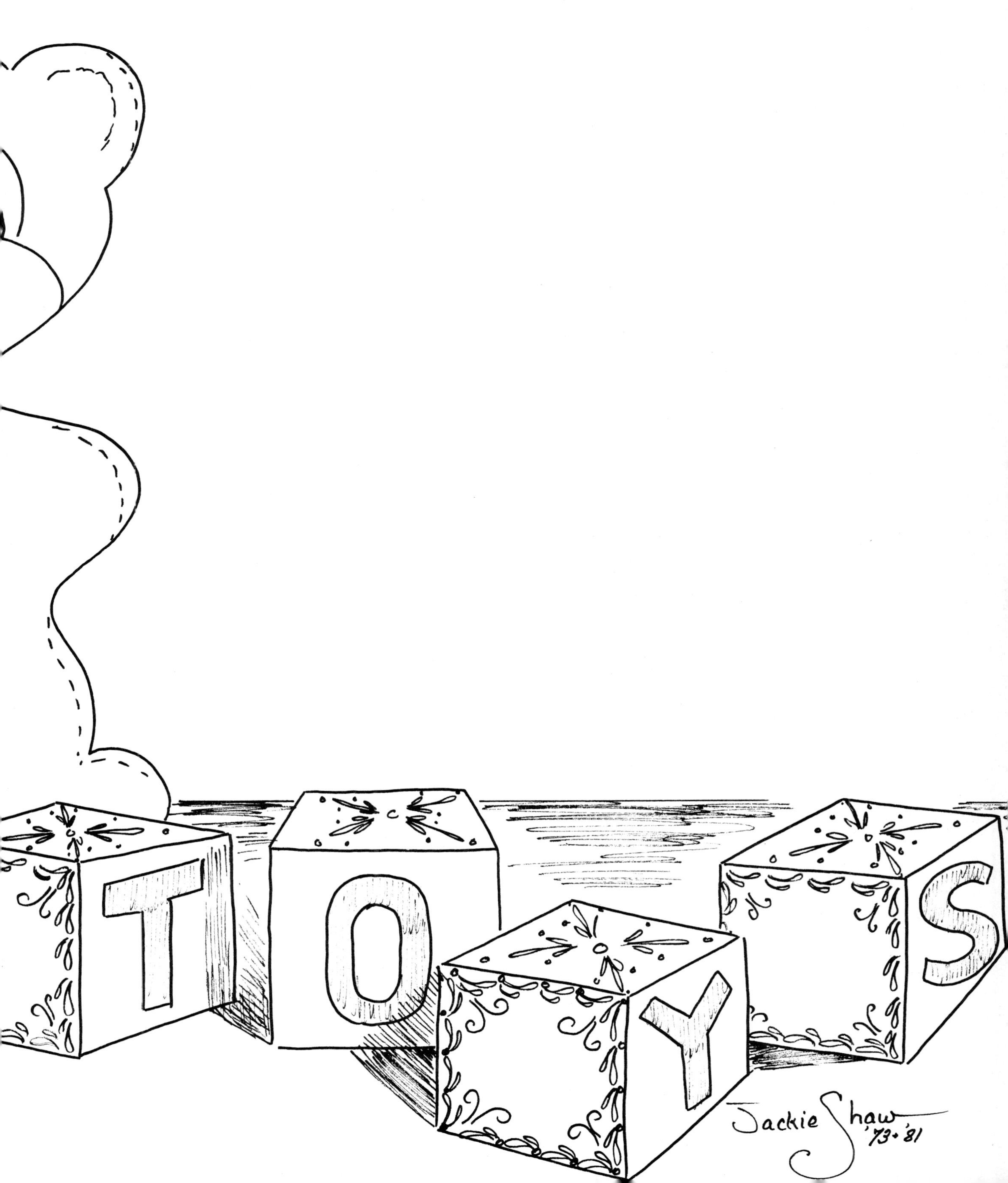
T
O
Y
S
Jackie Shaw
'73 + '81

ROLLY-SCROLLY

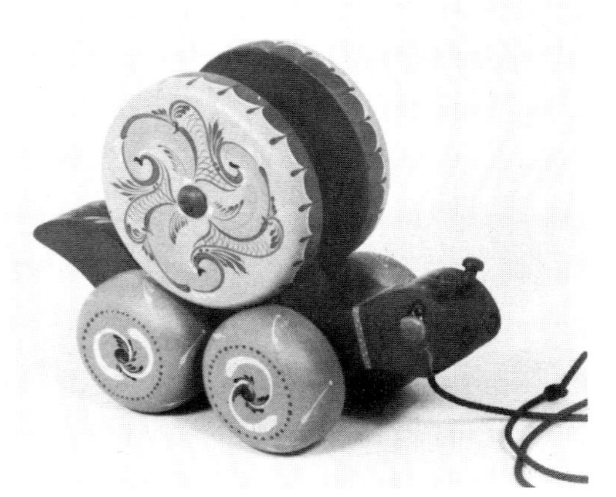

COLORS

Timberline
Red Tile
Old Parchment
Walnut
Vibrant Green
Black Green

PROCEDURE

Basecoat: Timberline - body
Red Tile + Old Parchment -wheels
Old Parchment + Walnut - shell (outside)
Red Tile - shell (inside)

CHEEKS. Sideload a #6 flat brush with the mixture of Red Tile + Old Parchment. Highlight with Old Parchment.

EYES. Outline with Walnut. Fill in with Old Parchment. Iris is Vibrant Green. Pupil is Black Green.

MOUTH. Paint a grin from cheek to cheek using a #2 liner and the Red Tile + Old Parchment mixture.

BOW TIE. Red Tile + Old Parchment.

ANTENNAE. Red Tile.

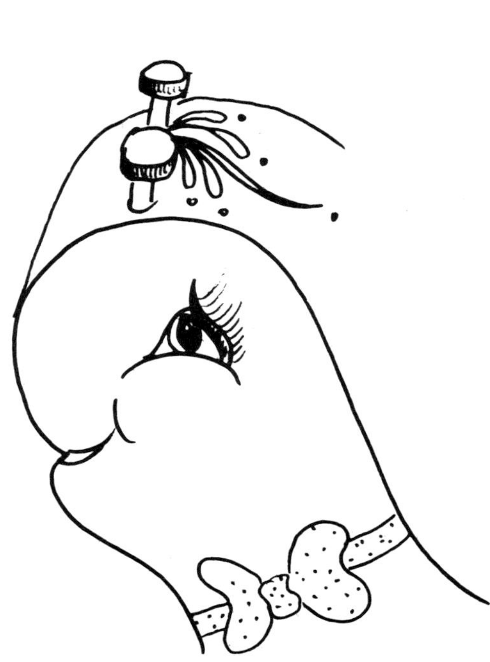

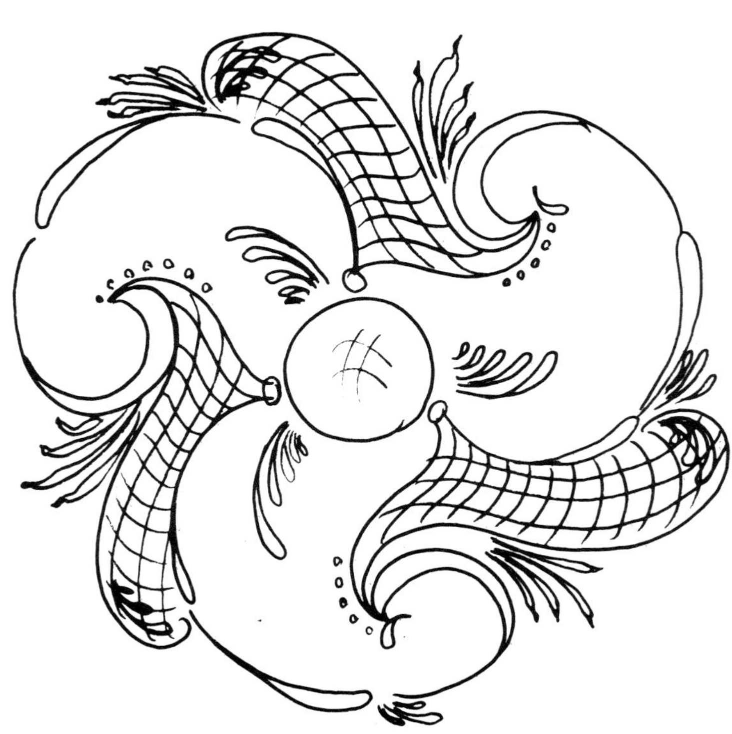

SHELL. Use chalk to divide it into thirds. Into each third, paint a large scroll using a 1/2" flat brush sideloaded with the Red Tile + Old Parchment mixture. Outline the scrolls with Red Tile. Connect the scrolls with detail liner and crosshatching. Trim the edges of the shell with a stroke border.

WHEELS. Decorate the wheels with curving comma strokes of Old Parchment. Add small Walnut teardrop strokes, and Vibrant Green centers shaded with Black Green.

SNAIL FEATHERS are Walnut. This little guy rates two sets, one on his head, one on his tail.

FORGET-ME-NOT

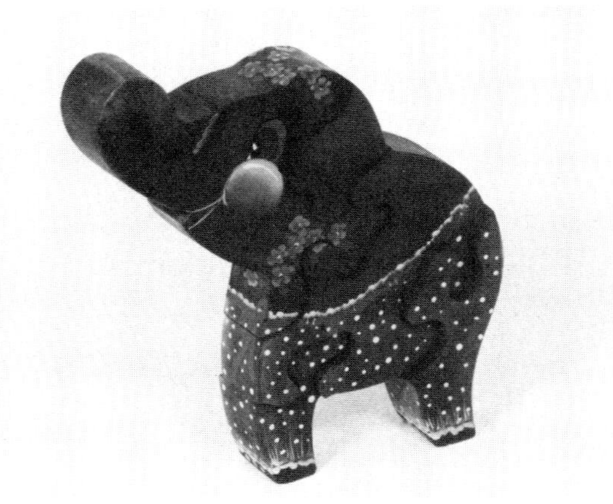

COLORS

Hammered Iron	Butter Yellow
Ivory	Seminole
Black	Copen Blue
Tompte Red	Coral

PROCEDURE

Basecoat the elephant entirely in Hammered Iron. Sketch her trunk, ears, cheek, eye, and waistband with chalk. Shade beneath the overlapping trunk and around the ears with Black in a sideloaded wash on a ½" flat brush. Highlight the top (bend) of the trunk and the top front edge of the ears with a very thin wash of Ivory + Hammered Iron.

FACE. Paint large cheeks Coral. Use a ½" flat brush, sideloaded. Blend the cheek out gently at the bottom edge. Outline the mouth with Coral, then fill in the inside with Tompte Red. Also fill in the edge of the trunk with Tompte Red + Coral. Forget-Me-Not's eyes are Copen Blue (to match her flowers and waistband). Follow the illustrated directions on page 56 for painting the eyes. Add long, curly Black eyelashes with the #2 liner. Paint thin Black crease lines in her trunk.

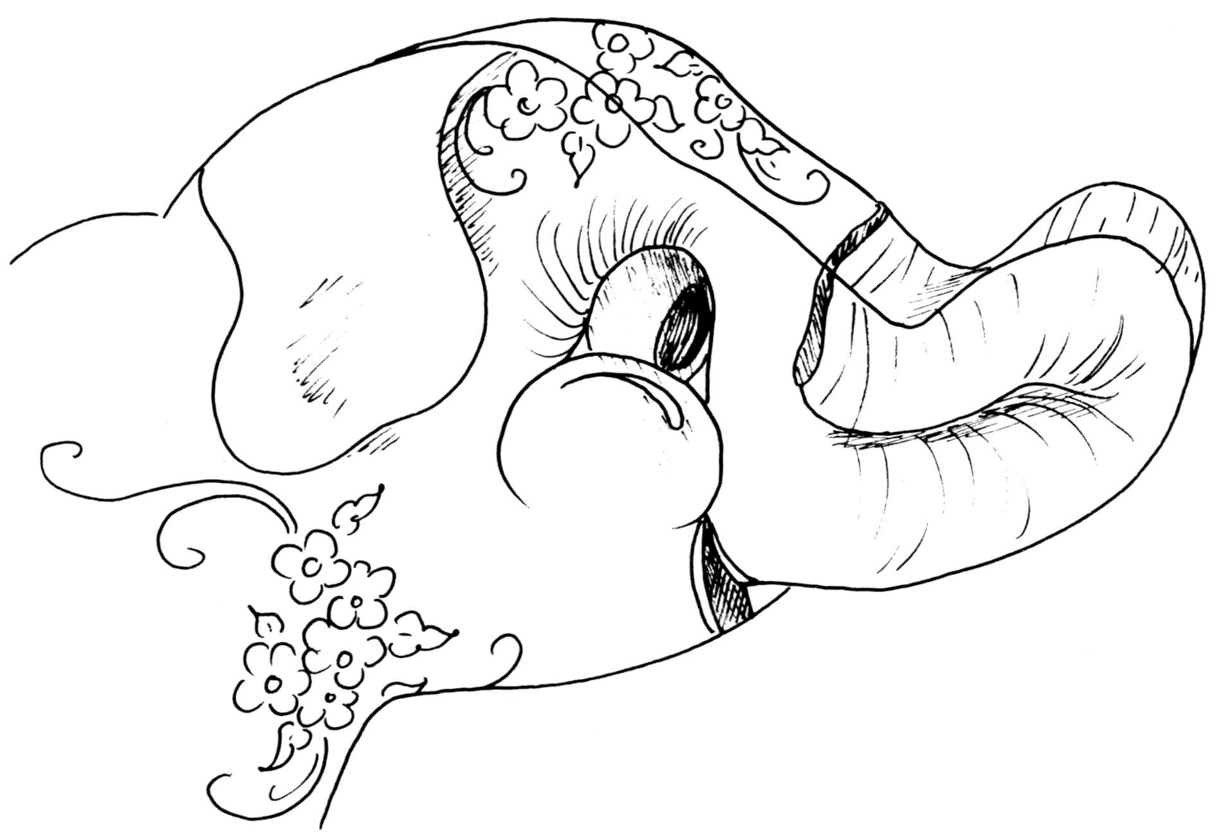

PANTALOONS. Use a ¾" or 1" flat brush and a very thin wash of Ivory to dress Forget-Me-Not in filmy lace-edged, dotted Swiss pantaloons. Paint the Ivory lace at the waist and cuffs with a sideloaded #2 flat brush. Add the polka dots with the handle end of the brush. Run Copen Blue stitching around the cuffs and a ribbon around the waist. Both accents are painted with the #2 liner. Add Ivory pucker wrinkles at the cuffs. See lace on page 15.

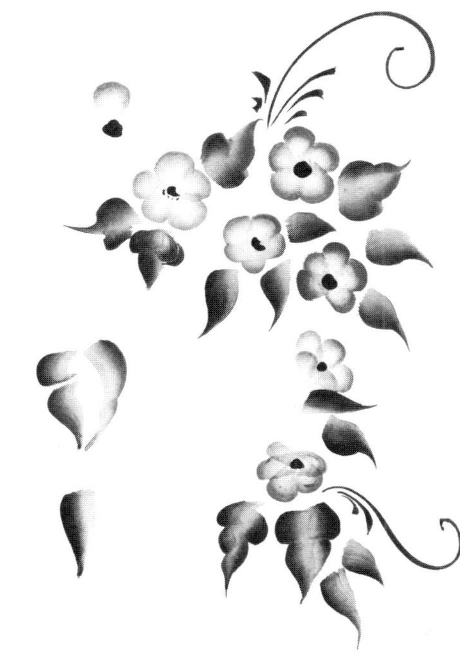

FORGET-ME-NOTS. Scatter these five-petaled little flowers around her neck and on her head. Double load a #2 flat with Copen Blue and Copen Blue + Ivory. Place the lighter value to the outside edge of each petal. Fill in the center with Butter Yellow and top with a Tompte Red dot. Paint Seminole leaves and scrolls with the #2 liner.

TAIL AND TOES. Paint a Hammered Iron + Black tail, and add round Coral toes.

"ELE-PHEATHERS" are on her back side in Copen Blue.

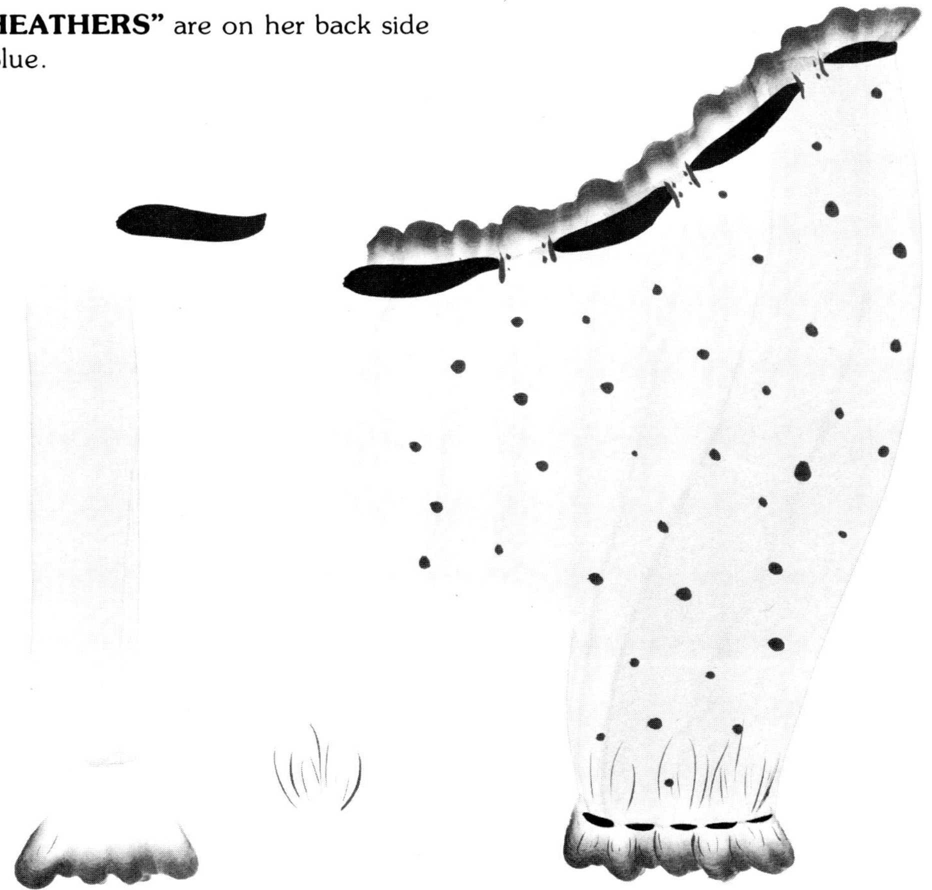

HONEY BEAR

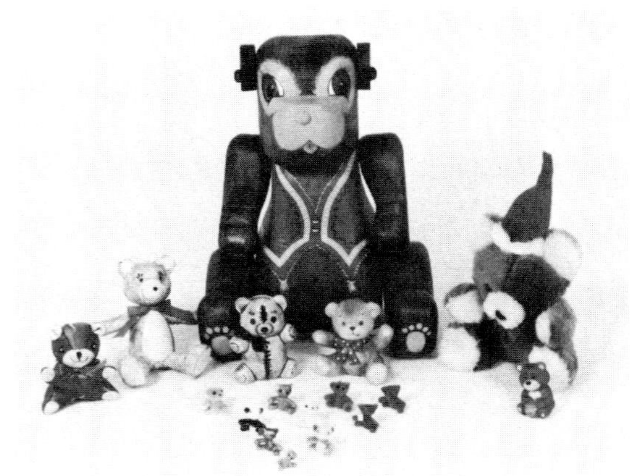

COLORS

Burnt Umber	Fiesta Pink
Light Chocolate	Tompte Red
Dark Forest	Red Iron Oxide
Black Green	Butter Yellow
Vivid Green	Woodland Night
Ivory	Seminole

PROCEDURE

Basecoat Honey Bear with a thin wash of Burnt Umber. Work quickly using a 1" or 1½" flat wash brush. (Note: to prevent color from "grabbing" too quickly, you may find that brushing on a thin layer of water prior to applying color will give you greater control.)

FACE. Basecoat the eyes and nose area with Light Chocolate using a ½" brush. Paint wispy lines of the Light Chocolate with the #2 liner around the edges of the face.

EYES. Follow the full color illustration on page 56. The colors used in Honey Bear's eyes are Dark Forest, Black Green, Vivid Green, and Ivory. Outline the eyes in Burnt Umber and add Burnt Umber lashes. For more explicit directions, refer to Sue Fle's eyes, page 20.

MOUTH. Paint Honey Bear's tongue Fiesta Pink. Sideload a #4 flat brush with Tompte Red. Shade along the top of the tongue. Place a thin Red Iron Oxide line down the center of the tongue.

EARS. Use a #10 flat brush sideloaded with Fiesta Pink to paint inside Honey Bear's ears.

VEST. There is no need to trace on a pattern. Just sketch an outline with chalk. Honey Bear's vest is painted Seminole. A Butter Yellow band embellished with Red Iron Oxide teardrops and Ivory dots trims the jacket. Woodland Night scrolls, Ivory zigzags, Butter Yellow fringe, and Red Iron Oxide buttons complete the decorations. But do not be overly influenced by the green. Maybe you would prefer a blue-eyed, blue jacketed bear. Or how about brown eyes and a red jacket. If you are really ambitious, try a plaid or patterned jacket. You might even consider a bow tie, suspenders, and britches; or, paint a mama bear with fringed shawl, curly locks and fingernail polish. Whatever you decide to do, have fun!

HONEY POT. This started out as an egg cup, but since everyone knows bears much prefer honey, it was decorated as a honey pot. Basecoated outside with Butter Yellow and inside with Red Iron Oxide, the honey pot was trimmed with lettering and detail strokes involving the colors already used in decorating the bear.

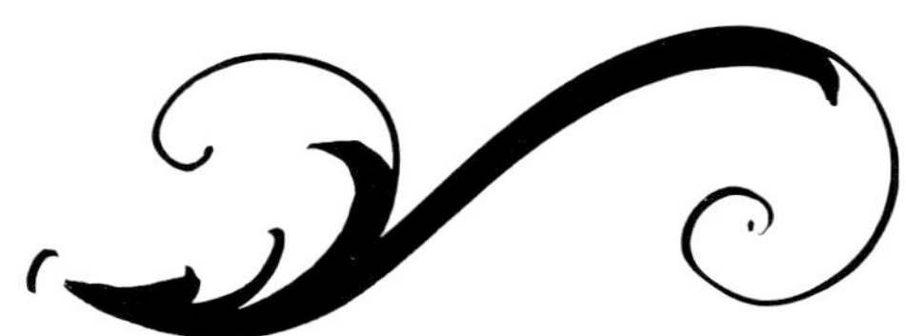

Our oldest daughter Kathy (age 16) has a growing collection of Teddy Bears, particularly miniature ones. Also in her collection is her Daddy's childhood stuffed Teddy which is as lovable as ever, 40 years later. When this marvelous wooden bear joined our family there was simply no question which child would claim it. Made from a thick block of wood, Honey Bear has arms and legs which move.

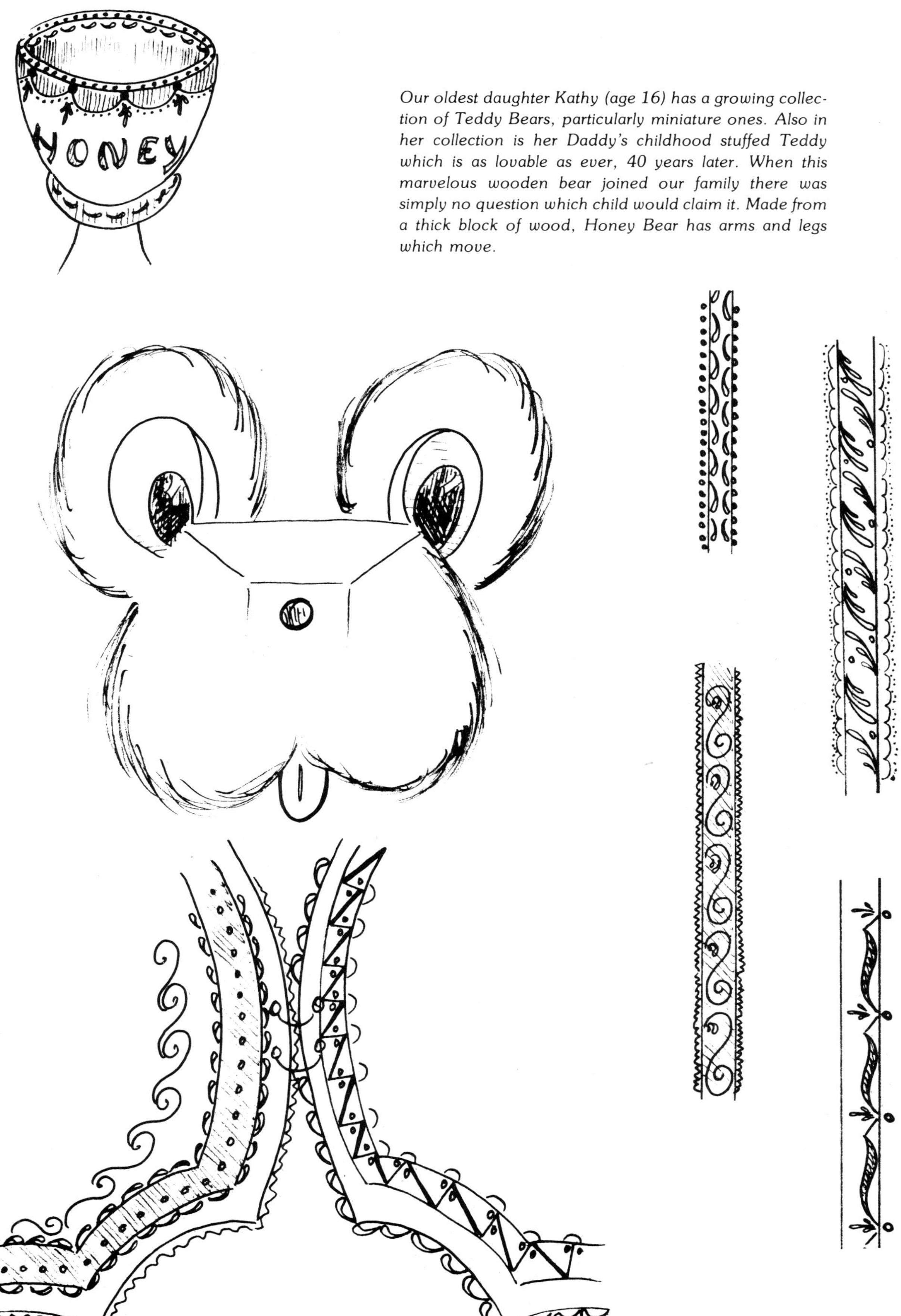

RYAN'S HORSE

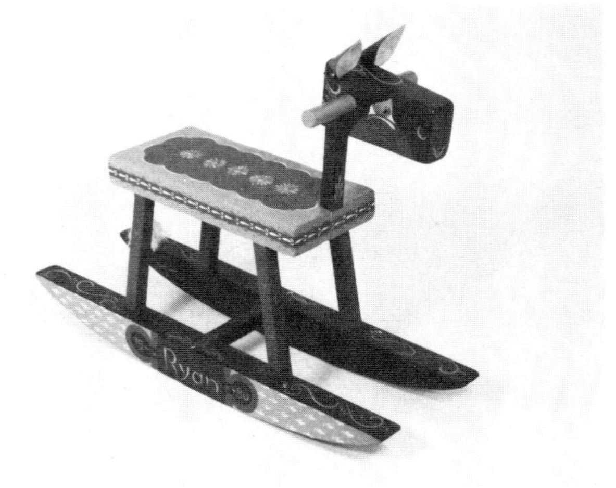

COLORS

Wedgewood Green
Salem Green
Dark Brown
Black
Coral
Timberline
Ivory

PROCEDURE

Basecoat as follows:

Dark Brown - head, neck, tops and insides of rockers
Wedgewood Green - seat, handlebars, outsides of rockers
Salem Green - legs, cheeks, seat inset and band, horseshoes on rockers

From this point on, it's just time to doodle, for this is where the fun begins. Use Ryan's horse only as a guide. Change the borders, substitute other flowers or design elements for the flowers illustrated. Refer to *Freehanding With Jackie* or *Rock 'N Tole,* or to other toys within this book for ideas. Tackle just one section at a time so as not to be overwhelmed. Relax and be *amused* with your efforts. If you have fun, a lively, happy quality will be reflected in your work. I've taught hundreds of these and similar child-sized horses in seminars and each student's horse has been uniquely different. Each developed a distinct personality and every one was a success. So you see, with such great odds in your favor, how could you fail? (Interesting note -nearly half of the horses painted were not intended as gifts for children. Instead, the painters had designated a particular place in the home for the horse to serve as a decorative accent, a plant stand, etc. Frequently heard was the admonishment, "No child had better try to ride on *my* horse." I guess we're never too old for toys.)

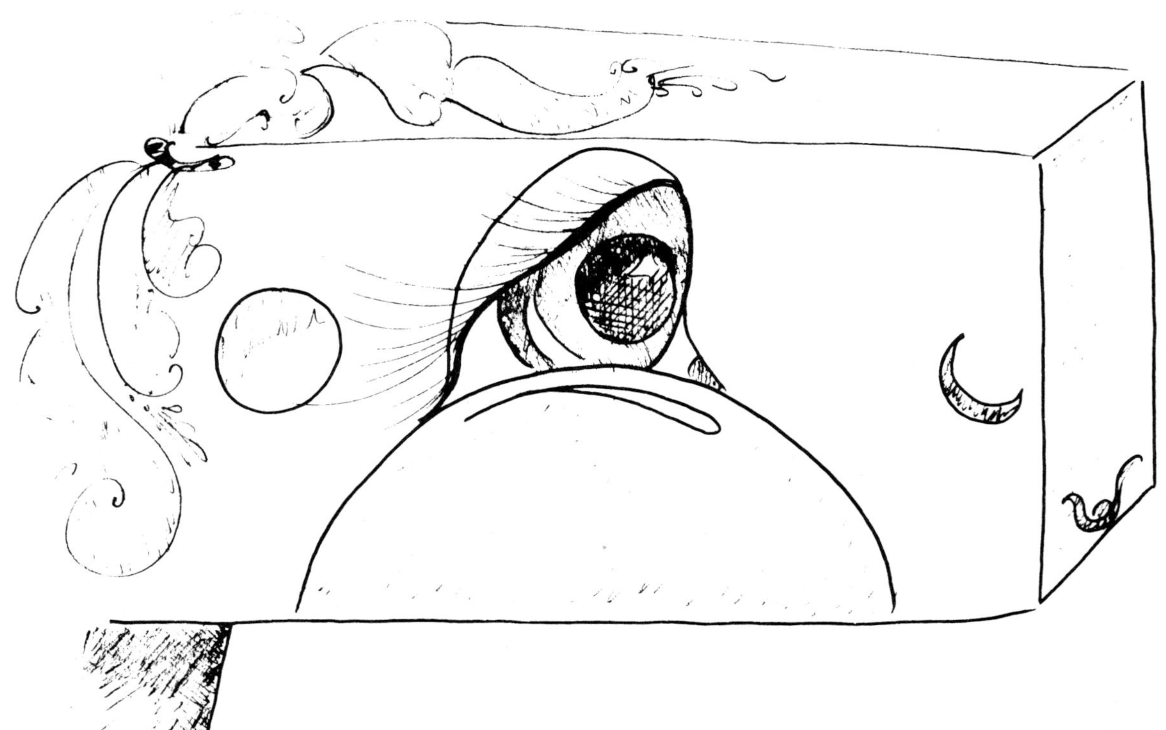

I don't know what kind of years 1980 and 1981 have been for wine, but they've been great years for babies and horses. Lots of our friends and relatives have been quite busy out there making babies and grandbabies. That keeps me busy painting horses. And I think we'll just keep things that way. This horse was painted to commemorate the birth of Ryan Newell Baum to our special friends, George and Julie. Although oodles of horses were introduced in Rock 'N Tole, *we just had to share another one with you because they are always such fun to paint.*

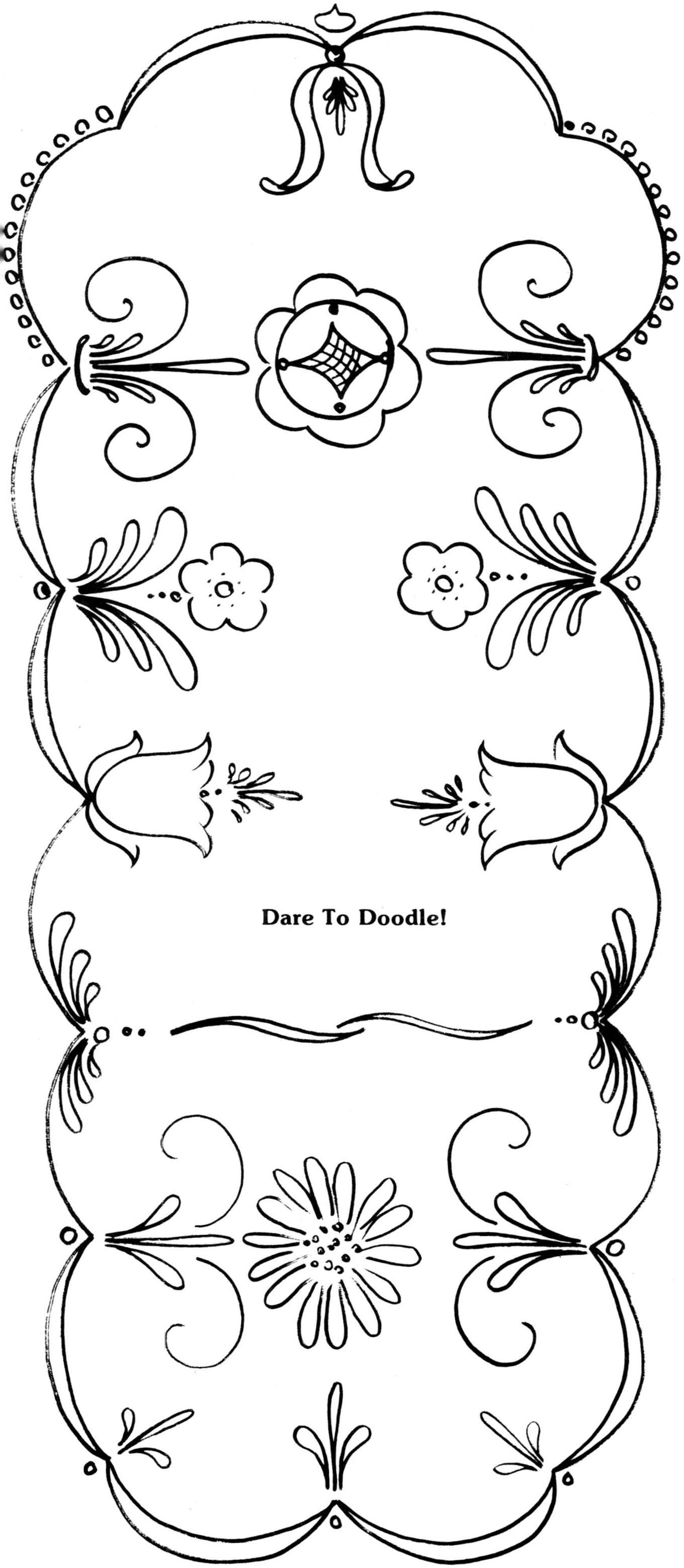

Dare To Doodle!

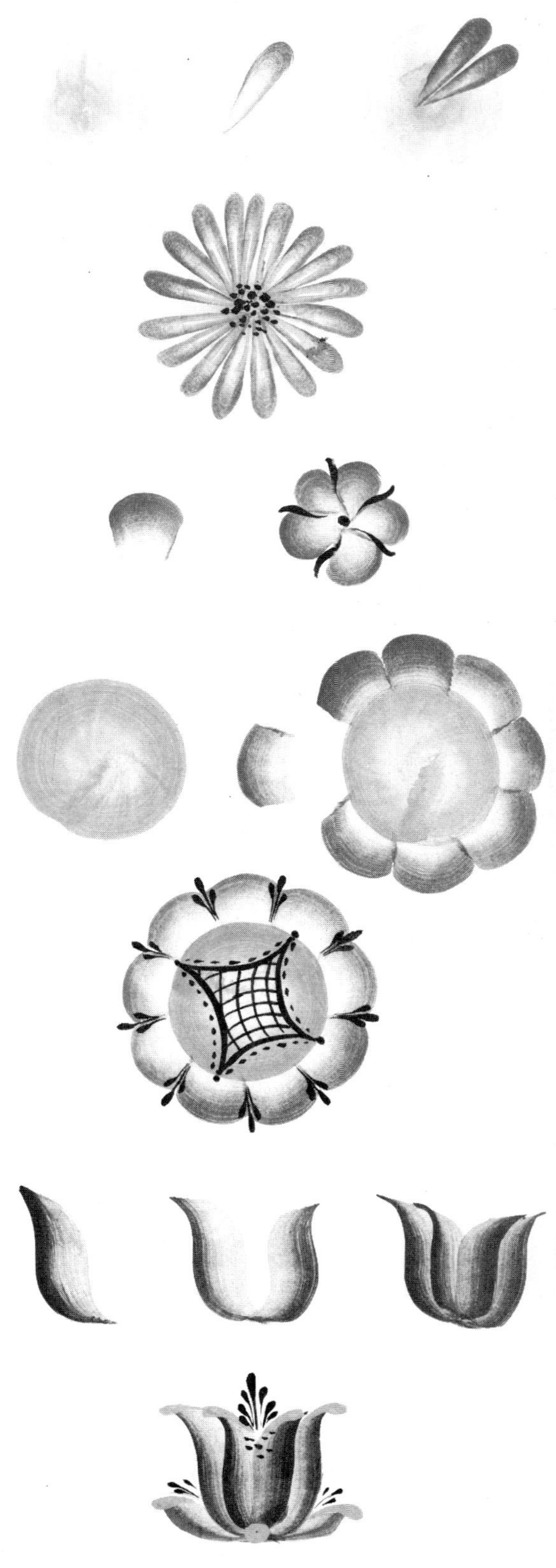

CHEDDAR

COLORS:

Butter Yellow
Hallingdal Red
Adobe
Black
Ivory
Cosmos Blue
Midnight

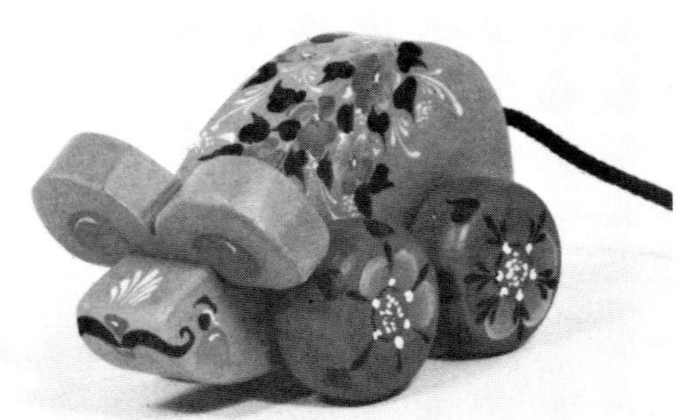

PROCEDURE

Mix Butter Yellow + Hallingdal Red to basecoat Cheddar's body and ears. Mix Adobe + Hallingdal Red to basecoat the wheels.

CHEEKS. Sideload a #6 flat brush with Adobe + Hallingdal Red. Paint a crescent stroke and blend out at the bottom. Add an Ivory highlight.

EYES. Use the handle end of your liner to paint a Black dot for each eye. Outline the back side of the eye with an Ivory "S" stroke. Add bushy Black eyebrows.

NOSE. With a #2 liner paint a "chocolate chip" in Hallingdal Red + Adobe. Add an Ivory highlight.

MOUTH. Use the Hallingdal Red + Adobe mixture and a liner to paint a sly grin.

MUSTACHE. We decided that for Cheddar to be a proper English mouse, he needed a proper mustache. So he was given a Black handlebar. (See page 15 for a selection of mustaches).

EARS. Paint the insides with crescents of the Hallingdal Red + Adobe mixture. Use a #6 flat brush. Embellish the backs of the ears with comma strokes in the same mixture.

FLOWERS. Using a #2 flat brush, scatter a bouquet of forget-me-nots across Cheddar's back. Don't worry about a pattern -- just begin. For each flower, give yourself a focal point -- a dot of chalk or paint -- around which the petals are painted. To make the flowers interesting, paint two or three of the petals in a darker value (Cosmos Blue) and the remaining petals in a lighter value (Cosmos Blue + Ivory). Additional pizzazz may be added to the flowers by painting Ivory highlights on the lighter petals with a sideloaded #2 flat brush. Add leaves. Fill in spaces among and around the flowers with Midnight leaves painted with a #2 flat brush. Finish off the floral grouping with scroll and detail strokes and dabbed flowers. See illustrations on page 23.

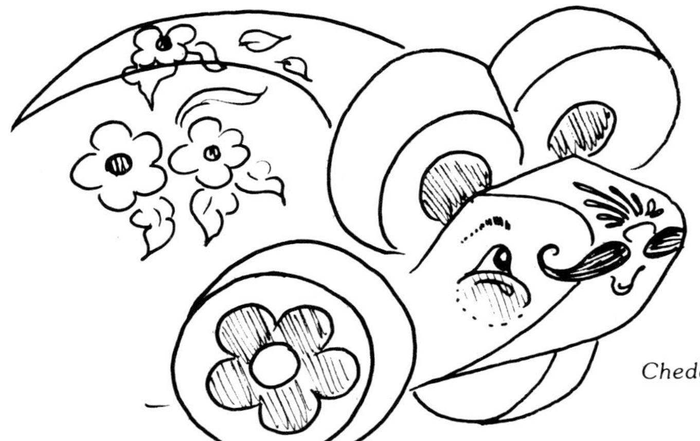

WHEELS. Divide the wheels into six sections. Paint a Cosmos Blue + Ivory crescent stroke in each section. Add dots and strokes to embellish.

MOUSE FEATHERS in Ivory ended up above Cheddar's nose.

Cheddar can be seen in color on page 49.

OUNCEMENTS

te

Bonnie Blue

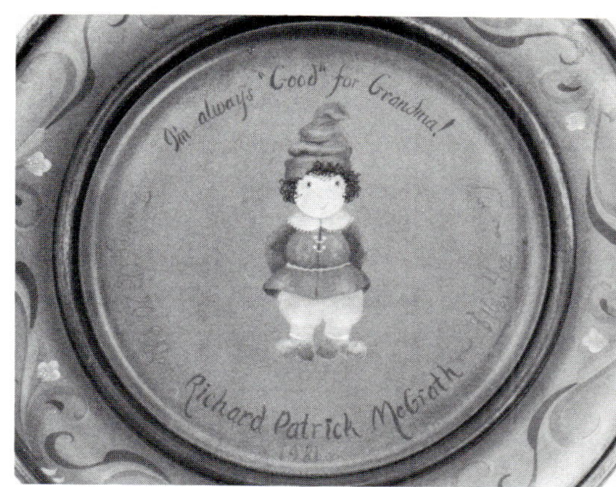

Kailian's Plate
Red Tile
Salem Green
Straw
Fiesta Pink
Ivory
Midnight
Fjord Blue
Hammered Iron
Autumn Brown

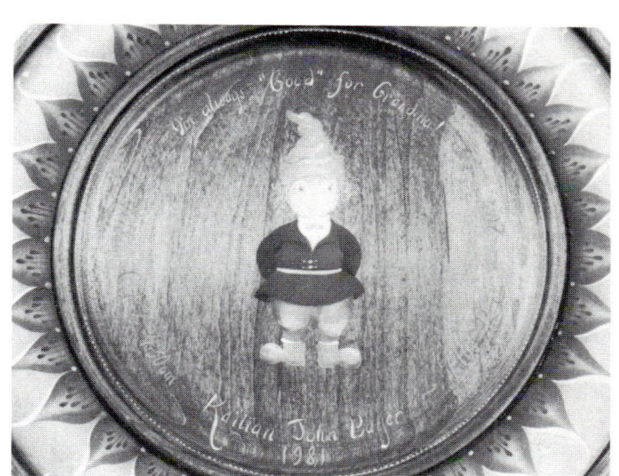

Adam's Drum
Red Tile
Midnight
Red Iron Oxide
Antique Gold
Ivory
Adobe
Norsk Blue
Fiesta Pink
Black
Hammered Iron
Maroon
Pineapple

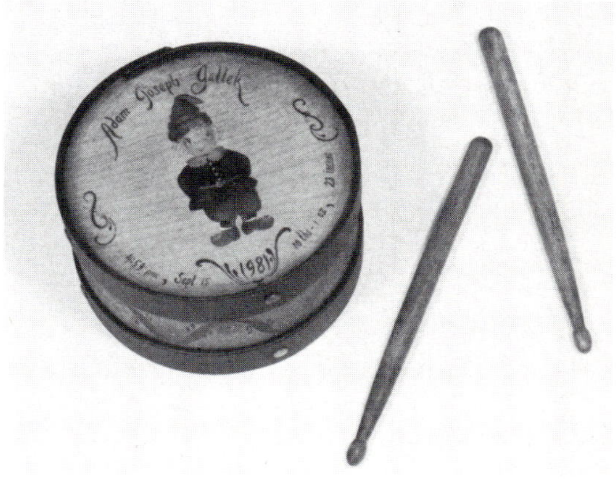

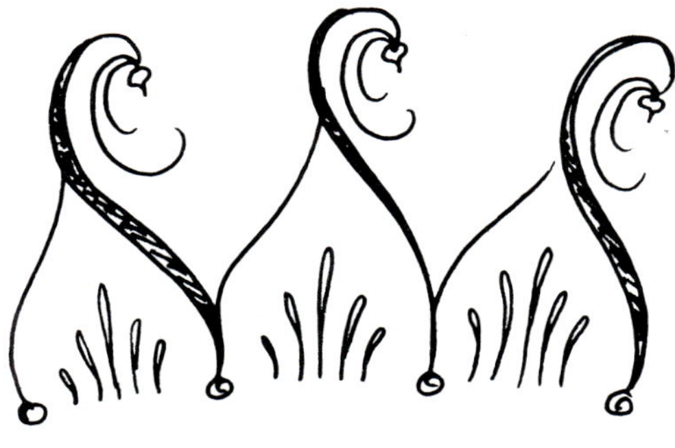

PROCEDURE

ADAM. Basecoat the bands of the drum with Midnight. The remainder of the decoration is done on sealed, unpainted wood.

RICHARD. Basecoat the plate with Red Iron Oxide, leaving the two beaded edges unpainted.

KAILIAN. Basecoat the border with Salem Green + Ivory. Paint Fjord Blue strokes trimmed with Ivory and Fiesta Pink.

FACES. Mix Red Tile + Ivory (or Old Parchment for a deeper color). Apply two coats for good coverage. When dry, apply a sideloaded wash of Adobe around the edge of the face, particularly along the hair line.

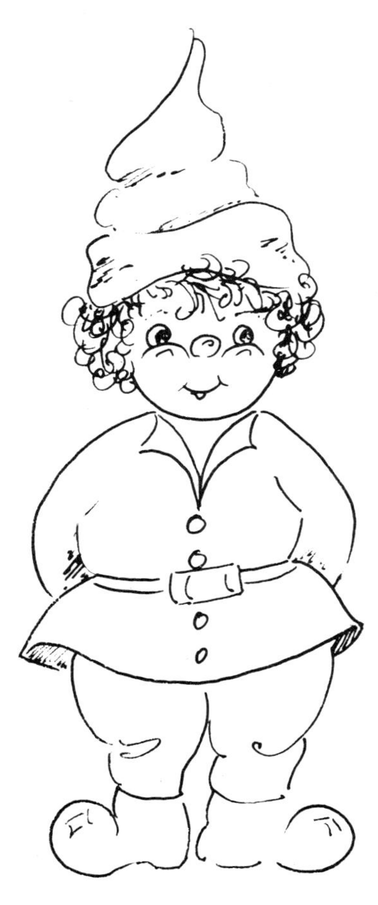

CHEEKS AND NOSES. Use Adobe (for Kailian, use Fiesta Pink), applied in a sideloaded wash with a #4 flat. Use just the corner of the brush for the nose. Add Ivory highlights.

EYES. Follow the step-by-step illustrations on page 15, using Midnight, Fjord Blue, Fjord Blue + Ivory, and Ivory for Richard and Adam. Substitute Salem Green + Ivory for Fjord Blue in Kailian's eyes. Use a #0 liner to outline the eyes in Black, and paint Black lashes.

MOUTHS. Adobe + Red Iron Oxide (Use Adobe + Fiesta Pink for Kailian).

HAIR. Richard - Black; Kailian - Autumn Brown with Straw highlights; Adam - Antique Gold with Pineapple highlights.

RICHARD'S CLOTHING. Hat and coat - basecoat with Fjord Blue. Shade with a Midnight wash sideloaded in a #4 flat; highlight with a Fjord Blue + Bonnie Blue mixture, barely dry - brushed on. Pants and collar - basecoat in Antique Gold; shade with an Autumn Brown wash; highlight with a thin Ivory wash.

KAILIAN'S CLOTHING. Hat and pants - basecoat with Salem Green + Ivory; shade with a wash of Salem Green; highlight with Ivory + Salem Green. Shirt - basecoat thinly with Ivory; sprinkle tiny Ivory dots liberally over the basecoat; add a Salem Green + Ivory tie.

ADAM'S CLOTHING. Hat and pants - basecoat with Red Iron Oxide; shade with Maroon; accent deeper shading with Maroon + very little Black; highlight with Fiesta Pink. Coat - basecoat with Midnight, shade with Midnight + Black; highlight with Norsk Blue. Collar -basecoat with Antique Gold; shade with Autumn Brown; add Ivory dots. Add buckles, buttons, belts and trims using colors to coordinate with the color scheme.

SHOES. Basecoat with Hammered Iron. Shade with Hammered Iron + Black. Highlight with Hammered Iron + Ivory.

SCROLLS ON RICHARD'S PLATE. Divide the plate into eighths. Begin with just two basic strokes, fitting each pair into one of the eight sections. Gradually add more and more strokes and overstrokes until your scroll border is as ornate as you want it. Use colors in the scroll border which were used in painting the little fellow (Midnight, Fjord Blue, Bonnie Blue). Embellish the design further with simple flowers and strokes in a contrasting color (Antique Gold, Autumn Brown, Ivory). See illustrations on page 15.

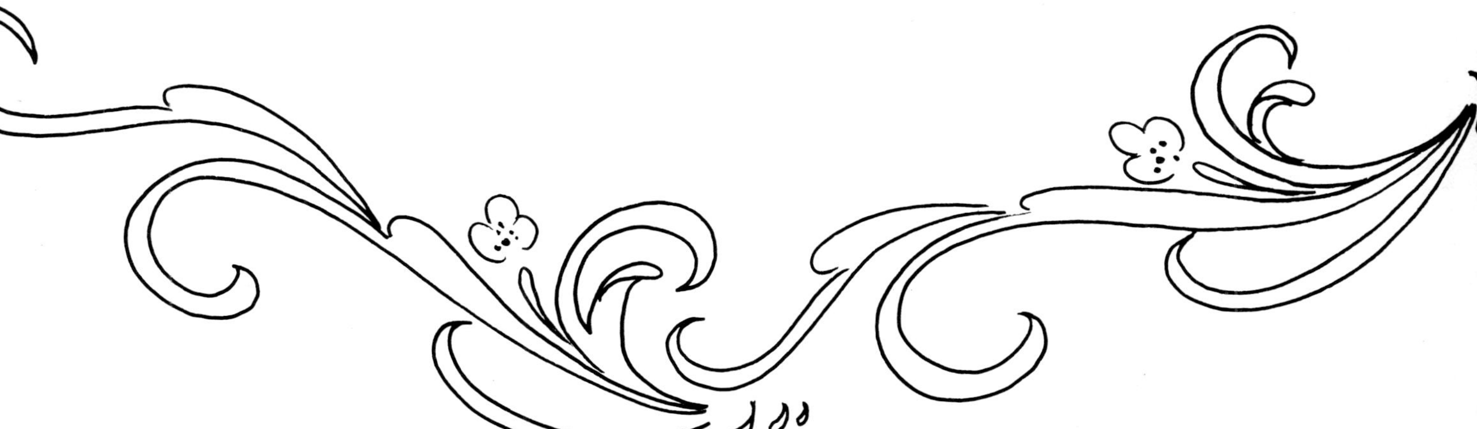

RIBBON BORDER ON ADAM'S DRUM. Paint "S" strokes with a #6 flat brush alternating between Maroon and Red Iron Oxide. Space an even number of "S" strokes around the drum. (I used 14). Embellish the ribbon with flowers of Antique Gold and Golden Brown. Forest Green comma or teardrop strokes suggest leaves.

LETTERING. Letter pertinent birth information evenly by first drawing chalk guidelines. Practice a couple of times with only water in your #2 liner to get an idea of how the word spacing will work out. When you're satisfied with your lettering, load the brush with paint and do it for real! The lettering on Richard's plate was done in Midnight and Fjord Blue with Bonnie Blue accents. On Kailian's plate, the lettering was done with Fjord Blue and Salem Green + Ivory. Lettering on Adam's drum was done with Midnight. All three projects were antiqued as described on pages 86 and 87 with Burnt Umber oils.

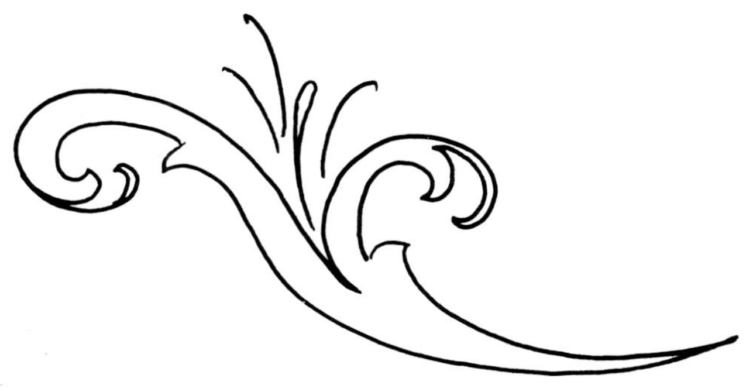

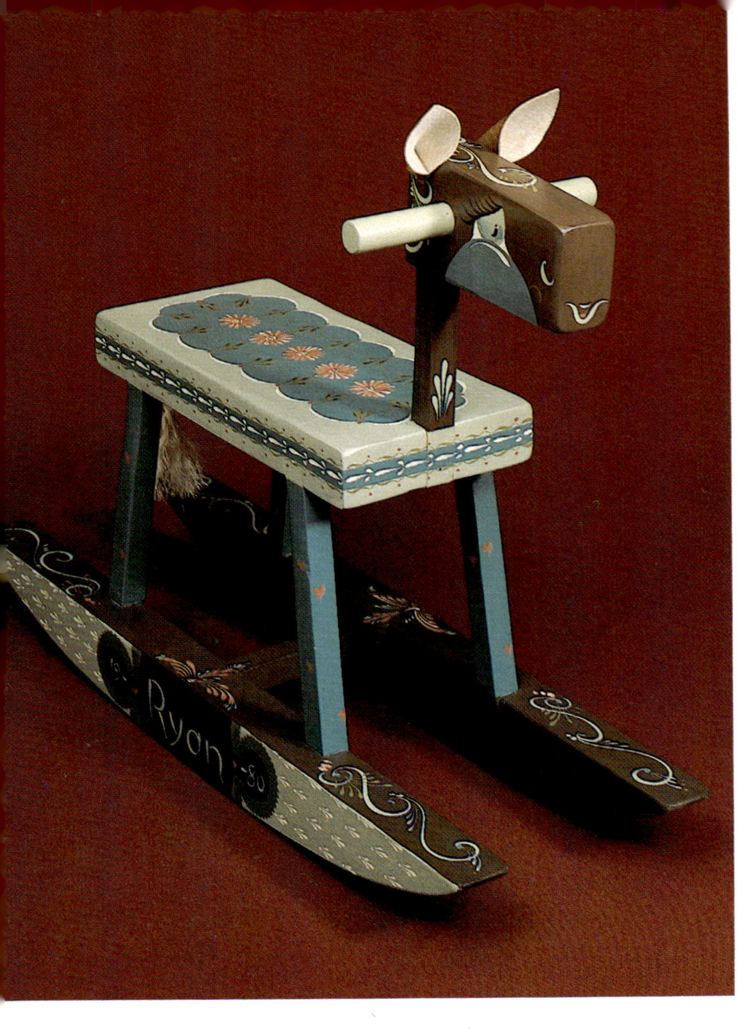
Ryan

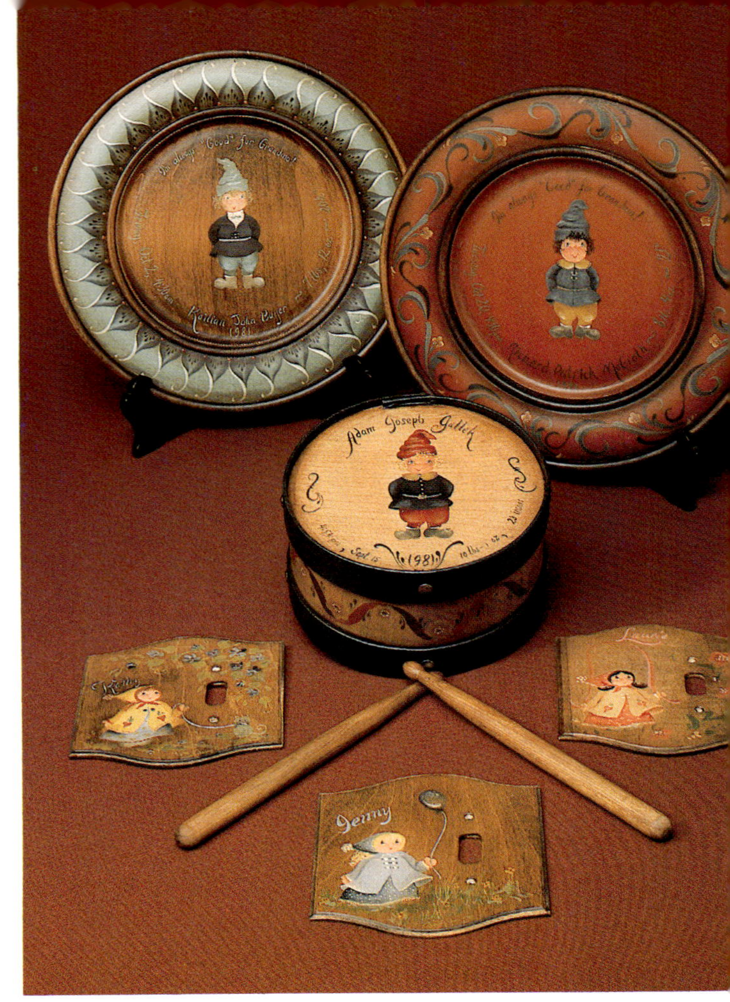
Adam Joseph Gellek
Sept. 15
1981
Jenny

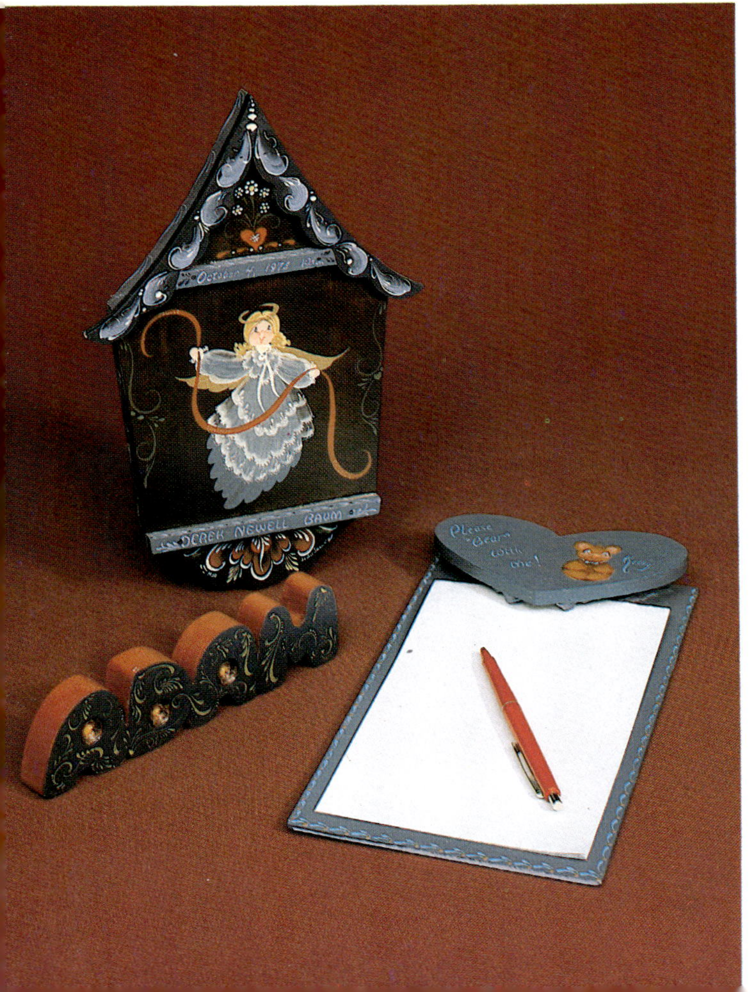
DEREK NEWELL BAUM
Please Bear with me!

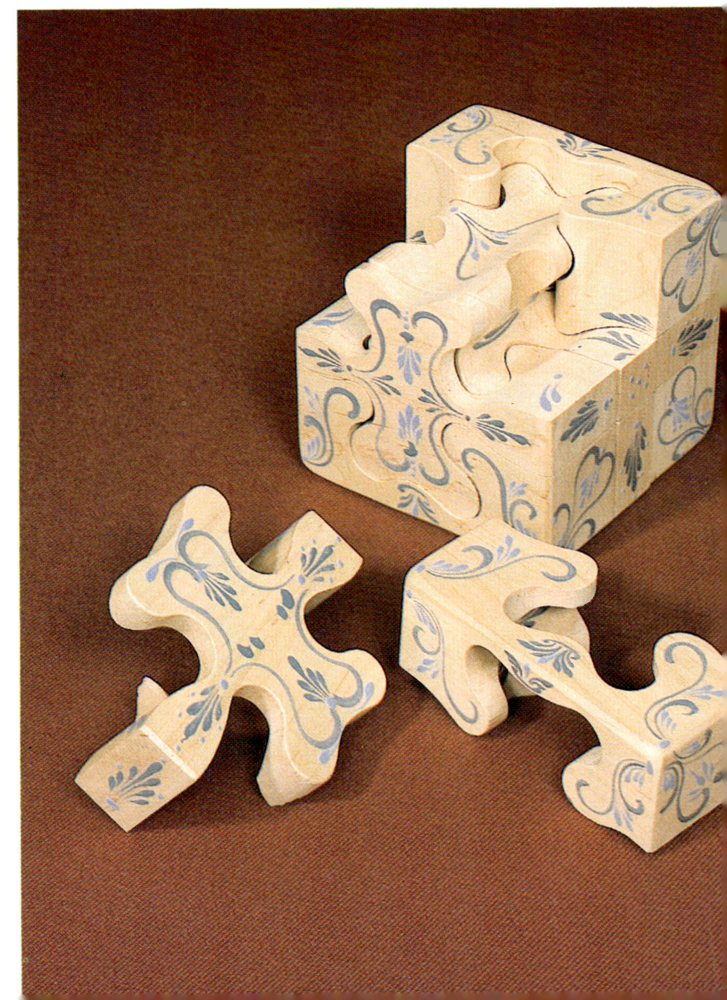

SWITCH PLATE COVERS

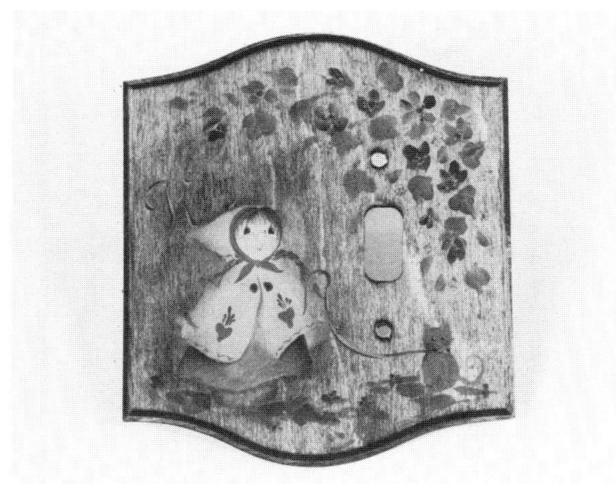

COLORS

Laurie
Fiesta Pink
Berry Red
Old Parchment
Burnt Umber
Forest Green
Hammered Iron
Midnight
Georgia Clay +
Old Parchment
(flesh color)

Jenny
Bonnie Blue
Fjord Blue
Midnight Blue
Ivory
Butter Yellow
Forest Green
Wedgewood Green
Hammered Iron
Georgia Clay +
Old Parchment
(flesh color)

Kathy
Straw
Golden Brown
Adobe
Bonnie Blue
Midnight Blue
Hammered Iron
Georgia Clay +
Old Parchment
(flesh color)

PROCEDURE

Follow the same general instructions as for painting the little boys on the birthplates and drum on pages 71-73.

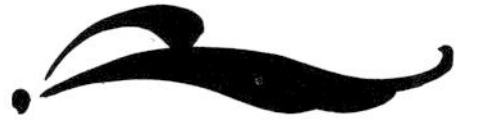

Hint: These make an ideal birth announcement gift. Include baby's name, birthdate, pertinent birth information.

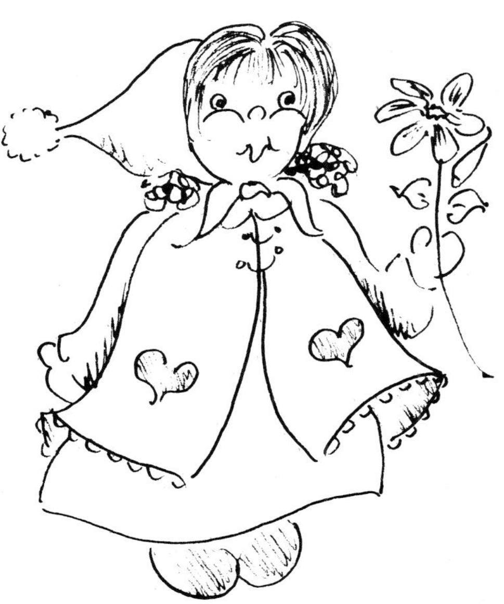

DABBLE DUCK

COLORS

Maple Sugar
Timberline
Red Tile + Old Parchment
Ivory

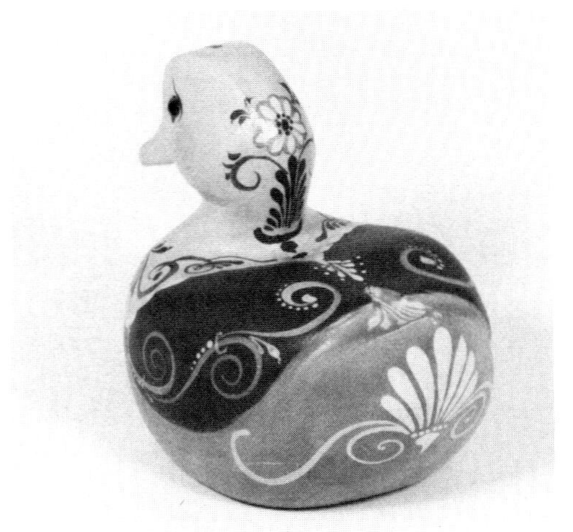

PROCEDURE

Using chalk or Conté pencil divide the duck into sections for basecoating. In the case of Dabble Duck, the head and chest section was basecoated in Maple Sugar. The wings were basecoated in Timberline. A mixture of Red Tile + Old Parchment was used on the rest of the body.

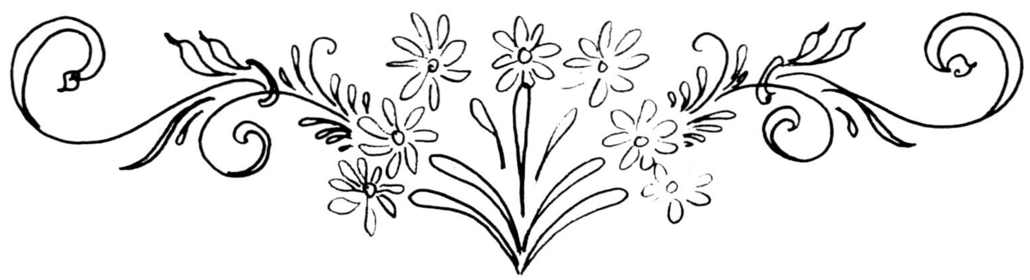

CHEEKS. Mix Red Tile + Old Parchment. Sideload this mixture into a #10 flat brush. Form the cheeks with a crescent stroke. Gently blend the bottom of the cheeks. Highlight with Ivory.

BODY. Using the three basecoat colors and the #2 liner proceed to dabble. Paint flowers, scrolls, strokes, crosshatching, whatever strikes your fancy.

DUCK FEATHERS. There are two sets on Dabble, one on the forehead, the other on the tail.

Look for the color plate of Dabble Duck on the back cover.

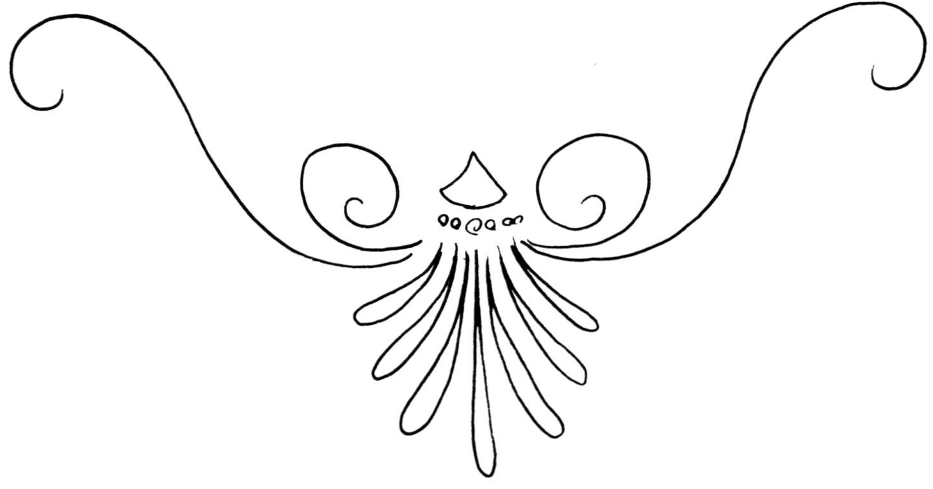

FLIP FLOP AND LITTLE FLOP

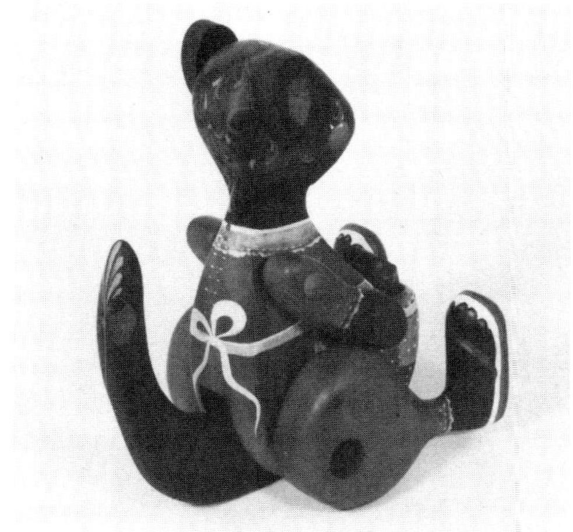

COLORS

Dark Chocolate	Black
Berry Red	Fiesta Pink
Ivory	Cloudberry
Norsk Blue	Maroon
Bonnie Blue	Red Tile
Midnight	

PROCEDURE

Basecoat head, ears, neck, forearms, feet and tail and Little Flop in Dark Chocolate. Basecoat pants and top in Berry Red.

Face, nose, and cheeks are Fiesta Pink highlighted with Ivory. Eyes are Norsk Blue and Midnight, highlighted with Ivory, outlined with Black. See page 56 for step-by-step full color illustrations of painting eyes and cheeks. Paint a big, cheerful smile in Berry Red, lightened with Fiesta Pink. Flip Flop's hair has just been "perm-ed" so give her lots of "S" and "C" curls in Red Tile "frosted" with Cloudberry. Tie a big Norsk Blue bow in her hair. Shade it with Midnight and highlight with Bonnie Blue. Flip Flop's ears are Fiesta Pink inside, lightly dabbed. Little Flop's face is painted with the same colors and technique as Mama, and just use a smaller brush.

Organdy apron, collar, and ruffles are painted with a very thin wash of Ivory. The pocket is given a second coat for more opacity. The ruffles are painted with a sideloaded #2 flat brush. Add detail stitching and dots with the #2 liner. Paint a band and bow on the apron with a #4 flat. Accent Flip Flop's outfit with buttons and bows of Norsk Blue shaded with Midnight highlighted with Bonnie Blue. Two sideloaded crescent strokes of Maroon, strategically placed, help give Flip Flop a maternal appearance.

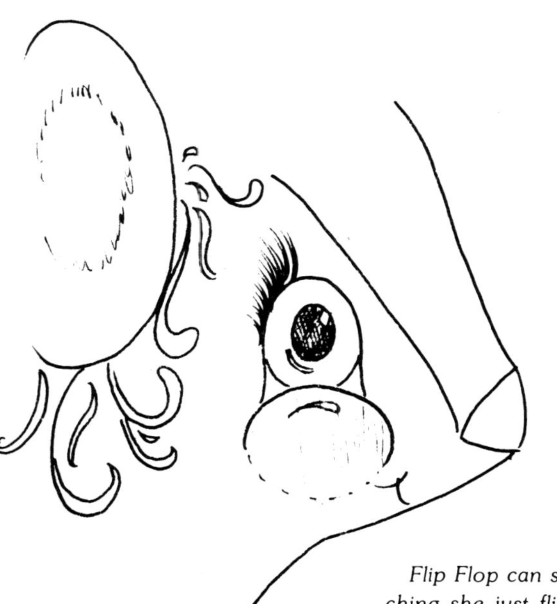

Flip Flop's flip flops are painted in cushiony layers of Cloudberry, Norsk Blue, Berry Red and Ivory. A fabric thong of Norsk Blue, shaded with Midnight and highlighted with Bonnie Blue holds them on her pedicured feet.

KANGA-FEATHERS appear on the tail in Red Tile and Cloudberry.

Flip Flop's choice of footwear was influenced by extended shopping trips with my two oldest daughters in the summer trying to find the "in" flip flops. Have you any idea how many ***not*** *"in" styles there are?*

Flip Flop can stand or sit, and sometimes when you're not watching she just flips over backwards with her head and feet both touching the floor. Little Flop generally stays in mama's pocket except when she flips, then he flops.

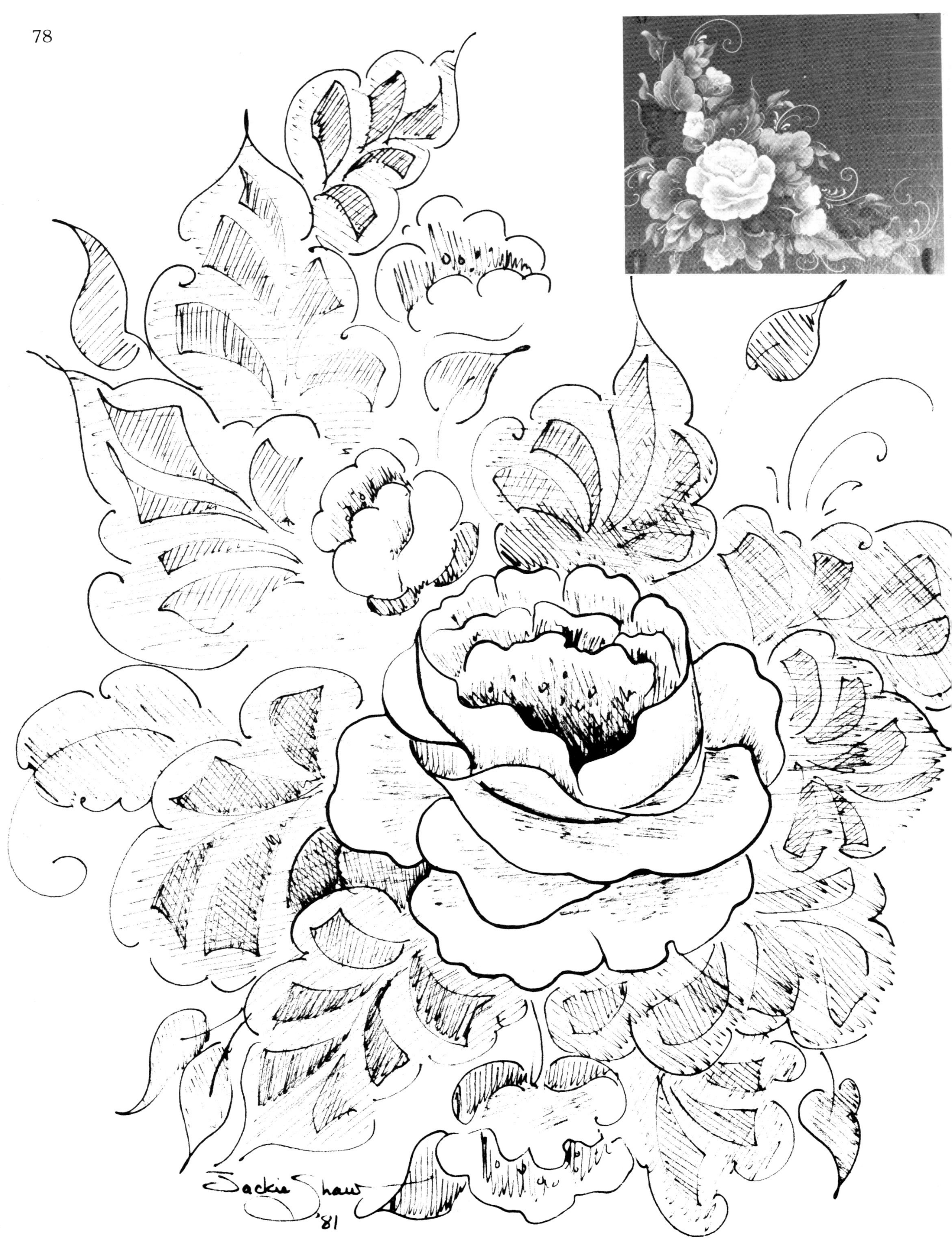
Jackie Shaw
'81

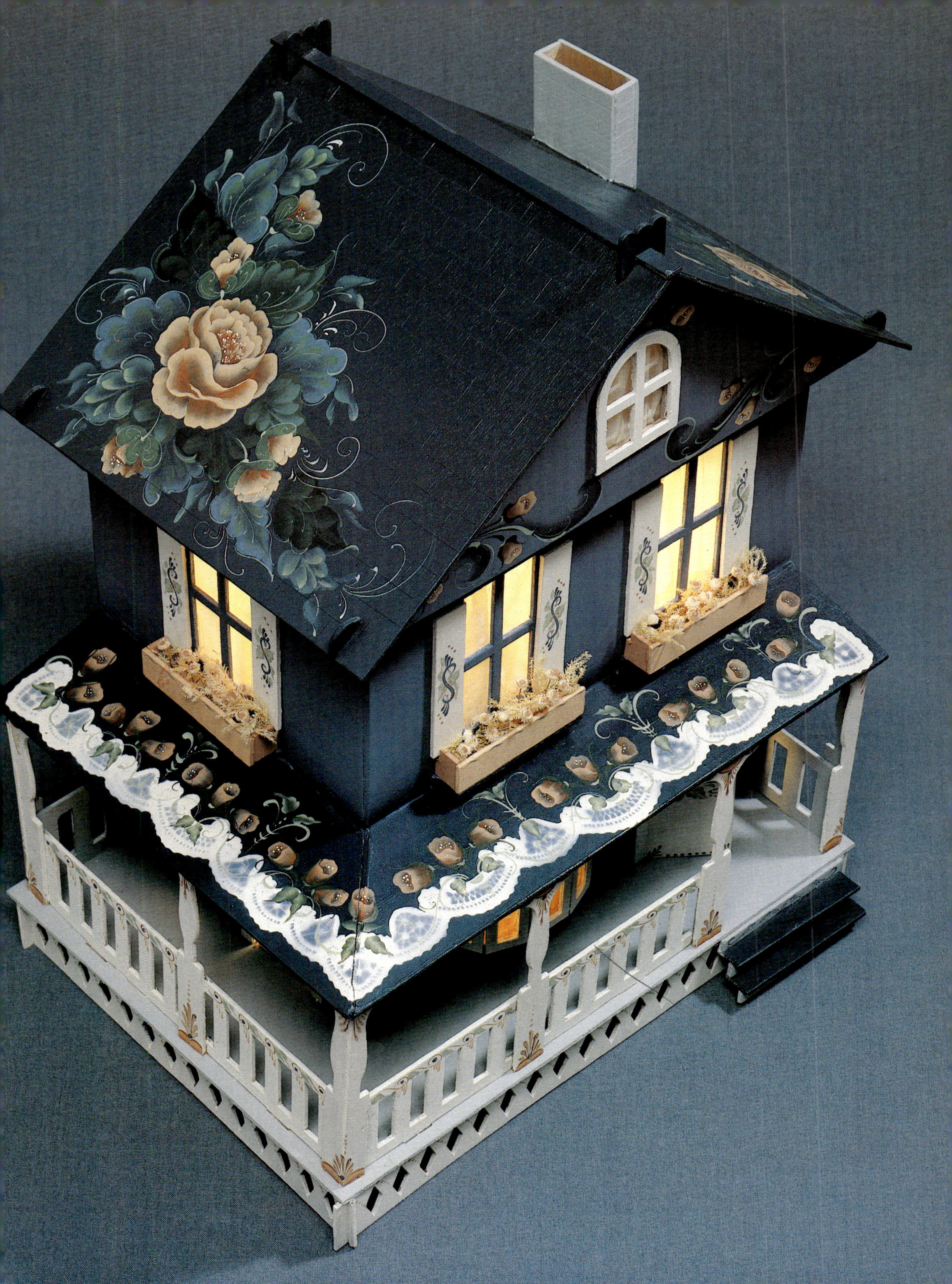

ROSE MANOR

COLORS

Midnight	Red Tile
Norsk Blue	Wedgewood Green
Lichen Grey	Black Green
Ivory	Dark Forest
CF Native Flesh	Blue Spruce

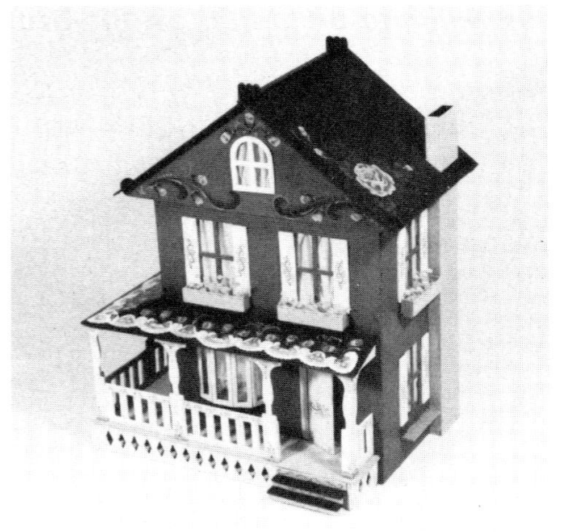

PROCEDURE

Basecoat as follows:

Midnight - top roof
Norsk Blue - house
Lichen Grey - porch, steps
Ivory - pillars, rails, lower roof, doors
CF Native Flesh - window boxes

LACE EFFECT ON LOWER ROOF. Here is an opportunity to experiment with a different technique. Basecoat the roof with whatever color you want the lace to be upon completion. In the sample, Ivory was used. When the basecoat is dry, tape sections of paper doilies to the roof. (Any mask can be used in place of doilies for special effects. Try rick-rack, very open-worked lace, pressed leaves or flowers, cut-out stencils, etc.) With an air-brush you can spray your own colors just as you have mixed them. (See pages 10 and 11 for tips on using the air brush.) The area which is masked by the lace will remain the basecoat color. It will be necessary to spray several coats to get ample coverage. When the unmasked area of the roof is solidly painted and dry, remove the doily or stencil. Use a small brush, if necessary, to touch up spots where tape held the doily in place, and any serious flaws. Do not worry about minor blurs or flaws. Attention will be detracted from these by all the doodling you will surely be compelled to do. The type of design and number and placement of flowers will depend upon the patterns created by the doily.

ROSES. Doubleload a ½" flat brush with CF Native Flesh and Red Tile. Follow the full color illustration on page 82. (Note: The color illustrations are much smaller than the roses in the patterns for Rose Manor, and were therefore painted with a smaller brush.)

LEAVES. After the rose is completed, surround it with leaves in assorted greens. See page 23 for other leaf techniques.

TRIM. Use any of the main colors to carry the color theme onto the pillars, rails, and doors with strokes, scrolls, and dots.

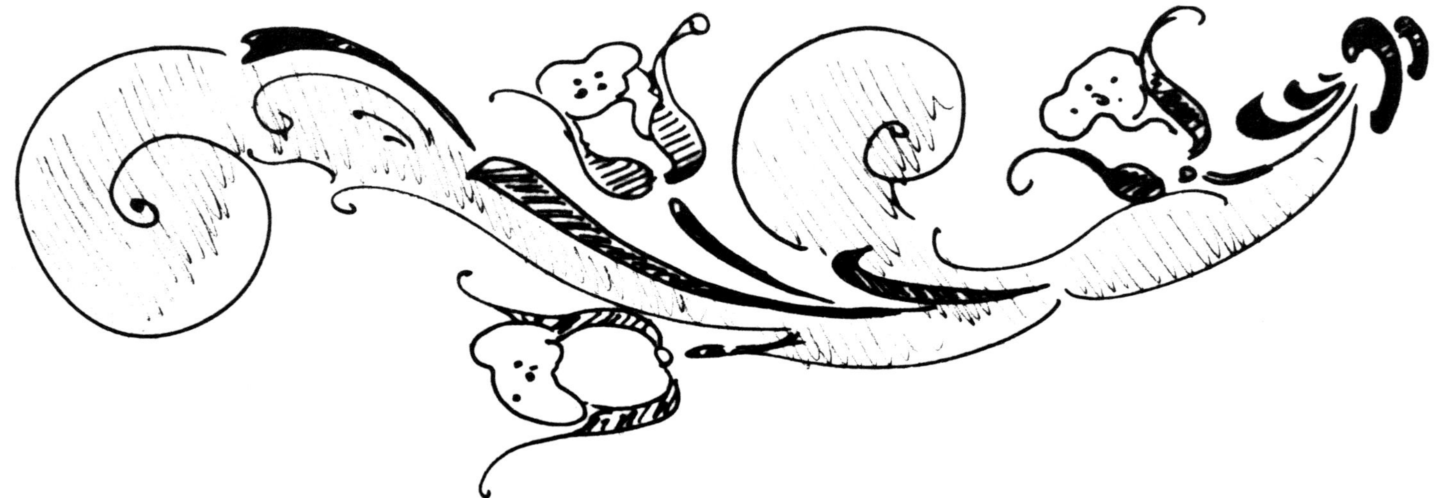

Some hints on using an air-brush:

1. You may use your acrylic colors in the air-brush. This is a real benefit since your color selection is so much wider than that available in spray cans. Since the Ceramcoat colors are already somewhat liquidified, we found that diluting them with 3-4 parts water to 1 part acrylic was a good proportion for the sprayer. If the mixture is too thick, the air brush will not spray.

2. Mix the paint into the water with a soft brush until it is thoroughly dissolved.

3. Protect surrounding areas from overspray.

4. Rinse the spray head and tube often to prevent clogging.

5. Work in a well ventilated area and wear a filter mask. (Check with your hardware store, or ask at your pharmacy for filters designed for coping with allergies.)

6. Spray several thin coats, rather than trying to achieve total coverage in one heavy coat. The latter effort causes drips, runs, and uneven coverage.

7. Plan to spray several items once you have your equipment and area set up. (Many of the toys, because of their compact construction and hard-to-get-to places are ideal candidates for air-brushing.

8. You can also use the air-brush for applying your favorite brush-on varnish. Thin the varnish according to manufacturer's directions. Then follow general directions on page 85 for spray finishing.

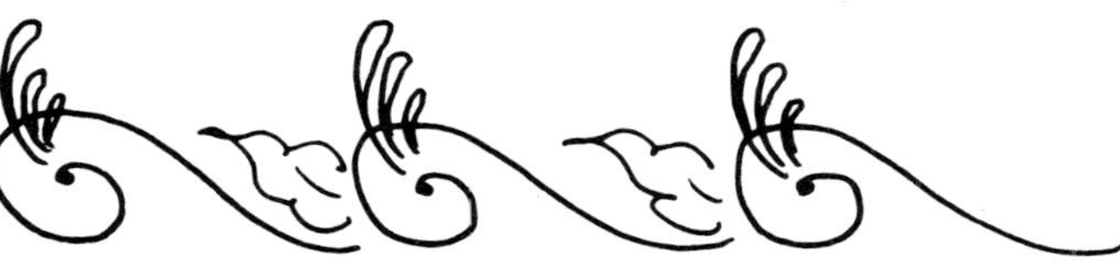

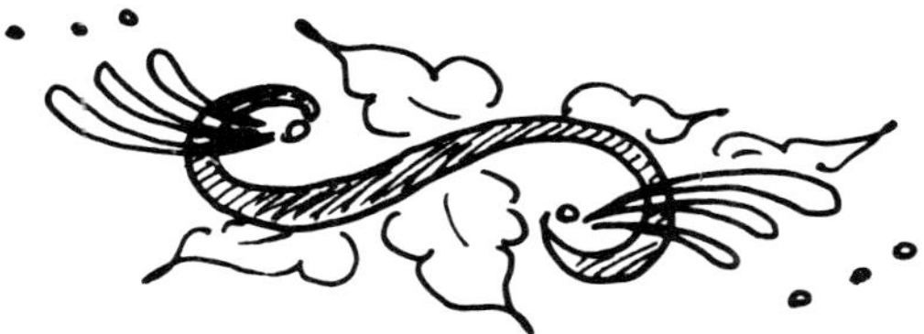

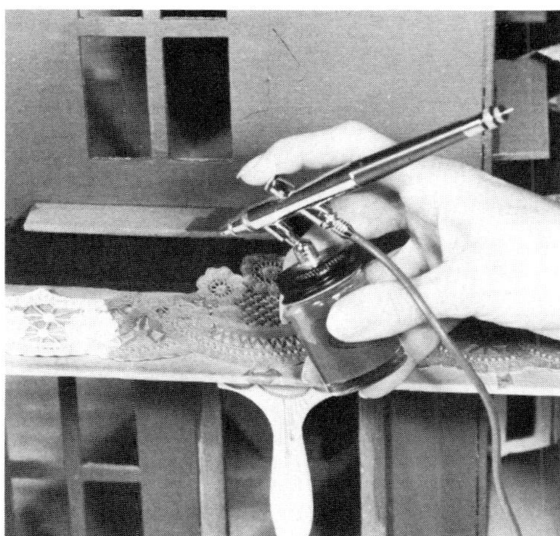

An airbrush is lightweight and convenient to use. It operates from small cans of compressed air or a small air compressor. It is particularly handy when many surfaces are to be prepared at once.

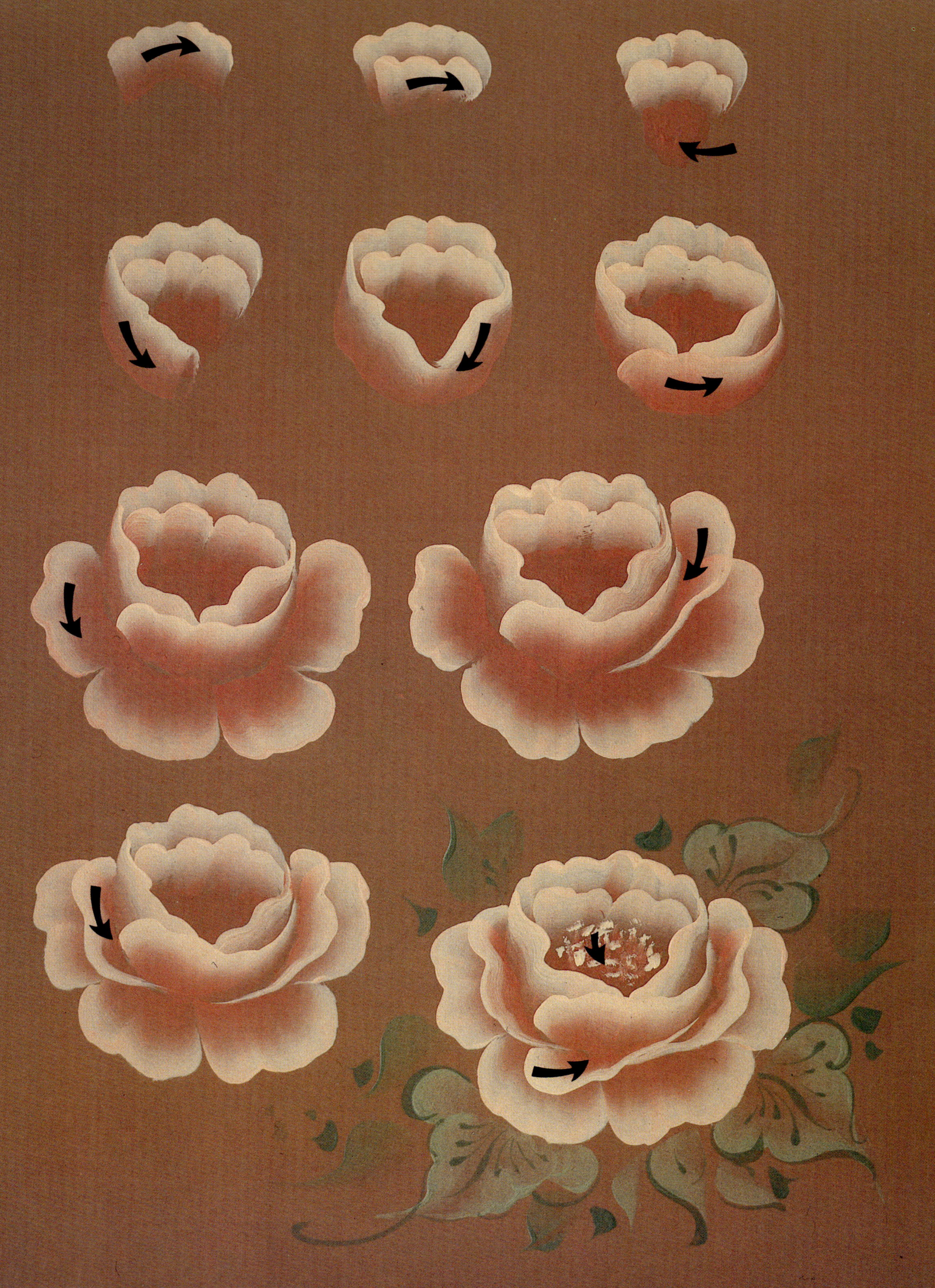

A house is not a home without a family in it. This dollhouse was a birthday gift to our 10-year old daughter, Jenny, who needed a home for her growing family of "Smerfs." Since "Smerfs" are blue and her room is blue, she wanted her house blue too.

Fully believing that a child who has the opportunity to share in the work of creation has a keen appreciation and respect for the final project, we encouraged Jenny to participate in the preparation. Little hands are quite capable of patching with wood filler, sanding (an emory board works great for edges and tight places), sealing, and some basecoat painting. In addition, our children frequently suggest ideas for the design and decoration of projects.

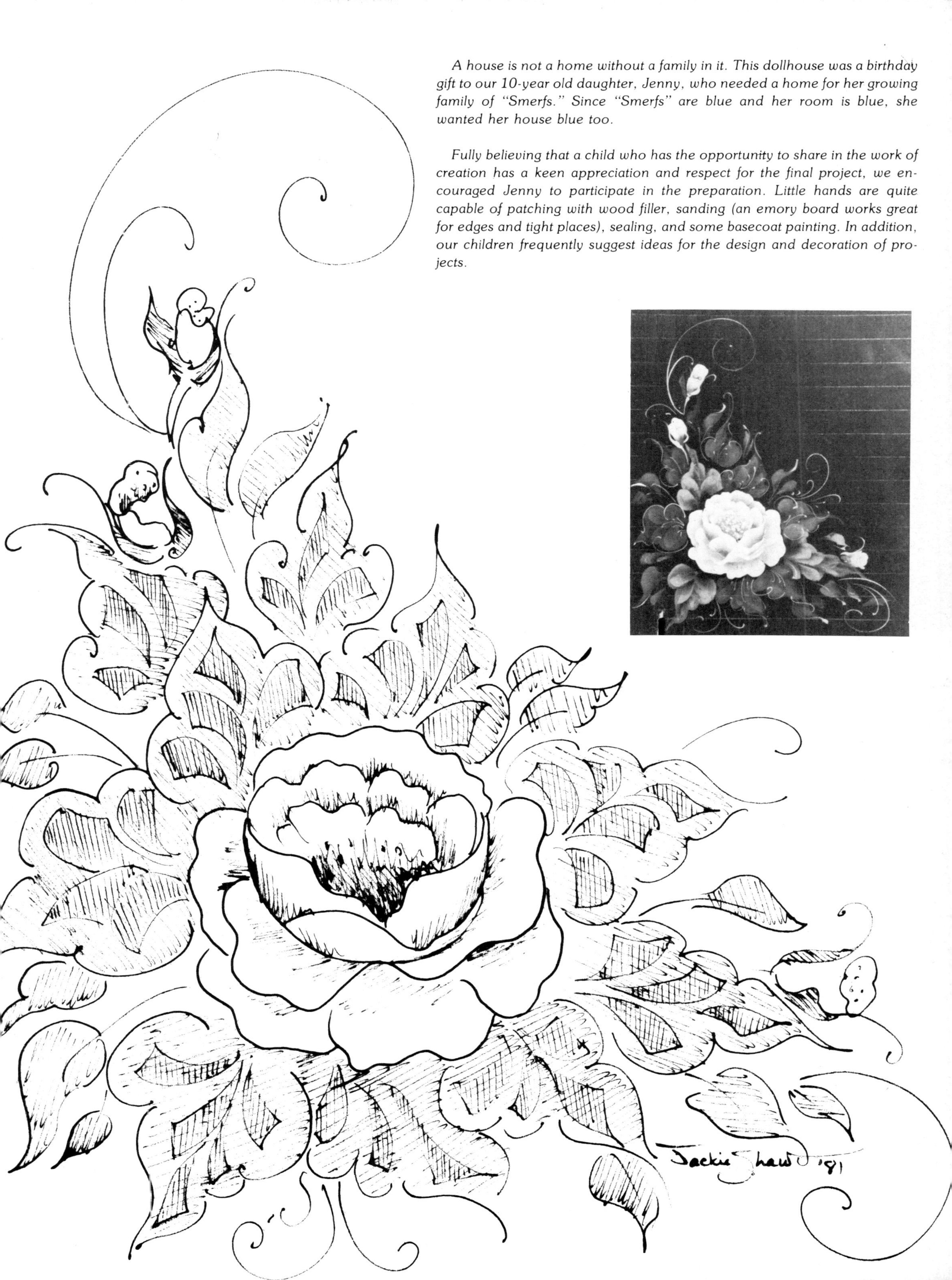

FINISHING TECHNIQUES

All projects (except those on fabric) should be given a protective coat once the painted design is dry. Here's how:

BRUSH ON VARNISH

1. Work in a warm, dust free room without moving air (good luck!).

2. Varnish (any satin finish variety) and object should be 72° or more. Cold varnish has a tendency to "crawl" away from the surface.

3. Apply varnish in fair weather to facilitate proper drying (which for oil based varnish requires 24 hours or more). Humid weather slows the drying process. For water based varnish, drying time is usually just a matter of minutes.

4. Before varnishing, remove dust from object by wiping with a tack rag (You can buy a tack rag or make one yourself. Dip a 12" square of cheesecloth in warm water. Wring out excess. Mix 2 teaspoons turp with 3 teaspoons varnish. Pour over, and work into, the cloth. Store in airtight container.)

5. Do not shake varnish. To do so causes unwanted bubbles. However, varnish should be thoroughly stirred to distribute the drying agent.

6. Never use old, thick varnish, and do not attempt to thin it for use. Such varnish would result in a disappointing finish. Throw it way.

7. Try to "flow" varnish on smoothly with a good quality varnish brush. Avoid wiping brush on lip of can, and do not brush excessively. Both gestures cause bubbles.

8. Place in a dust and draft free area to dry thoroughly.

9. Apply a second coat of varnish and let dry thoroughly.

10. With wet and dry sandpaper #600 sprinkled with water and a little liquid soap to reduce friction, or with steel wool #0000, sand VERY LIGHTLY after the second and any successive coats of varnish except the last one. Rinse off soap. Dry. Tack and varnish again, building up as many coats as desired.

FOR A HAND RUBBED FINISH (Optional)

After the last coat of varnish, dry 48 hours. Sprinkle surface with powdered pumice (4F dental grade is available from your drug store) or rottenstone and a little finishing oil (baby oil, linseed oil, or lemon oil will suffice). Then rub gently using the palm of your hand or a scrap of heavy felt to produce a satin finish.

Buff with a soft, clean, dry cloth.

SPRAY VARNISH

1. If you prefer to spray varnish, carefully follow the manufacturer's directions on the can. With some sprays, it is necessary to apply successive coats within a certain period of time to prevent crinkling of the finish.

2. Never combine different types of varnishes. Chemical incompatibilties often lead to disastrous results.

3. Varnish and project should be at room temperature. The first four principles listed above for brush on varnish also apply to spray varnishing.

4. Test the spray on a scrap to assure that the spray head is clean and operating properly.

5. Spray your project by beginning the spray off the edge then sweeping across the project all the way to the other side and off the edge. This prevents a drippy buildup at the beginning and ending points.

6. Spray lightly, several thin coats being preferable to one heavy coat. (Heavy sprays result in blobs and drips.)

7. It is possible to give a hand rubbed finish to sprayed pieces.

HINTS:

a. Finish the back of your project, removing any paint and varnish drips; paint or cover the back with wallpaper samples.

b. Pull-tabs from soda cans make handy hanging hooks.

c. For a weatherproof finish, use a marine varnish.

d. Heat and alcohol-proof varnishes are ideal for trays and heavy use items.

ANTIQUING / GLAZING

Some projects lend themselves nicely to antiquing or glazing. Use this technique as an enhancing measure only on those projects which are appropriate or would benefit from it. It is neither necessary nor desirable to get into the habit of antiquing everything you paint.

To antique a project, you will need a clear glaze (see recipe below), oil paints, palette knife, palette, cheesecloth, a mop brush, a sponge brush, and extra fine steel wool or a Home and Hobby Pad ("scrubby"). Plastic or rubber gloves are advisable as this technique tends to be a bit messy. (Lacking gloves, slip your hands into a couple of sandwich baggies.)

Mix a clear glaze medium as follows:

1 tablespoon varnish (I use McCloskey's)
3 tablespoons paint thinner or turpentine (dirty turp is great)
1-2 drops linseed oil

Proportions of the recipe may be varied to suit your preferences. (More turpentine makes the glaze thinner. More varnish accelerates the drying time. More linseed oil retards the drying time). Frequently, if I am out of my glaze, I will use the palette knife to scoop small amounts of the ingredients onto my palette - no calculated measurements - just rough proportions.

Select a color of oil paint to be mixed with the glaze. Gradually add glaze to the oil paint until the mixture is workable, but still fairly dense. Popular oil paint colors to use for antiquing include Burnt Umber, Raw Umber, Black, Prussian Blue, Burnt Sienna, Raw Sienna. These colors may be used individually or in mixtures. It is a good idea to make a test sample of your design colors for the purpose of experimenting to see which antiquing color or combination of colors you prefer over the designs.

It is also possible to glaze with other colors - such as red, yellow, green, etc. In such a case, the effect is not so much one of antiquity as it is an interesting treatment of color.

The full color illustrations on the facing page depict the changes in appearance of a project being antiqued or glazed.

The first section shows the original colors of the art work.

In section two, a heavy coat of the antiquing glaze was applied directly onto the unvarnished paintings. A foam brush works well for this step.

In section three, cheesecloth was used to wipe away the excess antiquing glaze. Afterwards a soft "mop" brush smoothed the glaze and "dusted" away distinct lines and abrupt changes in glaze coverage. The "mop" is especially useful on projects with corners, nooks, and crannies.

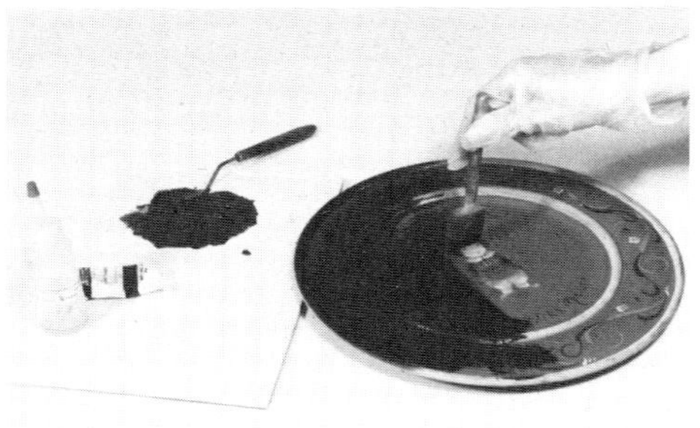

Brush heavy glaze mixture over the project. For large projects, work on one section at a time.

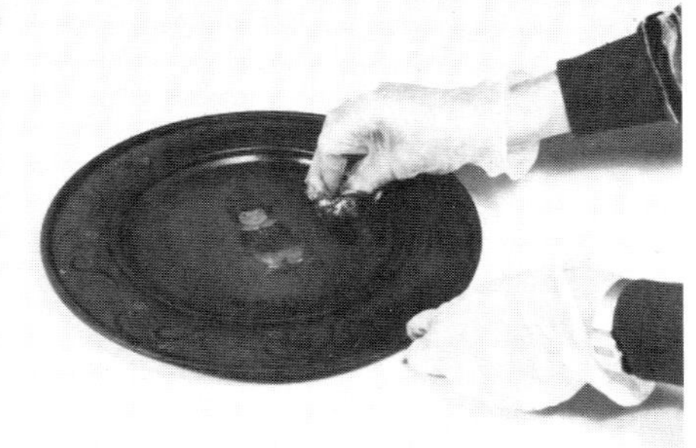

Excess glaze is removed with cheesecloth.

Section four shows the finished effect. After several days drying time, this area was gently rubbed with a "scrubby" pad (or fine steel wool) well lubricated with finishing oil or linseed oil. In doing this step, keep a lint-free, soft cloth handy to wipe away residue frequently in order to check progress. (It is possible to rub away an entire design if you're not careful.) The main effort here is to remove the antiquing glaze from all the raised areas. Textured stroke work creates exciting effects in this step.

Let this final stage dry overnight, then apply varnish. (See finishing techniques on page 84.) I prefer to use an oil based varnish, such as McCloskey's Heirloom Eggshell finish, on the antiqued or glazed pieces.

The sample on the facing pages was antiqued with Raw Umber. Other pieces in the book which were antiqued include the toy box, Speedy Van, the drum and birth plates, and the switch plate covers. These were all antiqued with Burnt Umber.

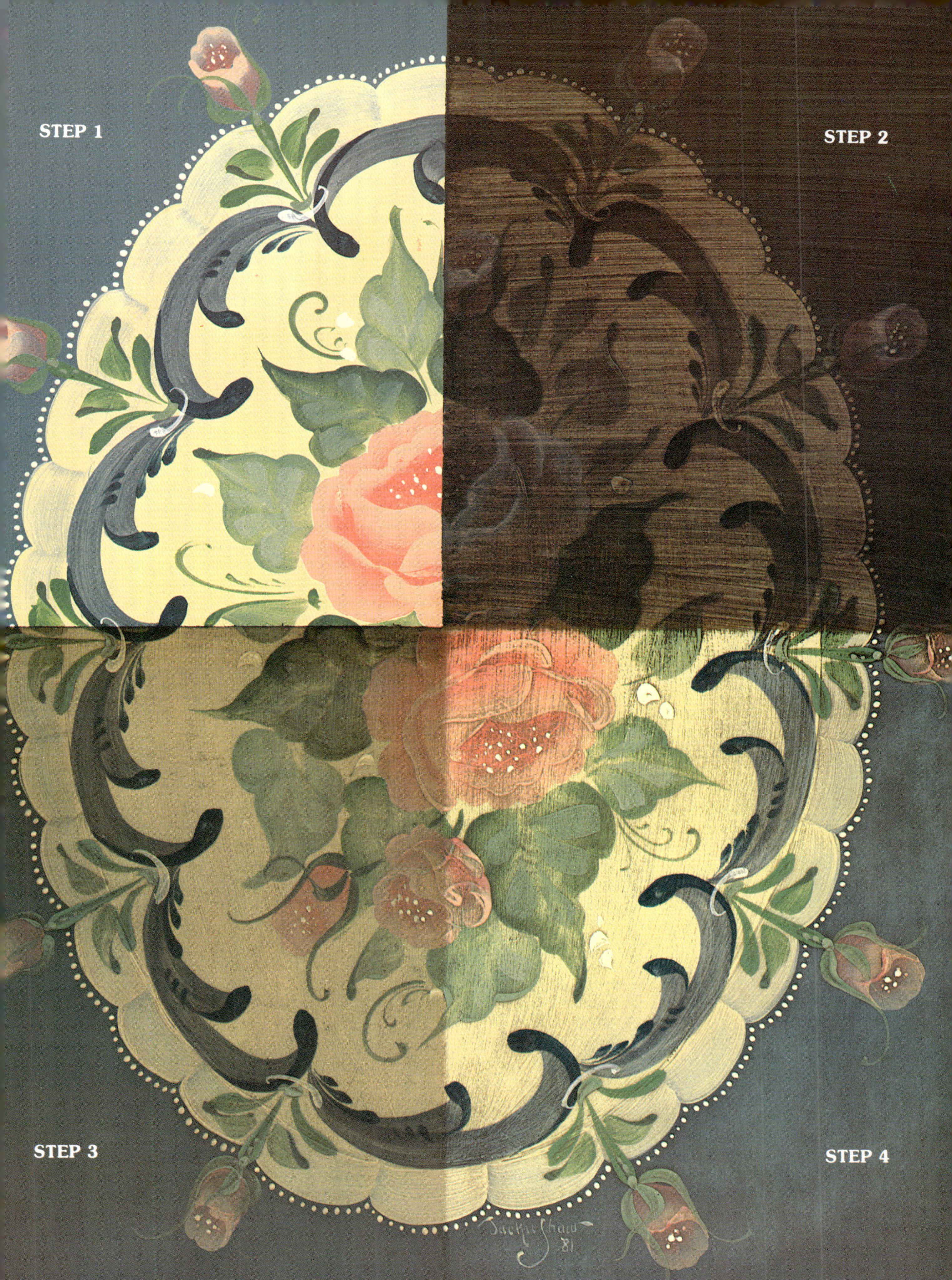
STEP 1
STEP 2
STEP 3
STEP 4
Jackie Shaw
81

SOURCES

The following companies and the marvelous people who run them are behind all the fun things that happened in this book. Special thanks to them all for their encouragement and support.

Product	Source
Honey Bear, Snap Dragon, Rainbow-Wow, Flip-Flop, Sue Fle, Stilts, Mental Block, P'Ony, Happy Little Yellow Car, Speedy Van, Cheddar, Charlie Charlie Tango, Rolly Scrolly, Mr. Alley Gator, Forget Me Not, Dandy Lion	Woodstock Toymakers 114 Marion Avenue Columbia, MS 39429
Toy Box	Treasures RR #2 Lake View, OH 43331
Ryan's Horse	Red Barn Distributors 16 Scott Street South Attleboro, MA 02703
Stuffed Unicorns	Bonnie's Babes & Things c/o Apt. PO9 3100 Shore Drive Virginia Beach, VA 23451
Magic Fairy Wand	Top Drawer P.O. Box 405 Newberg, OR 97132
Drum	Designs by Bentwood Box 1676 Thomasville, GA 31792
Rose Manor (dollhouse)	Greenleaf Products, Inc. P.O. Box 391 Cooperstown, NY 13326
Derek's Guardian Angel Plaque, Richard's & Kailian's Plates	Viking Woodcrafts 1317 8th Street, S.E. Waseca, MN 56093
Crayonasaurus	R & M What Knots Edmonds, WA
Cat Astrophy	Puzzle-In-Wood-Craft Alfred E. Knobler & Co., Inc. Moonachie, NJ 07074
Air Brush	Badger Air Brush Co. 9128 W. Belmont Ave. Franklin Park, IL 60131
Brushes	Loew-Cornell 131 W. Ruby Ave. Palisades Park, NJ 07650
Paints	Delta Technical Coatings, Inc. 11015 Rush St. South El Monte, CA 91733

Ask your favorite craft and hobby dealer for the products supplied by the above companies.